THE VOLVO TOUR
Y E A R B O O K

With Hewlett-Packard, the Tour are now calling the shots.

A major golf tournament calls for a computer that's on the ball.

A computer that can accurately and immediately present on your TV screen a wide range of information including leaderboards, hole statistics and individual scores.

Hewlett-Packard's fully integrated system knocks spots off the competitors.

Designed in conjunction with the PGA European Tour, it will reveal hole-by-hole results, order-of-merit ratings and even players' biographies at the touch of a button.

This on-site service graphically demonstrates the computer's capabilities. In a demanding situation, it's no wonder the PGA European Tour have designated Hewlett-Packard as their official computer.

If you'd like to know the score on Hewlett-Packard, call us in Bracknell, UK on (0344) 369369 or in Boeblingen, Germany on 49/7031 142610.

 **HEWLETT PACKARD**

THE POSSIBILITY MADE REALITY.

EDITOR
Chris Plumridge
PHOTOGRAPHIC EDITOR
Charles Briscoe-Knight
CO-ORDINATING EDITOR
Sue Rose
CONSULTANT EDITOR
John Hopkins

ART EDITOR
James Chambers

PUBLISHER
Eddie Southcombe
ACCOUNT HANDLER
Dieter Lloyd

PRODUCTION MANAGER
Ken Holt
PRODUCTION CONTROLER
Nicola Mirams
PRODUCTION DIRECTOR
John Petty

THE VOLVO TOUR YEARBOOK 1993 is published by HHL Publishing, Greater London House, Hampstead Road, London NW1 7QQ, England, on behalf of PGA European Tour Enterprises Ltd. Printed by Printer Portuguesa Lisbon, Portugal. © Headway, Home & Law Publishing. No part of this book may be reproduced, stored in a retrieval system of transmitted in any form or by any means, electronic, mechanical, photocopying, recording or otherwise, without prior permission in writing from Headway, Home and Law Publishing. ISBN 1-85386 281 9

INTRODUCTION FROM THE PGA EUROPEAN TOUR

The 1992 Volvo Tour will be remembered firstly for the supreme performances of Nick Faldo.

Four Volvo Tour victories, plus the World Match-Play Championship, included, of course, the 121st Open Championship to enable Nick to equal Severiano Ballesteros' modern European record of five major championships. Faldo's year once again installed him as the leading golfer world-wide and we remain fortunate in European golf to have such great champions, coinciding with Volvo's overall corporate sponsorship of the Tour.

Reference to this Volvo Tour Yearbook will reveal all sorts of record-breaking performances which bode well for the short and medium term future. Above all, in my opinion, are the stroke averages for the season which, led by Nick Faldo's remarkable 69.10 and Bernhard Langer's superb 69.91, indicate that it remains very possible to dominate our sport at a time of dramatic all-round improving standards.

There were many noteworthy performances during 1992 and I wish to single out our over 40s – Jose Maria Canizares, Christy O'Connor Junior and Vicente Fernandez whose victories very much emulated similar recent successes in the United States by Raymond Floyd, Tom Kite and Lanny Wadkins. Their performances also indicated that given dedication and discipline, careers can remain successful over two or more decades and I feel their experience can and will benefit our new generation of players.

May I express the PGA European Tour's continuing appreciation and admiration for Volvo's outstanding support – visible to all followers of European golf – at times which remain sensitive and difficult for many companies and countries.

KENNETH D. SCHOFIELD
EXECUTIVE DIRECTOR

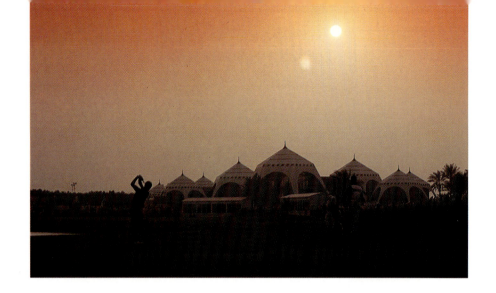

CONTENTS

A COMMON MARKET OF TALENT

BY MICHAEL McDONNELL

Facing page, Rookie of the Year Jim Payne finds his ball in another hole while, above, Barry Lane and Andrew Murray check on the seam.

In 1992 the great contemporaries of European golf completed their season of toil with justified satisfaction that they could still assert themselves in an arena that grows richer in talent – and tougher in attitude – with each year that passes. Even so, it was not an easy task.

The situation itself, of course, offers the best possible news for the future of the game; a winning formula which not only discovers and fosters new talent but also offers rich rewards and frequent opportunities to fulfil itself.

The elite coterie of superstars – Nick Faldo, Bernhard Langer, Seve Ballesteros, Sandy Lyle, Ian Woosnam and Company – will aver the gap between themselves and what used to be regarded as the chorus line of the Volvo Tour has narrowed to an almost negligible margin. Indeed, there was a time when the stature of a tournament, while never simply a private affair between these great players, was somehow accorded heavier importance if one of their names was engraved on the trophy. Not any more.

One of the strengths of the Volvo Tour and of the sucessful manner in which it has been marketed worldwide by its Wentworth-based officials, is the frequency of opportunity it has now given tournament professionals. In the 1992 season, there were 38 such winning chances from Bangkok, Dubai and throughout continental Europe – too many for the great

men to either seek or to monopolise – so that a new contingent of winners emerged to take their place on the roll of honour.

This winning experience is spreading more widely among the nationalities of professionals on the Tour so that the immediate result of the trend will almost certainly be to present a more disparate collection of players for Johnnie Walker European Ryder Cup skipper Bernard Gallacher to command next season at The Belfry against the Americans.

This common market of talent, after all, has always been the ultimate object of the exercise. Professional golf officially embraced the European concept almost a

quarter of a century ago although the spiritual affinity clearly stretches back to the days when J H Taylor was winning the 1908 French Open at La Boulie and George Duncan captured the 1912 Belgian Open in Brussels and Harry Vardon took the 1911 German Open at Baden-Baden. Moreover, the old theory that team spirit was somehow the exclusive prerogative of Anglo-Saxons and one that could never be really comprehended by those born elsewhere, has clearly been disproved by the unity that existed during the 1985 and 1987 Ryder Cup victories and subsequent encounters.

It is now clear, for example, that the strong Swedish presence established by Anders Forsbrand during the 1992 season as he finished fourth on the Volvo Order of Merit with two tournament wins as well as the movement of Per-Ulrik Johansson towards the top could be manifested in Ryder Cup team places. More than this, the spirit of camaraderie that comes from collective life under stress – be it warfare, global travel or the pressure of week to week tournament play – can only strengthen this bond and in the process serve to diffuse the outbursts of misplaced patriotism that have occasionally appeared in recent matches.

In the broader perspective the 1992 season was a heartening case of business as usual. Its itinerary refused to be

restrained by geography and ventured once again to the Far East on the inarguable premise that the Volvo Tour is defined only as the place where most of its members play – wherever it may be. The purses grew to over £20 million despite the general economic recession and at least one of the world's four major titles was captured by a member of the PGA European Tour for the ninth time in ten successive years and all tournaments, bar one, were won with sub-par scores. It all made good reading for the balance sheet but hid a more pivotal moment in the development of European golf.

Without question, the season earned additional significance because of the effect Nick Faldo had upon it. The champion himself had reached that most important milestone of all which marks the true point of greatness.

His stature was no longer dependent upon, nor measured by, the collection of titles. In short, with his fifth major victory, he had joined the great figures of the game and rightfully could be talked about in the same breath as Jack Nicklaus, Ben Hogan, Arnold Palmer, Lee Trevino and Gary Player.

His Open Championship win at Muirfield was drama of the highest quality in which he threw the title away and then found within himself the courage and resolve to retake it. There were other moments too, all characterised by curious hesitancy before he could re-focus his fierce concentration on the task of winning.

It happened in the Carrolls Irish Open, then too in the Scandinavian Masters. The GA European Open was a more confident display but the occasion that elevated Faldo into that rare class of distinction from which it is impossible to be removed came at the Toyota World Match-Play championship at Wentworth. Those who witnessed his display can be forgiven if they do not remember his winning margins, but they took away with them unforgettable memories a precision play the like of which has rarely been seen in championship golf as his long irons rarely wavered an inch from their target. This was Faldo at his very best as he underlined the merit of his blinkered dedication to his task. Truly, the world's best golfer was alive and well and playing in Europe, with no serious desire to pursue a career elsewhere. That too was tribute to the quality of the Volvo Tour in that this perfectionist could still find quality of competition from his peers to hone his game to its keenest edge.

In ecclesiatical terms, it has been a broad church which accommodated all manner of winners. Seven newcomers – Ian Palmer (Johnnie Walker Asian Classic), Daniel Silva (Jersey European Airways Open), Peter O'Malley (Bell's Scottish Open), Peter Mitchell (Mitsubishi Austrian Open), Miguel Angel Martin (Peugeot French Open), Jamie Spence (Canon European Masters) and Miguel Angel Jiminez (Piaget Open) made up the customary average of recent years.

There were 29 winners from 15 countries to underline the essential international flavour that gives the Tour its strength.

Christy O'Connor Junior wins
Dunhill British Masters.

Flamingo patrol holds up
Severiano Ballesteros in Dubai.

Bernhard Langer launches the Tour Physio Unit at the Volvo PGA Championship.

Bernard Gallacher and Andrea Matthews of British Airways with group of British Airways High Flyer Award winners.

Pensive pose from Rodger Davis and David Feherty.

Langer levitated into second place on the Volvo Order of Merit.

There were multiple winners too. Anders Forsbrand, Seve Ballesteros, Jose Maria Olazabal, Bernhard Langer, Sandy Lyle and Vijay Singh each won two titles apiece while Faldo collected five of the best.

Yet for all its great industry and growth, the Volvo Tour remains part of the entertainment business and offered some enchanting moments of drama and delight: the moment Christy O'Connor Junior ignored his advancing middle years and the hazards of Woburn to become Dunhill British Masters champion; the confident manner in which Tony Johnstone took on the mighty Wentworth West Course and golf's great stars to win the Volvo PGA Championship. But most of all, the style with which an England side — without Faldo — took on most of the best players the world could offer at St Andrews and beat them all in the Alfred Dunhill Cup.

In truth, Jamie Spence, David Gilford and Steven Richardson offered the ultimate proof that the gap has virtually closed on the great names and nobody can really detect much of a difference anymore. More to the point, it doesn't really matter anymore either.

A RAGE FOR PERFECTION

BY JOHN HOPKINS

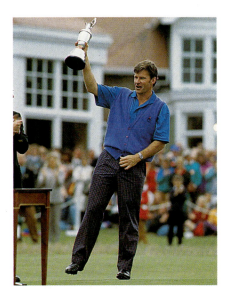

When Nick Faldo had won the Toyota World Match-Play Championship at Wentworth he sat talking to journalists. It was an autumnal day. Outside there was a chill in the air, a hint of mist, and leaves spiralled crazily to the ground. Faldo looked entirely at ease with himself, as well he might having just won £160,000.

It was his fifth victory in Europe this year and as his results are shown later it is sufficient to say here that he had a further 11 top ten finishes in the 22 events he had competed in on both sides of the Atlantic in 1992.

'Yes, this was a hell of a week,' he was saying. 'It has been a pretty satisfying year, actually. I am enjoying my golf and enjoying educating myself on golf as well. I am trying to keep on improving. I just have to keep working on my game. When I think things are going well I want to work harder.'

Someone asked if he felt he was the most complete golfer in the world. Faldo looked flustered. He shrugged his shoulders and flicked nervously at the cow lick of hair that tends to fall forwards from the crown of his head. It was a question he didn't want to answer and his reactions were significant. 'It is not for me to say,' he said with a hint of embarrassment. 'You guys know the score. You know who the good players are. All I know is you can't get cocky or over excited about this game. Just when you think you've got it, you have a bad day and it knocks you down again.'

Did he compare himself with Ben Hogan? Again a hint of a blush passed across Faldo's face. 'I am very honoured to be mentioned in the same breath as Hogan. We come from two different eras. To me it is one of the highest accolades I could be paid. I am not sure I deserve it.' I wondered, idly, why he was so flattered to be compared to Hogan, a man he had never seen play golf who won only nine major championships. Why wouldn't he want to be compared to Jack Nicklaus, whose tally of 20 major titles was more than twice as many as Hogan's, a man Faldo knew well and had played with and against. And then I realised: Faldo had never seen Hogan play, indeed never met him. There's nothing like a bit of mystique to catch the imagination.

We are all children of our parents. To understand Faldo it is necessary to know his parents just as it is illuminating in trying to cast some light on the motives that drove Ben Hogan so relentlessly to know a little about his mother and father.

Hogan's parents were poor. When he was nine his father, Chester Hogan, ill and with deep financial worries, shot himself in the heart. Much of Hogan's life was a triumph against the odds. As a caddie at a golf club in Fort Worth, Texas, Hogan was bullied because he was so small. His early days on the tour were so unsuccessful that he and his wife Valerie once went for a month eating only oranges. When they had $18 left to their name, a thief stole the tyres of their car.

Faldo's early life was pampered and sumptuous by comparison. His internal dynamic comes from his mother Joyce who believed that almost anything was possible for her son, their only child, and did all she could to help him achieve it. George Faldo is the rock on which the family was founded, the main breadwinner. Nick Faldo resembles his father in physique and temperament. Life was not easy for George Faldo. He had four brothers and sisters and they grew up in the East End of London in a flat that had no running water and a lavatory that had to be shared with neighbours.

Faldo is blessedly uncomplicated, unlike Severiano Ballesteros of whom it was once said is a riddle wrapped in a mystery inside an enigma! Golf is his game. It is practically all he cares about. He is reassured by his ability to make money but money as an end in itself has never been important to him. He has a rage for perfection. He has talked of wanting to hit shots so straight they didn't err more than a foot or two from their target and, at times, he has achieved

such accuracy. But the demons that make him work so hard to achieve this are the same ones that make him turn away in disgust when a shot of his ends 20 feet from the flag. Success is a fierce taskmaster.

As he looked back over the season, Faldo hardly dwelled on his play in Ireland, Belgium, France, in the US PGA, and in the Open at Muirfield. At all these events Faldo was sailing along serenely one minute, in hideous trouble the next. He has rationalised these lapses in his own mind as follows: 'If I get into contention every week I play then I am going to fall from grace from time to time. I can't win everything.' After Faldo's third round, a 76, in the US PGA he went to the practice ground for an urgent meeting with David Leadbetter, his coach. 'There is nothing wrong,' Leadbetter said. 'You are playing well, swinging well. It was just one of those days.'

There is a statistic about Nicklaus that Faldo likes to remember. It is not that Nicklaus has won 20 major titles but that he has come second or third in nearly 30 others. Faldo wants to be remembered for the quality of his golf. In days to come he wants people to ask one another: did you see Nick Faldo play golf? We saw him play in 1992 all right, in a way that no Briton has this century, not even Harry Vardon.

Faldo's results this year on both sides of the Atlantic are worth recording. They are: tied 21st in the Johnnie Walker Asian classic, fifth in the Dubal Classic, tied 17th in the Honda Classic, missed cut in the Nestle Invitational, tied second in The Players' Championship, tied sixth in the Freeport-McMoran, tied 13th in the US Masters, tied third in the Benson and Hedges International Open, second in the Peugeot Spanish Open, eighth in the Volvo PGA Championship, fourth in the

Dunhill British Masters, first in the Carrolls Irish open, tied fourth in the US Open, tied third in the Peugeot French Open, tied third in Bell's Scottish Open, first in the Open Championship, first in the Scandinavian Masters, tied second in the US PGA, first in the GA European Open, tied 17th in the Trophee Lancôme, tied fifth in the Piaget Open, first in the Toyota World Match-Play Championship and tied 23rd in the Volvo Masters. In sum that is five victories and a further 11 top ten finishes from 23 events.

In the 15 stroke-play events he completed in Europe, Faldo played 60 rounds and had a stroke average of 69.1. This compared with Ian Woosnam's 69.66 in 1990 and Ballesteros's 69.72 in 1991.

These are startling figures. It just shows how well he is playing and how he retains a starting sense of purpose and clarity. There is yet more to come from Nick Faldo.

Moments from a season of

dominance.

Mel Pyatt of Volvo congratulates

Faldo at the Volvo Masters.

CALLING ON ALL THE SHOTS

'If anyone can, Canon can' runs the advertising slogan and in 1992 the Canon Shoot-Out showed that it can provide excitement and entertainment on the golf course as well.

With a heavy worldwide involvement in Formula One motor racing, atheletics, ice-skating, soccer and tennis the Japanese company has also moved into mainline sponsorship of golf. In addition to giving financial backing to their season-long Shoot-Out series, the company now sponsors the European Masters, the former Swiss Open, at Crans-sur-Sierre.

It was at Crans, too, after their eight scheduled Shoot-Outs in France, Italy, Spain, England (twice), Austria, Holland and Germany, that Canon introduced their first Shoot-Out final to involve earlier season winners and a few top line guests to make up the field. Seve Ballesteros won high in the mountains above the Rhône Valley at the most spectacular of all Volvo Tour venues but before that 40 players had competed in the eight regular Shoot-Outs with Sandy Lyle and Steven Richardson involved in five of them and each winning one.

Throughout the season, 17 countries had representatives in the Shoot-Outs, the format for which is simple. Ten players line up to play nine holes – usually, but not always the back nine. At each hole

The Canon Shoot-Out Series drew on all the players' skills throughout the season

the player with the highest score drops out until at the final hole only two players are left to compete for a first prize, usually of £2,500 but sometimes much more if the Shoot-Out is tied up with a major charity event. In the event of more than one player having the highest score at a hole they shoot out until one player is left.

The referee has the right to decide the format of the shoot-out. He might decide that all players tieing should chip from the side of the green, or play shots out of a selected bunker around the green or

simply putt with the winner being the player whose ball finishes nearest the hole. It is simple. The spectators understand how it works and can enjoy the more relaxed atmosphere in which the event takes place.

There is the usual rivalry among the contestants that has over the years ensured ever-lowering standards of scoring in Volvo Tour events but there is more banter among the contestants than there is when the tournament begins. Various pre-tournament events are staged each season – challenge matches, mini-Ryder Cups, and even team events, but the Shoot-Out is always the most popular method of creating interest and pre-tournament publicity for the main event later in the week.

Throughout the season the nine Canon events, including the final at Crans, produced a total of 37 shoot-outs, eight of them in the competition held before the BMW International Open at Munich, won by Bernhard Langer. On just one occasion did the winner of the Shoot-Out go on to win the tournament and that was in Milan where Lyle followed up his Tuesday afternoon success at Monticello with his second career victory in the Lancia Martini Italian Open.

The series started at Cannes Mougins where a former Credit Lyonnais Cannes Open winner Paul Broadhurst proved

*Per-Ulrik Johansson featured
strongly in the Shoot-Out series.*

*Steven Richardson, facing page and
left, and charity won at Wentworth.*

before a huge crowd just how much he
enjoys playing the course. The series, in
fact, could not have made a more
dramatic start with Frenchman Jean Van
de Velde holing an outrageous chip to
beat Tony Johnstone in the first Shoot-Out
of the season. It was an indication of the
excitement that would follow through to
September. Van de Velde survived for
four more holes before bowing out and,
in the end, it was Broadhurst who won at
the last when Per-Ulrik Johansson was in
the water.

The following week in Milan, Sandy
Lyle teed up for the first time in 1992
remembering his last Canon Shoot-Out
appearance the previous year. That had
been in Munich where he went on to win
the title and end the form slump which
had been with him for almost three years.
Johansson, who had so nearly won in
Cannes was a first hole loser in Italy
where Lyle, helped by the most delicate
of chips down the green at the last, just
managed to edge out Johnstone.

Next stop was Madrid where the

venue should have been Club de Campo
in the heart of the city. A threatened strike
of club workers prompted the promoters
of the Peugeot Spanish Open to move the
tournament, lock, stock and barrel to the
RAC Club outside the city. Ballesteros
was, as always in Spain, the favourite to
win but although he holed a 30-yards
blind approach shot at the third of the
Shoot-Out holes, the Spaniard came a
cropper at the next and was
followed into the clubhouse in quick
succesion by four of his Ryder Cup
team mates – Ian Woosnam, Steven
Richardson, David Feherty and Nick
Faldo. At the last the defending Peugeot
Spanish Open champion Eduardo
Romero and Lyle again were left. This
time Romero holed from 40 feet to win
but, unlike Lyle in Italy, the popular
Argentinian did not go on to win the
Spanish title for a second year running.

The next Shoot-Out was an eight-
man affair prior to the Volvo PGA
Championship at Wentworth where the
contestants were trying to win the biggest
share of a £30,000 jackpot for the

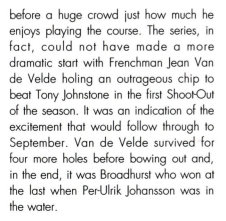

John Paramor explains the format to Bernhard Langer,
Anders Forsbrand and Steven Richardson.

Star-studded Shoot-Out line-up at
the Volvo PGA Championship.

charity of their choice. The holes selected were the first three and the last four on the West course, and the big winner for the Cystic Fibrosis Trust was Richardson who beat Langer with a chip to two feet in their last hole shoot-out. Richardson handed over a £12,000 cheque to June Reynolds of the Trust while Langer made £6,500 for the Diabetic Care Unit at Charing Cross Hospital, his chosen charity. Faldo finished third having narrowly lost a shoot-out at the penultimate hole. He made £3,500 for his own Rainbow House charity which benefited by over £40,000 later in the year when his wife Gill and Cathy Chapman, wife of Roger, were the guiding lights in a hugely successful fashion show and dinner.

Gary Nicklaus, second youngest of the four sons of Jack Nicklaus, designer of Gut Altentann, venue of the Mitsubishi Austrian Open, competed in the fifth Canon Shoot-Out but did not win. It was third time lucky for Johansson who splashed expertly out of a bunker at the last to beat reigning Austrian champion Mark Davis to the £2,500 prize.

With defending champion, American

Payne Stewart, former Open champion Ian Baker-Finch, Langer, Jose Maria Olazabal and Lyle in the line-up for the sixth Shoot-Out at Noordwijkse before the Heineken Dutch Open, the chances of local star Chris van der Velde winning should have prompted longish odds from any bookmakers around but the Dutchman survived to win at the last with a 70 foot putt which finished off Baker-Finch effectively enough.

There were just two more Shoot-Outs before the big final at Crans and the seventh of the season at Munchen Nord-Eichenreid in Germany provided another home winner. In the end Langer found himself up against the American Tour's top shoot-out expert Corey Pavin, a winner of the German Open in the early 1980s when he played regularly in Europe. Langer had survived seven of the eight shoot-outs at earlier holes before producing the *coup de gras* – an eagle at the difficult par five last. Later in the week Langer would be involved in the five way play-off won by Pavin's Ryder Cup team mate Paul Azinger, something of a course expert with a win and second-place finish

in previous years.

Bad weather prompted a reduction of the final Canon Shoot-Out at The Belfry prior to the Murphy's English Open to just seven holes with two players being eliminated at the first two holes.

So far two Englishmen, Broadhurst and Richardson, a Scot, Lyle, an Argentinian, Romero, Swede, Johansson, Dutchman van der Velde and a German, Langer, had won to ensure the 1992 Shoot-Out series had been a truly international affair. And a new nationality was added to the winners' roll when Australian Rodger Davis took first prize when he managed a superb birdie at the famous tenth hole at The Belfry which Johansson could only par.

So to the grand final, and a class winner in Ballesteros, back in action after a much-needed three-week break from golf. He was at his most ebullient and, in the end, claimed long-time rival Langer as his final victim in a last hole shoot-out to win the £16,000 prize and bring another successful Canon Shoot-Out series to an impressive finish in outstandingly beautiful surroundings.

ON THE LEARNING CURVE

This year's Apollo Week at the San Roque Club in Spain near Gibraltar, served to confirm just how precarious the career of a Tour professional can be.

By its very nature, the seven-day training seminar for Volvo Tour professionals attracts many newer members of the Tour. Typically, they are young, tasting life on the Tour for the first time, burning with ambition.

So called because it is sponsored by the shaft manufacturer of that name, the Apollo Week has been held annually for the past four years and offers the players expert advice and training in all aspects of tournament golf.

Present this year were coaches Bob Torrance – mentor of Ian Woosnam, Sam Torrance and David Feherty – Tommy Horton, the former Ryder Cup player, and Gary Smith, a member of the David Leadbetter coaching team. Alan Fine, a noted sports psychologist was also on hand to offer advice regarding the mental approach to the game and Ted Pollard, an acknowledged expert in physical fitness, held daily training sessions. John Paramor and his team from the PGA European Tour were also there to extend the players' knowledge of the Rules.

So what could be better for a young player on the brink of a successful new career? Already blessed with enough natural ability to make it to the Tour, the Apollo Week offers them a chance to hone their skills still further with some of the top coaches, and it provides them with a week away in the sun.

The Apollo Week at the San Roque Club provided some solid grounding for the aspirants on the Volvo Tour

'It's great,' enthused Stephen Field. 'Alan Fine has really helped me with some thoughts for when I'm playing badly, and I've been very impressed with Gary Smith this week. He seems to make a lot of sense.'

Yet the presence of some more experienced players among the field of 23 was a stark reminder of what might lie ahead. These players were attending the Apollo Week in the hope of picking up a vital tip that would make a welcome improvement in their game during the coming year.

They included Philip Parkin, who's played the PGA European Tour since 1984 and is desperately seeking ways of making more than four cuts in 12 months,

as he did in 1991, and Jeremy Robinson, who turned professional in 1987 and has returned to the PGA European Tour Qualifying School every year since then.

And the presence of two players who have previously shown some winning pedigree – albeit at the PGA European Tour Qualifying School – also highlighted how quickly fortunes can change.

One was Andrew Hare, the promising 24-year-old embarking on his first season on the Volvo Tour after winning last year's PGA Qualifying School in Montpelier. The other was Heinz-Peter Thuel, who came top of the class three years ago.

Hare must be hoping that any similarities between his career and Thuel's end there, for the German has just £17,000 in career earnings to show for eight years of hard grind.

Since first qualifying for the Tour in 1983 he has had to return to the Qualifying School every year. In 1990, the year following his first place at the Qualifying School, Thuel finished in 189th position on the Order of Merit – well outside the top 120 exempt places. 'I played some of my best golf at the Qualifying School in 1989 and I hoped to keep that level up – that was my big mistake,' he recalled.

Hare has experienced the downside of professional golf, too, and has been forced to come to similar conclusions about the game. He failed to claim one of the 50 cards that were on offer at the

Qualifying Schools in 1989 and 1990 by finishing 98th and 59th respectively. He puts that down lack of experience in handling professional golf pressures. 'I've probably taken a while to mature in that respect,' he said. 'But I've since learnt that I must take each day as it comes.'

Like Thuel, he sees the Apollo Week as an ideal opportunity to get his game into the best possible shape for the coming season, although he knows he cannot be falsely optimistic. 'I'm really glad I·came out here,' he said. 'I hope it will boost my year but I don't really set myself any targets; I just go out to do my best. To keep my card will be nice – anything else will be a bonus.'

Part of the reason for the optimism, felt Hare, is that he is one of a new breed of golfer emerging from the increasingly competitive amateur scene. 'The amateur game has improved vastly and is now more geared towards turning pro. The top amateurs are as good if not better than the average Challenge Tour player now. There are some tremendously talented individuals at the top end.'

And Hare's amateur track record takes some beating. He played for England Boys' and Schools' in 1983, was Captain of both in 1984. He gained Youths' honours in 1987 and, in 1988, full England honours. In 1989 he represented Great Britain and Ireland in the victorious Walker Cup team.

Yet Hare believes that if he does avoid a fate similar to Thuel's, it will be down to his experience of the Challenge Tour, where his results were rather more modest, rather than his seasoning as an amateur. 'My two years' experience on the Challenge Tour were invaluable,' he said. 'You play week in, week out against a lot of guys who are very good. And the scores are nearly the same as those on the Volvo Tour. I finished 15th and 16th the past two years on the Challenge Tour and last season I counted 398 guys on the Tour, so it's good competition. Playing it has without doubt made me a harder, better player.'

It was a sentiment that was expressed by other players at Apollo Week, too. 'I think the players from the Challenge Tour are so strong enough that 20, not ten, should qualify for the Volvo Tour,' noted the young Swiss player, Paolo Quirici.

The players believe the Challenge Tour

Rules queries are handled by the Tour's John Paramor.

should continue to grow and gain in stature. 'In the long term it would be good for the game to have a stronger Challenge Tour,' said Hare. 'I don't think David Jones has had the coverage he should have done for winning the Challenge Tour last year, because it is a year's golf.'

There is no doubt that the Challenge Tour and events like Apollo Week are helping reduce the element of luck in a professional's career by increasing the quantity and the quality of available training and preparation.

'I've had a quiet winter because I've had no chance to hit balls with the weather we've had back home,' noted Stephen Field. 'It's my first time at Apollo Week but I'll be coming back.'

Paolo Quirici also believed Apollo Week had enhanced his preparations for this year. 'Apollo Week is a good thing because it gives me the chance to see people like Bob Torrance and to talk with Alan Fine about my mental attitude for the coming season,' he said.

So even if these young hopefuls don't know what the future holds for them, they can take some comfort from the fact that they are better prepared for the rigours of the Volvo Tour than the players before them.

Tommy Horton instructs on the short game.

PALMER
IN CHARGE

Another Palmer rose to the top when the 1992 Volvo Tour commenced in steamy Bangkok

O ut of Africa, into Asia, and straight to the top of the Volvo Tour rankings is an achievement that Ian Palmer will savour for the rest of his golf career.

It was certainly not the expected scenario when the 1992 Volvo Tour began in Bangkok with Johnnie Walker's lavish Asian Classic at the Pinehurst club, especially as five of the world's top ten and eight of the 1991 Johnnie Walker European Ryder Cup team were assembled in the Thai capital.

The world-beating quartet of Seve Ballesteros, Ian Woosnam, Nick Faldo and Bernhard Langer and Volvo Masters champion Rodger Davis were rightly regarded as the leading contenders for the £83,330 first prize. Should they falter, Steven Richardson, Colin Montgomerie, Paul Broadhurst and Sam Torrance were ready to stake their claim for early honours and a place in Johnnie Walker's end-of-season World Championship. Ronan Rafferty, already a winner in Australia, and Mike Harwood and Peter Senior, the former Volvo PGA and GA European Open champions, had also flown in from 'down under' to complete a formidable line-up which also contained Japan's legendary Isao Aoki, and the best Thai players Boonchu Roengkit and Suthep Meesawat.

But Palmer, a 34-year old from Johannesburg who had graduated in ninth place from the previous November's PGA European Tour Qualifying School at Montpellier, had brought his own script. When he found a golf course with barely a tuft of rough, fairways half a mile wide,

and slow, grainy greens, his spirits leapt like a springbok. Neither was he bothered by the 90 degree heat and humidity which hit the unacclimatised Europeans, notably Woosnam who went down with heat exhaustion and a stomach upset after his first round. He was in such distress that he had to be taken to hospital and fed an intravenous drip, happily recovering quickly to complete all four rounds.

For Palmer, the Bangkok Pinehurst was just like home and he fulfilled to the letter Langer's prediction that a 20-under par

total would be the winning score. His experience of greens that exasperated most of the 100-strong European contingent proved invaluable and, when he also displayed a sound temperament, even the German's flair for the big occasion failed to dislodge Palmer from the head of the field.

Langer was making his first appearance since finishing runner-up to Fred Couples for the Johnnie Walker World Championship in Jamaica. Could Europe's man for all seasons go one better this time, even though his preparation had been somewhat unusual? The German golfer had spent the previous week skiing in the sub-zero temperatures of a Colorado resort and, not surprisingly, took time to adjust. Had he been just a trifle sharper he might well have atoned for his Caribbean near miss, but it was short, rather than long iron play that mattered most on the flat Thai course. He began well enough with a 67 that contained six birdies in his first 11 holes, but it still left him four shots off the lead.

That was taken by Richardson who had spent the previous two weeks in South Africa. A readjustment of the distinctive putting style that had taken the Hampshire golfer to second place in the Volvo Order of Merit in 1991 brought an immediate benefit. He firmed up his stroke by tucking his right arm closer to his body, and birdied six of his first eight holes to get out in 30. His 63, matched by Australian Peter O'Malley in the second round, secured them the

first Johnnie Walker Tour Course Record Award of the new season.

Sweden's Mats Lanner, who had spent the previous ten weeks campaigning on the Australian circuit, also began with a flurry of birdies, claiming seven in a 65 that gave him a share of second place with Ballesteros. Next day Lanner delivered another 1992 Volvo Tour first, hitting a perfect five-iron shot to the 16th, that arrowed in on the flag and rolled gently into the cup. Lanner's first ace on Tour won him a cash award of one million bahts, or £23,000 sterling.

Ballesteros had been forced to cut short his preparation because of a sore back which he deemed a legacy of the long flight from Spain. He accepted the offer of a local back specialist to cure his pain – and then wished he had kept silent. The Spaniard described the treatment as being worse than the pain after the Thai medic had put him through an ordeal by fire. 'He filled a glass with alcohol then set fire to it before putting the rim of the hot glass on my back,' reported Seve, as he revealed a kaleidoscope of circular scarlet weals on either side of his spine. He declined the offer of a second session and turned instead to the gentler ministrations of Paul Ankers, the physiologist who had been working on Faldo's wrist and elbow problems.

The quality of Ballesteros's putting had not deteriorated and five birdies plus an eagle three at the 14th enabled the

European number one to present a 65. He and partner Rafferty, who opened with a 67, consumed almost two dozen half-litre bottles of water.

Rafferty talked later about the wall of exhaustion that hit them both after 14 holes. 'After that it was very difficult to summon the effort and concentration and it was just a question of whether you could hang on to the score you had already made,' he said.

That wall fell on Ballesteros in round two when he took 39 strokes for the

inward half in a return of 74, and was effectively out of the hunt. A still woosy Woosnam improved to a 69 and defending champion Faldo to 67 after getting his caddie Fanny Sunesson to squat behind him to check his putting alignment. She moved smartly aside before he began the stroke in order to avoid infringing the rules.

O'Malley's 63 and Brett Ogle's 66 moved them to within a shot of halfway leaders Langer, Richardson and Palmer, who had started the second day with a blistering onslaught. When the later starters arrived Palmer was already 13-under par after 24 holes, having begun with four successive birdies, an eagle, then another birdie. Seven under after six was sensational stuff but then the dream shattered! A bunkered drive at the seventh and three putts at the ninth meant an outward 31. He was home in level par to be 11-under at the midway point.

A third day of oppressive heat resolved itself into a battle of wills

Bernhard Langer, above, at full stretch. Right, hole-in-one beneficiary Mats Lanner and below, Ian Woosnam receives oxygen.

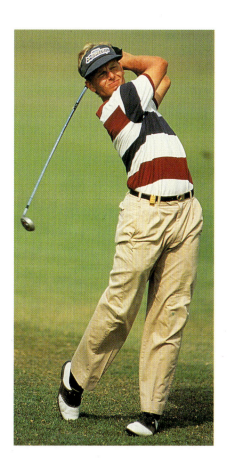

between the ice-cool Langer and the imperturbable South African, with Ogle rapidly making up ground. The slim Australian went out in 33 and the trio were level at the turn at 13 under. Then Langer holed three successive putts of 12 feet for birdies from the 11th only to see Palmer respond with his own birdie hat-trick from the 12th. They stayed level until the 18th where the German three-putted to hand Palmer a priceless one-stroke lead for the final leg. The South African commented: 'It was difficult to play with someone you only see on television but Bernhard was so calm he made me relax. I always felt comfortable and just played it shot for shot.'

For the last round Langer was in the penultimate match and set out with the intention of posting a target the rest could not match. So did Rafferty who had won in Queensland a fortnight before with a closing 65. The Irishman birdied four of the first seven holes to get out in 32, while Langer, three ahead of him at the outset, birdied four of the first five to reach 19 under.

Three putts at the sixth pegged the German to an outward 33, but another birdie from six yards at the tenth left him poised for a victory sprint. Rafferty was also racing, birdies at the tenth and 14th taking him to 18 under, but he could manage only one more in the last four holes, missing from eight feet at the 16th but succeeding from the same range at the long 17th. His splendid 65 for 269 was to leave him just one tantalising stroke short.

Langer's putter also turned tepid when he most needed it, and he missed every birdie chance in the last eight holes. 'I left all the putts into the grain short of the hole,' he lamented.

Behind him, Palmer and Ogle had both gone out in 35, reaching 19 and 18 under with birdies at the 13th. Then Palmer holed the vital putt at the short 16th where his six-iron shot left him 15 feet from the hole. Ogle birdied the 17th which Palmer could not after finding sand from the tee and there was just one stroke between them as they reached the last.

Both drives were perfect and their short iron approaches landed within five yards of the flag. Palmer had no need for heroics but Ogle had to convert his birdie chance to force a play-off. When his putt slid wide the Tour school's old boy had won his colours with remarkable aplomb.

'It's nice to be back with a bang, exclaimed Palmer who played in Europe from 1982 to 1985. 'I have had too many seconds in my career, so to beat so many great players gives me a big thrill. Maybe my best golfing days are not yet over.'

Langer, Rafferty and Ogle tied second with Lanner adding another £21,200 to his hole-in-one award by taking fifth place ahead of Richardson. Ballesteros, Faldo and Woosnam retired to lick their wounds, but at least the Welshman departed with a rare honour.

As a mark of his achievement in capturing the US Masters title of 1991 he was made an Honorary Life Member of the Tour, only the tenth man to be so recognised. It means that Woosnam will be excused in future from paying his annual subscription which currently stands at £117.50.

Last round 65 left Ronan Rafferty one stroke shy.

POS	NAME	CTY	1	2	3	4	TOTAL	PRIZE MONEY
1	Ian PALMER	SA	66	67	67	68	268	£83330
2	Brett OGLE	Aus	68	66	67	68	269	37283
	Bernhard LANGER	Ger	67	66	68	68	269	37283
	Ronan RAFFERTY	N.Ire	67	68	69	65	269	37283
5	Mats LANNER	Swe	65	71	67	67	270	21200
6	Steven RICHARDSON	Eng	63	70	69	69	271	17500
7	Peter SENIOR	Aus	67	71	67	67	272	15000
8	Mike McLEAN	Eng	67	69	66	71	273	11825
	Paul WAY	Eng	71	67	69	66	273	11825
10	Danny MIJOVIC	Can	69	69	68	68	274	8470
	John MORSE	USA	69	69	65	69	274	8470
	Mike CLAYTON	Aus	68	69	69	68	274	8470
	Ross McFARLANE	Eng	69	67	67	71	274	8470
	Peter O'MALLEY	Aus	71	63	71	69	274	8470
	Anders FORSBRAND	Swe	68	68	69	69	274	8470
16	Sam TORRANCE	Scot	70	68	71	66	275	6900
	Boonchu ROENGKIT	Thai	68	69	68	70	275	6900
18	Gordon J BRAND	Eng	69	69	68	70	276	6216
	Frank NOBILO	NZ	69	72	64	71	276	6216
	Daniel SILVA	Port	68	71	69	68	276	6216
21	Suthep MEESAWAT	Thai	68	69	72	68	277	5325
	Jorge BERENDT	Arg	70	66	72	69	277	5325
	Sang Ho CHOI	Kor	71	70	69	67	277	5325
	Mike HARWOOD	Aus	68	70	68	71	277	5325
	Wayne RILEY	Aus	71	69	67	70	277	5325
	Wen Teh LU	Tai	69	70	68	70	277	5325
	Colin MONTGOMERIE	Scot	68	69	72	68	277	5325
	Nick FALDO	Eng	71	67	72	67	277	5325
29	Adam HUNTER	Scot	66	70	70	72	278	4187
	Aaron MEEKS	USA	70	70	70	68	278	4187
	Rodger DAVIS	Aus	69	69	70	70	278	4187
	Frankie MINOZA	Phil	68	72	66	72	278	4187
	Phillip PRICE	Wal	67	71	67	73	278	4187
	Chih-Chen LIN	Tai	68	69	73	68	278	4187
	Hideki KASE	Jap	67	71	70	70	278	4187
	Nandesena PERERA	Sri	69	68	68	73	278	4187
37	Liam WHITE	Eng	70	70	71	68	279	3400
	Vijay SINGH	Fij	68	67	71	73	279	3400
	Paul McGINLEY	Ire	69	70	71	69	279	3400
	Eoghan O'CONNELL	Ire	70	70	70	69	279	3400
	Jose COCERES	Arg	72	69	69	69	279	3400
	James SPENCE	Eng	70	65	74	70	279	3400
	Prayad MARKSAENG	Thai	69	70	67	73	279	3400
44	Marimuthu RAMAYAH	Mal	69	71	69	71	280	2750
	Patrick HALL	Eng	72	67	72	69	280	2750
	Barry CONSER	USA	68	70	67	75	280	2750
	Jimmy HEGGARTY	N.Ire	70	70	72	68	280	2750
	Stephen McALLISTER	Scot	69	70	68	73	280	2750
	Seve BALLESTEROS	Sp	65	74	69	72	280	2750
50	Desmond TERBLANCHE	SA	70	70	70	71	281	2100
	Miguel Angel JIMENEZ	Sp	70	66	70	75	281	2100
	Steven BOWMAN	USA	69	69	71	72	281	2100
	Kyi Hla HAN	Bur	69	71	69	72	281	2100
	Gerry NORQUIST	USA	69	68	75	69	281	2100
	Gary EVANS	Eng	70	71	69	71	281	2100
	Roger CHAPMAN	Eng	75	65	70	71	281	2100
57	Tony MALONEY	Aus	71	70	69	72	282	1533
	Jim RUTLEDGE	Can	71	70	72	69	282	1533
	Robert KARLSSON	Swe	71	66	68	77	282	1533
	Isao AOKI	Jap	69	71	71	71	282	1533
	Per HAUGSRUD	Nor	70	69	74	69	282	1533
	Ian WOOSNAM	Wal	71	69	71	71	282	1533
63	Ross DRUMMOND	Scot	69	71	71	72	283	1300
	Peter LONARD	Aus	69	71	73	70	283	1300
	Orrin VINCENT III	USA	72	68	71	72	283	1300
66	Robin MANN	Eng	69	71	72	73	285	748
	Wen-Sheng LI	Tai	71	67	76	71	285	748
	Chris MOODY	Eng	71	70	71	73	285	748
69	Paul MOLONEY	Aus	72	69	71	74	286	744
70	Kevin DICKENS	Eng	68	73	71	75	287	741
	David J RUSSELL	Eng	68	71	73	75	287	741

COURSE: PINEHURST G&CC   DATE: 30.1-2.2   YARDAGE: 6851   PAR: 72

JOHNNIE WALKER AND THE RYDER CUP

The Ryder Cup, first played for in 1927, has become the world's most prestigious team golf event now contested by the top professionals from Europe and the USA.

BALLESTEROS STORMS TO DESERT VICTORY

Severiano Ballesteros made it 50 PGA European Tour titles in 17 years when he edged out Ronan Rafferty in a play-off over the Emirates course

Using his number two golf swing, because he had left number one behind on the practice ground, Seve Ballesteros demonstrated in the Dubal Desert Classic tournament in Dubai how sheer determination and will-power sometimes drive him on to victory against seemingly impossible odds.

Ballesteros had set his heart on winning the Desert Classic title on the fabulous Emirates GC course and not even a brilliant spell of golf from the in-form Ronan Rafferty, who birdied two of the last three holes, could stop him. Seve wanted that title badly and he produced a devastating display of putting in the final round to close Rafferty out in extra time.

It gave the proud Spaniard his 50th victory in Europe, his 87th in all, and extended his own Volvo Tour record of winning a tournament in each of his last 17 seasons. But those achievements, magnificent as they are, were not behind his burning desire for victory that particular week in the desert sands of the United Arab Emirates.

The desire was to prove to himself that he could still win against a top quality field with a game in far from peak condition. Indeed, Ballesteros readily admitted he had been looking ahead to the US Masters in Augusta by experimenting quite drastically with his swing and practising for hours to perfect a right-to-left tee shot. This, he said, was the secret to winning a third Masters because right-to-left tee shots reduced all the par five holes to two-shotters.

So with his mind very much on Augusta in the early February sunshine of Dubai, Ballesteros spent hours hitting right-to-left driver shots on the Emirates practice ground. Those who had watched him, including many admiring professionals, conceded they were probably watching this week's winner. But those who then followed him to the first tee for the start of the third round, as Welsh World Cup player Philip Parkin had done, saw a different side to the man widely regarded as the finest golfer in the world.

Ballesteros, after a couple of majestic practice swings, snap-hooked his opening third round tee shot to within four feet of the out-of-bounds fence and told faithful caddie Billy Foster: 'It's not working. We've got to re-think our ideas and play with what we've got.'

That's where his number two swing came in handy. Although Ballesteros had continued to mould his number one Augusta swing on the practice ground, once he stepped onto the first tee he reverted to the method which had earned him tournament victories all over the world. His Desert Classic examination was as difficult and as searching as any he was likely to face in the Volvo Tour season because the quality of the field was superb. Sony Ranking number one and US Masters champion Ian Woosnam was there, plus double Open champion and double US Masters winner Nick Faldo – and another eight current Johnnie Walker Ryder Cup players.

All of Europe's leading players expressed their pleasure at being back in Dubai for the third Desert Classic following the cancellation of the 1991 tournament because of the Gulf War. The Emirates GC course, the first grass course to be built in the Gulf States, opened in 1988 and won instant world-wide acclaim for its condition, practice facilities and climate. To a man, the players heaped praise on their own PGA

European Tour officials for arranging a tournament on such a fine course so early in the season.

Most arrived in Dubai via Bangkok, where the opening Volvo Tour event had been played. Others drifted in from various parts of the world to start the new season. Defending champion Eamonn Darcy was flown from London to Dubai by his caddie, Emirates Airline captain Mike Sadler, while the first Desert Classic winner, Mark James, suffered a gruelling three-day journey from his home in Yorkshire because of the unpredictable English weather. He was not at all optimistic about his chances following a three-month break from competitive golf and declared himself to be rusty and jaded. Yet he was quickly off the mark with a run of seven birdies in the space of 11 holes in the first round en route to a 67, which he followed with a 68. David Curry, the former Amateur champion, had two 68s. Anders Forsbrand started with a 68 and then added a 66.

But they were clutching at Ballesteros's slipstream. He led after 36 holes, with rounds of 66 and 67. To the end he would maintain that he lacked confidence, yet he played some wonderful strokes, strokes that were hardly those of a diffident man. The first was a 180-yard bunker shot to within six feet in his first round. He sank the putt.

Next day he demonstrated more of the same. He hit a four iron from 180 yards so close to its target the ball was left hanging over the lip of the hole. On the ninth he hit a three iron to within a few feet so a birdie was a formality. There was no doubt this was to be Ballesteros's week, particularly after he recovered from that potentially disastrous opening tee shot in the third round to record a 69.

The final round, played beneath clear blue skies in a warm, gentle breeze, was full of drama. Again, Ballesteros was quickly in trouble, hooking his three-iron tee shot out of bounds at the second and soon seeing his one-stroke lead become a two-stroke deficit, benefiting playing companion Rafferty. It was at that point that Ballesteros began to draw on all his reserves and skills and set about the task

Ronan Rafferty and Severiano Ballesteros keep their hands in.

Clubhouse at the Emirates GC.

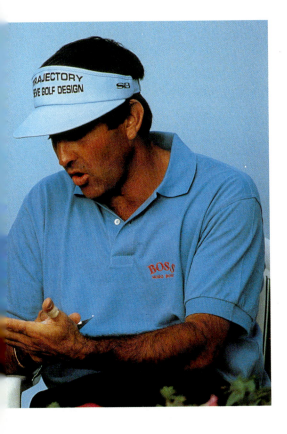

Left, Isao Aoki thinks Ballesteros used to be much taller. Below, Nick Faldo and Mark James discuss damaged ball.

Ballesteros was beached on the 10th.

of winning the tournament. With six holes to play, he was still two shots behind Rafferty and he effectively single-putted them all to tie on 16-under-par 272 and force a play-off. Rafferty, remarkably, had birdied two of the last three holes yet was about to finish a runner-up.

The play-off holes were the 17th and 18th. The first was halved in par but at the long 18th it was Ballesteros again who secured the crucial birdie four, this time for a £58,330 victory. Rafferty, for the second time in half-an-hour had taken a regulation par five, and for the second week running had finished a runner-up.

Many a professional golfer might have

been devastated by the experience of losing a title after scoring two birdies in his last three holes on his way to a closing 69. But not Rafferty. This exceptionally talented Northern Ireland professional, back on song after a miserable 1991 season, not only accepted defeat with good grace, he actually told the world's Press that he thought Seve Ballesteros was the best golfer in the world.

Third placed David Feherty
recovers from sand.

'With all respect to Ian Woosnam and the world rankings, Seve is the best as far as I'm concerned,' he said. 'He's a wonderful strokemaker and pulls out all the shots when he needs them. Even when he's playing badly, he's so graceful on the ball.'

Those who saw Ballesteros maintain his 17-year winning record could not have agreed more.

Top, Rafferty looks to Mecca.

Above, 'What, no coffee?' as the

winner examines his prize.

COURSE: EMIRATES G. C. DUBAI	DATE: 6-9.2		YARDAGE: 72				PAR: 72	
POS NAME	**CTY**	**1**	**2**	**3**	**4**	**TOTAL**	**PRIZE MONEY**	
1 Seve BALLESTEROS	Sp	66	67	69	70	272	£58330	
2 Ronan RAFFERTY	N.Ire	66	70	67	69	272	38880	
3 David FEHERTY	N.Ire	69	69	68	69	275	19705	
Mark JAMES	Eng	67	68	71	69	275	19705	
5 Nick FALDO	Eng	70	68	69	69	276	14830	
6 Mike McLEAN	Eng	67	71	68	71	277	9830	
Ian WOOSNAM	Wal	70	67	70	70	277	9830	
Barry LANE	Eng	69	69	72	67	277	9830	
Isao AOKI	Jap	68	69	73	67	277	9830	
10 Jorge BERENDT	Arg	70	70	69	69	278	7000	
11 David CURRY	Eng	68	68	71	72	279	6030	
Anders FORSBRAND	Swe	68	66	73	72	279	6030	
Peter BAKER	Eng	74	71	66	68	279	6030	
14 Per-Ulrik JOHANSSON	Swe	67	70	72	71	280	5036	
Stephen McALLISTER	Scot	68	74	68	70	280	5036	
Stephen BENNETT	Eng	68	70	71	71	280	5036	
Gordon BRAND Jnr	Scot	68	71	71	70	280	5036	
18 Joakim HAEGGMAN	Swe	71	71	69	70	281	4351	
Jose COCERES	Arg	67	70	71	73	281	4351	
James SPENCE	Eng	68	70	71	72	281	4351	
21 Glen DAY	USA	70	74	66	72	282	3832	
Roger CHAPMAN	Eng	72	70	70	70	282	3832	
Anders SORENSEN	Den	71	70	70	71	282	3832	
Russell CLAYDON	Eng	72	68	70	72	282	3832	
David GILFORD	Eng	71	71	70	70	282	3832	
Des SMYTH	Ire	67	69	75	71	282	3832	
27 Andrew MURRAY	Eng	71	72	69	71	283	3360	
Miguel Angel JIMENEZ	Sp	74	71	64	74	283	3360	
Steven RICHARDSON	Eng	72	70	72	69	283	3360	
30 Peter TERAVAINEN	USA	75	68	71	71	285	2775	
Ross DRUMMOND	Scot	71	74	69	71	285	2775	
David J RUSSELL	Eng	69	68	76	72	285	2775	
Patrick HALL	Eng	68	69	75	73	285	2775	
Paul WAY	Eng	69	73	71	72	285	2775	
Mats HALLBERG	Swe	73	70	73	69	285	2775	
Jose Manuel CARRILES	Sp	69	71	74	71	285	2775	
Steen TINNING	Den	72	72	72	69	285	2775	
Vijay SINGH	Fij	71	68	75	71	285	2775	
Paul BROADHURST	Eng	68	73	70	74	285	2775	
40 Robert KARLSSON	Swe	70	75	70	71	286	2275	
Colin MONTGOMERIE	Scot	73	68	73	72	286	2275	
Rick HARTMANN	USA	71	71	72	72	286	2275	
Carl MASON	Eng	71	68	70	77	286	2275	
44 Gordon J BRAND	Eng	71	72	72	72	287	2030	
Mark ROE	Eng	71	73	71	72	287	2030	
Bill MALLEY	USA	68	71	73	75	287	2030	
47 Lucien TINKLER	Aus	71	72	71	74	288	1715	
Per HAUGSRUD	Nor	72	73	75	68	288	1715	
Marc FARRY	Fr	71	73	70	74	288	1715	
Phillip PRICE	Wal	73	69	72	74	288	1715	
Chris VAN DER VELDE	Hol	69	73	70	76	288	1715	
Darren CLARKE	N.Ire	73	71	75	69	288	1715	
53 Paul McGINLEY	Ire	70	72	71	76	289	1400	
Glenn RALPH	Eng	74	71	72	72	289	1400	
Magnus PERSSON	Swe	72	73	72	72	289	1400	
56 Fredrik LINDGREN	Swe	72	72	76	70	290	1141	
David WILLIAMS	Eng	72	73	71	74	290	1141	
Roger WINCHESTER	Eng	68	74	76	72	290	1141	
David R JONES	Eng	71	73	72	74	290	1141	
John HAWKSWORTH	Eng	74	70	75	71	290	1141	
61 Paul LAWRIE	Scot	70	72	79	70	291	980	
Michael ARCHER	Eng	75	70	75	71	291	980	
Mats LANNER	Swe	68	74	73	76	291	980	
64 Malcolm MACKENZIE	Eng	73	71	76	72	292	770	
Christy O'CONNOR Jnr	Ire	69	70	75	78	292	770	
Brian BARNES	Scot	73	72	68	79	292	770	
67 Bernard GALLACHER	Scot	72	73	77	71	293	522	
Jim PAYNE	Eng	73	71	73	76	293	522	
69 Martin GATES	Eng	75	70	71	78	294	519	
70 Kevin DICKENS	Eng	75	70	75	76	296	517	
71 Jeremy ROBINSON	Eng	69	71	82	75	297	515	

SINGH'S 66 SWINGS IT

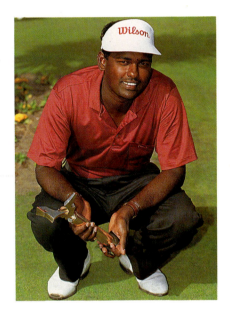

A final round of 66 was enough to give Vijay Singh the third Volvo Tour title of his career

Spain was a sporting paradise in 1992 and golf was at the forefront of the Iberian international celebrations. Barcelona staged the Olympic Games, Seville had its stunning Expo, and the capital Madrid rejoiced as Europe's City of Culture in marking the Quincentenary of the discovery of the New World by Columbus.

Yet it was golf, as played by the best on the Volvo Tour which provided the overture and gave the other Spanish regions their chance to join in the sporting fiesta.

Tourism is the nation's biggest industry so it was a natural step, even in a time of recession, for the Spanish National Tourist Board to make the commitment that justified the PGA European Tour's faith in early season events in southern Europe.

The Turespana circuit of five tournaments was launched with the Turespana Masters – Open de Andalucia, the first of the joint ventures between the national and regional governments. The pattern was repeated in Tenerife, Valencia, the Balearics and finally Catalonia, with the Tourist Board investing over £2 million during 1992, and promising a similar sum in the subsequent two years. Along with the tournaments went follow-up promotions in the northern European nations. The Turespana initiative was given enthusiastic support by Spain's incomparable golf ambassadors, Severiano Ballesteros and Jose Maria Olazabal, who both competed at the Paradores Club de Campo in Malaga.

Ballesteros had arrived on the wings of

a hard-won 50th European victory in the Dubai Desert Classic at the Emirates club. It was the 11th play-off of his illustrious career and he was rapidly installed as favourite for the first Spanish 'Masters'. His Arabian achievement was marked by the presentation of a celebration cake by Tournament Director Andy McFee, but Ballesteros found the Malaga course much less appetising after the lush oasis of Dubai.

The transition to a bouncy, narrow links-type course was a near impossibility

and he finished 25th. His consolation after an opening round of 78 was that his cheque for £2,835 was enough to make him the first player to win £3 million on the European Tour.

Olazabal was making his first appearance of the year after a two months' break during which he had spurned chances to play in South Africa and in the new Johnnie Walker World Championship in Jamaica. He had undergone acupuncture treatment in Japan for a neck muscle injury and it still bothered him when he began practice early in the new year. He tied for 17th place, one shot better than Ballesteros on 289.

The re-emergence of England's Richard Boxall also created considerable interest. He had been forced off the Volvo Tour for seven months after suffering a stress fracture of his left leg during the third round of the Open Championship at Royal Birkdale. Not surprisingly the popular 'Boxy', who had won the Lancia-Martini Italian Open two years previously, was apprehensive as he embarked on his comeback. 'I felt very edgy and it was very difficult to commit myself,' he said. 'I was scared of hitting that first shot.' Boxall exceeded his expectations by completing all four rounds, his best being a four-under-par 68 on the second day.

Another English golfer, one with much less experience but a similar background, was to make a major impact on an event in which the outcome was in doubt until the closing holes. The title was taken by Fiji's Vijay Singh, but Gary Evans from Worthing, shortly to celebrate his 23rd

Anders Forsbrand in supplicatory mode after missed putt.

birthday, almost made it a rookie triumph in what was only his third Volvo Tour professional event.

The blond Evans showed that the 1991 PGA European Tour Qualifying School may be remembered for a vintage crop of graduates when he shot a record 65 in the third round containing eleven birdies. Ten of them came in the space of 11 holes after he had dropped three shots to the card in the first three through misdirected drives. His round won him the Johnnie Walker Tour Course Record Award of £4,000.

'Good Evans' said the headlines as Gary revealed that the putter he had employed with such panache had once been used by Tony Jacklin. The youngster who had played in the previous season's Walker Cup match and then finished fourth in the School at Montpellier had acquired it during a schoolboy tournament at Valderrama when the former Open champion was based there. 'I wanted to buy a Ping Anser and they took it out of Tony's own golf bag' he recalled. 'I am sure he does not know that it ended up with me.'

Evans went on to be runner-up, quickly ensuring he would retain his Volvo Tour place for 1993 with a cheque of more than £33,000 and was followed by Andrew Hare, who had played in the winning 1989 Walker Cup team against the USA and had won the 1991 School. It was significant that both had learned their golf at seaside courses, Evans on the Channel coast at Worthing, and Hare at Sleaford.

Wind was to be a factor from the start as the 'terral' from the Malaga mountains had the big names running up big scores in the first round. It blew strongly across most holes and the combination of narrow fairways and small greens led to numerous tales of woe. Ballesteros began with a six, ended with four bogeys in a row and counted five triple

Severiano Ballesteros in silhouette.

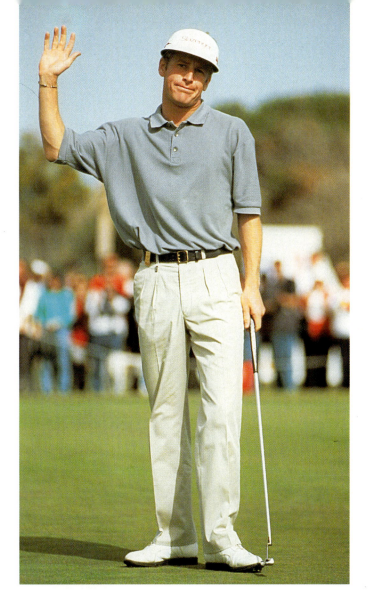

*Richard Boxall, centre,
returned to the fray.*

*Gary Evans, left, took the Johnnie
Walker Tour Course Record Award.*

*Sign language from local
steward.*

putts. Steven Richardson, second on the Volvo Order of Merit to the Spaniard in 1991, began with an 82 and Colin Montgomerie, who was fourth, had 80. A total of 240 strokes for such a trio made the pace-setting 68 by Michael McLean look positively inspired.

Richardson three-putted on six occasions while Montgomerie had four putts on the short ninth before withdrawing because of influenza symptoms.

McLean's two-shot lead over the Dutch-American Chris Van der Velde owed everything to his first professional hole-in-one at the 214-yards 11th with a two iron, to which he added three birdies in the last five holes. Sweden's Anders Forsbrand was the only other player to better the par of 72.

Mark James had emerged from his winter hibernation to share third place in Dubai but the problems of chipping from bare lies to the small firm greens, and his inconsistent putting when he got there, led him to withdraw despite having qualified for the final 36 holes. Five putts on the fifth green were probably instrumental, but James took advantage of a change in the

regulations that permits such withdrawals.

Evans, who had opened with rounds of 73 and 69, made the course look easy on a sunny Saturday, twice narrowly failing to equal two of Europe's scoring records. He had seven birdies in a row from the eighth to the 14th, one less than the best at that point shared by Ballesteros, Tony Johnstone, and Ian Woosnam. His grand total of 11 birdies was one below the round dozen recorded by Fred Couples in the inaugural Scandinavian Masters. Evans's record enabled him to begin the last round with a three-stroke lead over Anders Forsbrand and Singh and Hare one stroke further back at five under par.

One birdie and one bogey in a regulation outward 35 kept the English rookie in front, but Forsbrand and Singh were both out in 33 and the tall Fijian closed the gap when he birdied the 13th and 14th. The title was then effectively decided at the 16th, a reachable par five directly towards the shore.

Singh was home with a two iron and holed from some ten yards for an eagle three whereas Evans cut his long iron approach into the bunker short of the green. He thinned his recovery over the green and took three more to get down.

The three shot swing left Singh with the simplest of tasks to record his second success in Spain – he had won the El Bosque Open two years previously – although he had an alarm at the 17th. There he hooked into the base of a bush and looked set to drop at least one stroke. Fortunately for Singh, a television gantry was between his ball and the green and he was able to claim, and receive, line of sight relief under the standing local rule covering such matters.

He made his par four, and although Evans birdied the hole, Singh had no difficulty in securing par at the last to win by two strokes. Hare and Forsbrand tied

ESPAÑA

Pass for life

Spanish favourite Ballesteros

drives in wooded setting.

Third place for
Andrew Hare.

Vijay Singh lined up
another title.

third, one ahead of American Jay Townsend who followed an opening 75° with three rounds of 69.

Experience had once again triumphed over the exuberance of youth, but Evans was unabashed. 'I have learnt a lot and my day will come' he declared.

			COURSE: PARADORES CLUB DE CAMPO DE MALAGA					
			DATE: 13-16.2		YARDAGE: 6751		PAR: 72	
POS	**NAME**	**CTY**	**1**	**2**	**3**	**4**	**TOTAL**	**PRIZE MONEY**
1	Vijay SINGH	Fij	72	70	69	66	277	£50000
2	Gary EVANS	Eng	73	69	65	72	279	33330
3	Anders FORSBRAND	Swe	71	70	69	71	281	16890
	Andrew HARE	Eng	75	70	66	70	281	16890
5	Jay TOWNSEND	USA	75	69	69	69	282	12700
6	Mike MCLEAN	Eng	68	72	72	71	283	10500
7	Marc FARRY	Fr	73	75	68	68	284	8250
	Jose Maria CANIZARES	Sp	75	72	68	69	284	8250
9	Paul BROADHURST	Eng	75	72	71	67	285	6690
10	Jean VAN DE VELDE	Fr	73	78	66	69	286	6000
11	Fredrik LINDGREN	Swe	74	70	74	69	287	5025
	Jose DAVILA	Sp	74	76	68	69	287	5025
	Malcolm MACKENZIE	Eng	75	74	68	70	287	5025
	Russell CLAYDON	Eng	76	72	68	71	287	5025
15	Christy O'CONNOR Jnr	Ire	72	72	74	70	288	4320
	Daniel SILVA	Port	73	68	74	73	288	4320
17	Ricardo GONZALEZ	Arg	77	71	70	71	289	3592
	Jose Maria OLAZABAL	Sp	75	71	73	70	289	3592
	Liam WHITE	Eng	81	68	73	67	289	3592
	Silvio GRAPPASONNI	It	76	71	74	68	289	3592
	David A RUSSELL	Eng	74	72	72	71	289	3592
	Miguel Angel JIMENEZ	Sp	78	68	72	71	289	3592
	Jon ROBSON	Eng	77	70	72	70	289	3592
	Antonio GARRIDO	Sp	77	73	70	69	289	3592
25	Thomas LEVET	Fr	76	72	71	71	290	2835
	Seve BALLESTEROS	Sp	78	69	73	70	290	2835
	Jose ROZADILLA	Sp	77	70	75	68	290	2835
	Steen TINNING	Den	73	73	72	72	290	2835
	Jeremy ROBINSON	Eng	75	72	71	72	290	2835
	David GILFORD	Eng	73	71	73	73	290	2835
	Gordon BRAND Jnr.	Scot	73	69	74	74	290	2835
	Mark ROE	Eng	76	67	73	74	290	2835
33	Jim RUTLEDGE	Can	75	75	71	70	291	2370
	Chris VAN DER VELDE	Hol	70	75	75	71	291	2370
	Glen DAY	USA	77	71	72	71	291	2370
	Santiago LUNA	Sp	76	72	72	71	291	2370
37	Peter BAKER	Eng	76	69	75	72	292	2190
	Peter SMITH	Scot	79	71	76	66	292	2190
39	Francisco NAVARRO	Sp	77	71	72	73	293	2070
	Olle NORDBERG	Swe	74	70	76	73	293	2070
41	Grant TURNER	Eng	72	72	76	74	294	1920
	Peter TERAVAINEN	USA	75	73	73	73	294	1920
	Derrick COOPER	Eng	76	72	70	76	294	1920
44	Paul LAWRIE	Scot	72	72	76	75	295	1740
	Alfonso PINERO	Sp	80	70	73	72	295	1740
	Mike MILLER	Scot	77	72	72	74	295	1740
47	Heinz P THUEL	Ger	80	71	75	70	296	1440
	Juan QUIROS	Sp	76	69	78	73	296	1440
	Andrew SHERBORNE	Eng	78	69	74	75	296	1440
	Mariano APARICIO	Sp	79	70	75	72	296	1440
	David J RUSSELL	Eng	74	74	73	75	296	1440
	Jose RIVERO	Sp	76	74	74	72	296	1440
	Lucien TINKLER	Aus	72	71	77	76	296	1440
54	Ian SPENCER	Eng	78	73	79	67	297	1170
	Barry LANE	Eng	75	74	76	72	297	1170
56	Patrick HALL	Eng	78	71	76	73	298	926
	Manuel PINERO	Sp	77	74	75	72	298	926
	Eamonn DARCY	Ire	77	73	75	73	298	926
	Robert KARLSSON	Swe	78	72	74	74	298	926
	Stephen FIELD	Eng	74	77	73	74	298	926
	Mats HALLBERG	Swe	72	72	79	75	298	926
	John McHENRY	Ire	77	69	77	75	298	926
	Anssi KANKKONEN	Fin	75	71	76	76	298	926
64	Jose Manuel CARRILES	Sp	79	72	72	78	301	765
	Richard BOXALL	Eng	79	68	78	76	301	765
66	Glenn RALPH	Eng	78	71	79	74	302	449
	Desmond TERBLANCHE	SA	77	74	75	76	302	449
68	Brian MARCHBANK	Scot	74	76	75	78	303	446
69	Mark JAMES	Eng	72	76	W/D		148	444

OLAZABAL MAKES IT TWO OUT OF THREE

Jose Maria Olazabal left a trail of admiration when he walked off with the Turespana Open de Tenerife at Golf del Sur. In one of those rare examples of ascending majesty he began by beating par, then further improved by three and two strokes before departing in a blaze of glory with a record 63.

That gave him a five shot victory over fellow Spaniard, Miguel Angel Martin, with Jose Rivero completing a clean sweep for the home team with a last round 64 that gave him a share of third place with England's Michael McLean. Olazabal's decision to spurn the chance of huge pay-days in South Africa and particularly the first Johnnie Walker World Championship in Jamaica in favour of a long winter break had raised eyebrows among his colleagues.

He did not touch a club for six weeks, spending his rest and recuperation by going hunting in the hills, playing soccer with his friends, visiting the cinema and watching television.

Olazabal does his pre-season training in France, on two of the best seaside courses above Biarritz, at Seignosse where he works on his iron play, and at Hossegor where the springy turf is ideal for fairway woods. Both courses are just a short drive across the Spanish border.

His hands, which have been likened to those of a concert pianist because of his slender fingers, had bled after three weeks on the practice grounds. They were still uncomfortable during his first sortie at Malaga but by the time he

*With a record 63 in
the final round,
Jose Maria Olazabal
captured his second
Tenerife title
in three years*

reached Golf del Sur, Olazabal was ready to start honing his game for another assault on the Volvo Tour.

Yet it was not the Basque who made the fastest start, but Madrid rival Miguel Angel Martin, who started at the tenth on a windy morning with a scarcely believable run of eagle, birdie, bogey followed by a trio of birdies. Martin went on to return a 69 which gave him a one-stroke lead over Argentinian Jorge Berendt and Bill Longmuir, with Malaga runner-up

Gary Evans, Michael McLean, and Olazabal among the other five players to beat par with 71. Olazabal had to thank two putts of 30 feet in his last three holes for bettering the card.

The holiday-making gallery shivered again on Friday when it was almost as windy and the rains came too. It made little difference to the 28-year old Martin who had an eagle and four birdies for the second day running. Three previous second places on the Volvo Tour, most recently in the 1991 Madrid Open to Andrew Sherborne, had left him determined to shrug off his bridesmaid's label. To that end he had recently acquired the same brand of Mizuno clubs as Nick Faldo and declared he was hitting the ball 30 yards further from the tee with a new 'high-tec' driver.

Martin added a 68 to reach seven under at the halfway mark, but was almost caught by Australian Peter Lonard who had a best of the day 67. Lonard from Sydney had survived for another season of exploits in Europe by the slenderest of threads after winning an eight-hole, three-man play-off for the 40th and final card at the previous November's PGA European Tour Qualifying School at Massane. Evans, still on a crest after his outstanding effort in the previous week's Turespana Masters, and that man Olazabal both had 68 to share third place on 139.

Among the flurry of birdies was one of the cheekiest from Ireland's Philip Walton at the par five ninth. He deliberately drove his ball down the road flanking the fairway, reasoning that it would be sure to bounce high enough to clear a low retaining wall and return to grass. Walton's geometric theory proved correct and when he measured his drive at 320 yards he was able to cover the remaining 230 yards to the green with his three wood – QED.

Evans, who was 15 under par for his last five rounds, put his success down to not being overawed by players like Ballesteros, Woosnam and Olazabal, and to his experience of seaside golf gained in his formative years at Worthing. 'I just concentrated on doing the same thing as I learned there,' he said, 'and that is to be sure of hitting the greens.'

For the former Boys', Youths' and Senior England amateur international, the Volvo Tour was a further step in his progression, even if the memory of the many nights he spent stacking shelves in a supermarket was still fresh in his mind. He was already well on the way to Rookie of the Year acclaim.

For Steven Richardson, the sensation of 1991, things were going nowhere near so well. 'I am not at the races at the moment,' he admitted after scrambling past the halfway cut which had claimed him in Malaga. Richardson then showed the form that took him to second place in the Volvo Order of Merit the previous year, by clipping ten shots off his third round score with a last day 64.

Martin's golf was assured once more as he again succeeded in beating his previous round, adding a 67 to reach a 12-under-par 204 after 54 holes. Four birdies in his first seven holes underlined his determination to secure that elusive first title. Olazabal responded with an eagle and six birdies to catch him, but then presented Martin with a lead of one for the last leg by missing the final green. The nearest challengers, McLean and Lonard, were three and five strokes further back with Evans tumbling back into the pack with a run of four bogeys in a 72.

The two Spaniards fought a thrilling duel for supremacy before an enthralled last day audience. Between them they had eight birdies in the first nine holes

which both covered in 33 strokes, Olazabal turning 14 under and Martin 15 below the card. Neither did the pace slacken over the next six.

Olazabal eagled the tenth to draw level, only for Martin to birdie the short 11th and regain the lead. A fourth Olazabal birdie at the 12th put both on 17 under, then came the acceleration into overdrive that sent 'Chema' hurtling to his 12th European victory.

Martin could not match his birdie four at the 14th or another birdie at the almost driveable 15th where Olazabal's chip finished two feet from the hole, and his opponent's scooted to the back of the green. Few can give Olazabal a two stroke leeway for the final three holes, and Martin was not among them. When he drove into sand from the 16th tee and gained only 30 yards with a recovery that needed to hit the green his paella was well and truly cooked. A bogey there and another at the short 17th where his long iron drifted on the wind into sand left Olazabal with a four-stroke lead when he stepped on to the last tee.

It was all over bar the flourish expected of a champion and Olazabal pro-

duced it in the manner of a matador delivering the final thrust. From a fairway bunker some 130 yards from the target, he punched a six-iron level with the flag. Richardson and Rivero, who had got home in 31, had just shot matching records of 64. Olazabal trumped them both with a putt of 25 feet for his seventh birdie of the afternoon to breeze back in 30 for a 63. That gave him victory by five strokes plus £2,000 for the Johnnie Walker Tour Course Record Award.

'It is almost impossible for me to play any better than that,' exclaimed Olazabal. 'But Miguel deserved enormous credit. He gave it everything and would have won any other tournament. He pushed me to the limit and I would not have played so well but for him.'

Martin, consigned to the runner-up role for the fourth time had a look of resignation. 'Maybe I am just unlucky,' he said. 'Chema made so many threes that anyone would think we were playing a par-three course. He was brilliant.'

First hole at Golf del Sur.

*Fly-past
over the course.*

Miguel Angel Martin finished runner-up, right, while Gary Evans, below, had another top ten finish.

POS	NAME	CTY	1	2	3	4	TOTAL	PRIZE MONEY
1	Jose Maria OLAZABAL	Sp	71	68	66	63	268	£50000
2	Miguel Angel MARTIN	Sp	69	68	67	69	273	33330
3	Jose RIVERO	Sp	75	72	69	64	280	16890
	Mike McLEAN	Eng	71	70	67	72	280	16890
5	Joakim HAEGGMAN	Swe	74	71	69	67	281	10733
	James SPENCE	Eng	72	72	67	70	281	10733
	Stephen FIELD	Eng	73	72	67	69	281	10733
8	Philip WALTON	Ire	77	70	68	67	282	7095
	Gary EVANS	Eng	71	68	72	71	282	7095
10	Peter LONARD	Aus	71	67	72	73	283	5760
	Peter MITCHELL	Eng	73	72	71	67	283	5760
12	Mats HALLBERG	Swe	73	70	75	66	284	4995
	Alfonso PINERO	Sp	73	72	66	73	284	4995
14	Costantino ROCCA	It	75	74	69	67	285	4230
	Miguel Angel JIMENEZ	Sp	73	72	73	67	285	4230
	Des SMYTH	Ire	71	73	70	71	285	4230
	Patrick HALL	Eng	76	74	65	70	285	4230
	Roger CHAPMAN	Eng	73	72	66	74	285	4230
19	Manuel PINERO	Sp	72	73	72	69	286	3720
20	Manuel MORENO	Sp	72	71	72	72	287	3375
	Anders SORENSEN	Den	73	74	68	72	287	3375
	Grant TURNER	Eng	77	71	73	66	287	3375
	Ignacio GERVAS	Sp	74	71	73	69	287	3375
	Eamonn DARCY	Ire	74	69	72	72	287	3375
	Russell CLAYDON	Eng	77	72	71	67	287	3375
26	Bill LONGMUIR	Scot	70	76	68	74	288	2835
	Steven RICHARDSON	Eng	78	72	74	64	288	2835
	Mark DAVIS	Eng	74	71	76	67	288	2835
	Peter TERAVAINEN	USA	76	71	71	70	288	2835
	Chris VAN DER VELDE	Hol	73	72	72	71	288	2835
	Gordon J BRAND	Eng	72	78	70	68	288	2835
32	Jimmy HEGGARTY	N.Ire	73	73	72	71	289	2490
	Lucien TINKLER	Aus	74	73	71	71	289	2490
34	Ole ESKILDSEN	Den	74	74	72	70	290	2190
	Antonio GARRIDO	Sp	78	69	71	72	290	2190
	Daniel WESTERMARK	Swe	77	70	74	69	290	2190
	Charles COX	Eng	76	72	71	71	290	2190
	Jose Manuel CARRILES	Sp	77	72	72	69	290	2190
	Neal BRIGGS	Eng	72	75	72	71	290	2190
	Jean Francois REMESY	Fr	74	74	71	69	290	2190
	Ronald STELTEN	USA	76	72	72	70	290	2190
42	David GILFORD	Eng	80	69	73	69	291	1890
	Ross DRUMMOND	Scot	74	75	73	69	291	1890
44	Christy O'CONNOR Jnr	Ire	74	76	71	71	292	1560
	Ricardo GONZALEZ	Arg	75	75	70	72	292	1560
	Santiago LUNA	Sp	77	72	77	66	292	1560
	Mike MILLER	Scot	73	72	75	72	292	1560
	Paul AFFLECK	Wal	77	70	76	69	292	1560
	Ricky WILLISON	Eng	77	70	74	71	292	1560
	Stephen HAMILL	N.Ire	74	74	69	75	292	1560
	Chris WILLIAMS	Eng	79	71	72	70	292	1560
	Heinz P THUEL	Ger	75	70	74	73	292	1560
53	Jorge BERENDT	Arg	70	76	75	72	293	1200
	Anssi KANKKONEN	Fin	80	69	71	73	293	1200
	Robert LEE	Eng	74	74	74	71	293	1200
56	Manuel CALERO	Sp	76	73	72	73	294	1050
	Thomas LEVET	Fr	72	75	74	73	294	1050
58	Andrew MURRAY	Eng	72	74	74	75	295	960
59	Nick JOB	Eng	74	72	78	73	297	915
	Mariano APARICIO	Sp	77	73	75	72	297	915
61	Paolo QUIRICI	Swi	76	74	74	74	298	870
62	Keith WATERS	Eng	75	74	77	73	299	840
63	Kevin DICKENS	Eng	72	76	82	71	301	795
	Dennis EDLUND	Swe	72	78	76	75	301	795
65	Colin GILLIES	Scot	75	74	78	76	303	750
66	Magnus PERSSON	Swe	74	73	74	RETD	221	450

COURSE: GOLF DEL SUR   DATE: 20-23.2   YARDAGE: 6384   PAR: 72

— **41** —

OLAZABAL AT THE DOUBLE

Jose Maria Olazabal made it two victories in a row when he outdistanced the field in Valencia

Like the classic mile runner, Jose Maria Olazabal timed his sprint for the line until the last lap was well under way in the Open Mediterrania at El Bosque. He did not take up the undisputed lead until he had played 11 holes of the final round, then with majestic contempt defied the pursuing pack to come and get him. Not one of them had the heart or the lungs to do it.

The day before the tournament started, Olazabal predicted that it might be won with a total of around 12 under par. He then went out and proved that in addition to his sublime gifts on the golf course he was no slouch as a forecaster, winning with a total of 276 – and that, it almost goes without saying, was 12 under par. It went as it had been written.

In winning for the second week running, Olazabal took his season's earnings to more than £120,000, and brought his career prize money in Europe alone to almost £1.9 million – more than Sam Torrance, more than Mark James, more even than Sandy Lyle, prolific winners all of them – and the sobering thought was that the Spaniard was at the time not yet a month past his 26th birthday.

This was his 13th European victory, and if his final round of 68 was not quite the exercise in total domination that his closing 63 had been the week before in Tenerife, it was still a pretty conclusive performance as he picked up the £66,660 first prize by a couple of strokes from Jose Rivero.

Rivero produced a performance on the demanding El Bosque course that would have won many a tournament. He had a chance to win this one, too; he had to birdie one of the last two holes to force a play-off. Instead, he failed to get up and down from a greenside bunker on the 17th and dropped a shot. Ollie was home and hosed.

Like Severiano Ballesteros, his illustrious compatriot, Olazabal's name alone is becoming enough to freeze the vitals of even the most sanguine of opponents. Who can tell what Rivero might have done on those last two holes had Olazabal not trod that way a few minutes

before? One thing is certain – the bogey-yielding Rivero of the dying half-hour of the tournament was not the rock-solid Rivero who had led going into the last day.

Olazabal's experience was in vivid contrast to that of Ian Woosnam, who had won this tournament in the two years it had previously been staged. Woosnam came to El Bosque feeling just about as disenchanted with his form as it was possible to be. It all stemmed from his putting, he said, and if that was off kilter, everything else was liable to go wonky, too.

He also said that if he lasted the four rounds, he would be much more likely to finish 12 over par. Well, he did, and he didn't quite, but the only time he really hit the headlines throughout the four days was when he was fined £500 by John Paramor, the Tournament Director, for refusing to speak to the press following an unhappy 74 in the first round.

It was a depressed man who fled to the sanctuary of his hotel room that night after scattering putts all round the course with an increasingly desperate prodigality. He finished in 285, three under par but nine shots off the pace – temporarily, at least, the fire had gone out under the little Welshman's boiler.

Another to finish down among the journeymen at the final throw was one Eric Giraud, but the young Frenchman had his moment of glory on the first day as he finished with a 67, including an eagle and three birdies. That was good enough to lead by a stroke from five others, including Olazabal, who offered some high entertainment comprising five birdies and a warmly contested tiff with a spectator on the seventh fairway, who decided he knew more about the game than Olazabal. 'I gave him an ironic reply,' Olazabal said. So that's what they mean by irony.

Giraud went backwards the next day as Rivero, who had had a 69 in the first round, improved by a shot to share the lead with Eamonn Darcy, who equalled the course record with a 66, and Vijay Singh, who had already demonstrated a liking for El Bosque by winning a tournament at the club a couple of years before. They were two shots ahead of Olazabal, who produced a round of 71 that was solid rather than spectacular, but the abiding feeling as darkness fell was that he was still the man to beat.

He looked likely to prove it, too, as he stepped on to the 17th tee the next day level with Rivero at ten under par. However, a flirtation with the siren charms of out of bounds – his ball left the course after a fierce duck hook, hit a tree and bounced back into a hazard – brought a double bogey six, leaving Rivero still in the lead by two and thanking his lucky stars.

All week Rivero had been using a putter that Olazabal had designed and

was preparing to put into production, so there was some satisfaction, however small, to be derived by Olazabal whether he won or lost on the morrow. In the event, defeat was never on the agenda. Challengers came and went as the final day unwound. Christy O'Connor Junior, who had quietly put himself into a challenging position with a pair of 67s in the second and third rounds, looked for a while as though he might steal the candy, only to drop five strokes in four holes coming home. Brett Ogle came in with a 69, Joakim Haeggman a 68. All had their chances, all failed to take them.

Olazabal, meanwhile, was putting five birdies on his card, but could not clock off for the week and take the applause, the trophy and the money while Rivero was still on the course. In the end the 17th, the all-important 17th where the day before he had flirted with disaster and survived, brought his friend and rival to his knees. We should have known. All week Olazabal had been been calling the big plays; he even told us the winning score and acheived it. That's confidence.

Panoramic view of the 18th at El Bosque.

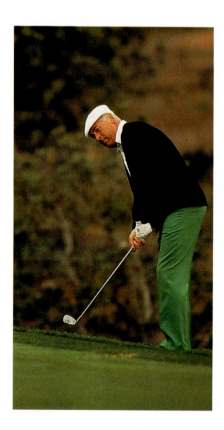

Christy O'Connor Junior chipped into contention. left. Far right, runner-up Jose Rivero.

Peter Baker, Mark Roe and Jose Maria Olazabal in anxious conversation.

								PRIZE
POS	**NAME**	**CTY**	**1**	**2**	**3**	**4**	**TOTAL**	**MONEY**
1	Jose Maria OLAZABAL	Sp	68	71	69	68	276	£66660
2	Jose RIVERO	Sp	69	68	69	72	278	44440
3	Joakim HAEGGMAN	Swe	70	69	72	68	279	25040
4	Costantino ROCCA	It	73	70	67	70	280	16980
	Vijay SINGH	Fij	70	67	71	72	280	16980
	Brett OGLE	Aus	69	71	71	69	280	16980
7	Alberto BINAGHI	It	70	71	67	73	281	12000
8	Christy O'CONNOR Jnr	Ire	74	67	67	74	282	9460
	James SPENCE	Eng	72	68	70	72	282	9460
10	Miguel Angel JIMENEZ	Sp	73	69	69	72	283	6960
	Eamonn DARCY	Ire	71	66	72	74	283	6960
	Mike MCLEAN	Eng	70	69	71	73	283	6960
	Peter BAKER	Eng	69	70	73	71	283	6960
	Colin MONTGOMERIE	Scot	71	73	71	68	283	6960
15	Andrew SHERBORNE	Eng	71	69	74	70	284	5520
	Steven RICHARDSON	Eng	70	71	69	74	284	5520
	Chris VAN DER VELDE	Hol	68	73	73	70	284	5520
	Per-Ulrik JOHANSSON	Swe	71	74	66	73	284	5520
19	Jesper PARNEVIK	Swe	70	74	70	71	285	4688
	Jean VAN DE VELDE	Fr	68	72	73	72	285	4688
	Ian WOOSNAM	Wal	74	70	71	70	285	4688
	Jay TOWNSEND	USA	74	70	69	72	285	4688
	Jose Manuel CARRILES	Sp	71	67	71	76	285	4688
24	Jonathan SEWELL	Eng	74	70	69	73	286	4260
	Jose ROZADILLA	Sp	72	73	70	71	286	4260
26	Martin POXON	Eng	71	73	70	73	287	3840
	Mark DAVIS	Eng	73	71	74	69	287	3840
	Mark ROE	Eng	69	70	73	75	287	3840
	Gordon BRAND Jnr	Scot	74	68	74	71	287	3840
	Glenn RALPH	Eng	74	68	72	73	287	3840
31	Anders FORSBRAND	Swe	73	71	70	74	288	3420
	Steven BOWMAN	USA	72	72	74	70	288	3420
33	David J RUSSELL	Eng	71	71	72	75	289	3080
	Stephen McALLISTER	Scot	74	71	70	74	289	3080
	Barry LANE	Eng	72	70	73	74	289	3080
	Stephen HAMILL	N.Ire	73	70	70	76	289	3080
	Glen DAY	USA	74	68	75	72	289	3080
	Magnus SUNESSON	Swe	72	69	75	73	289	3080
39	Heinz P. THUEL	Ger	71	70	71	78	290	2640
	Santiago LUNA	Sp	72	70	76	72	290	2640
	Peter MITCHELL	Eng	77	68	74	71	290	2640
	Jon ROBSON	Eng	74	69	74	73	290	2640
	Martin GATES	Eng	72	71	73	74	290	2640
44	Antonio GARRIDO	Sp	72	71	74	74	291	2280
	Sam TORRANCE	Scot	74	70	71	76	291	2280
	Daniel SILVA	Port	74	69	72	76	291	2280
	Fredrik LINDGREN	Swe	68	73	75	75	291	2280
48	Jimmy HEGGARTY	N.Ire	69	73	81	69	292	2000
	Gary EVANS	Eng	73	71	73	75	292	2000
	Darren CLARKE	N.Ire	74	71	76	71	292	2000
51	Peter SMITH	Scot	69	76	73	75	293	1640
	Mark MOULAND	Wal	72	72	77	72	293	1640
	Jose DAVILA	Sp	72	71	79	71	293	1640
	Jorge BERENDT	Arg	73	72	74	74	293	1640
	Eric GIRAUD	Fr	67	71	81	74	293	1640
	Andrew HARE	Eng	73	70	77	73	293	1640
57	Jose COCERES	Arg	71	74	78	71	294	1293
	Gavin LEVENSON	SA	74	71	73	76	294	1293
	Robert LEE	Eng	74	70	77	73	294	1293
60	Bill MALLEY	USA	70	72	80	73	295	1160
	Eoghan O'CONNELL	Ire	74	71	76	74	295	1160
	Rick HARTMANN	USA	76	69	78	72	295	1160
63	Brian BARNES	Scot	70	74	78	74	296	930
	Wayne STEPHENS	Eng	72	73	79	72	296	930
	David R JONES	Eng	72	72	77	75	296	930
	Alfonso PINERO	Sp	71	72	78	75	296	930
67	Roger CHAPMAN	Eng	70	74	74	79	297	596
	Richard BOXALL	Eng	70	73	81	73	297	596
	David A RUSSELL	Eng	75	68	74	80	297	596
70	Mark JAMES	Eng	70	75	73	80	298	592

COURSE: EL BOSQUE GOLF & COUNTRY CLUB, VALENCIA
DATE: 27.2-1.3   YARDAGE: 3505   PAR: 72

BALLESTEROS TRIUMPHS AFTER MARATHON PLAY-OFF

It took Severiano Ballesteros six extra holes before he could shake off Jesper Parnevik and win his third Balearic title

Recalling the words of Jack Nicklaus some 20 years before, Severiano Ballesteros allowed his genial mask to slip briefly during the Turespana Open de Baleares. For a moment there was a glimpse of the pressures the great Spaniard feels each time he tees up. 'I'm playing quite well,' he said after a third round three-under-par 69 placed him threateningly a stroke behind the leaders, 'but there are a lot of players here. And all of them against me.'

The Turespana Open de Baleares had become a case of Seve taking on all-comers. 'It is not easy to win. I have played well for three rounds...,' a pause before the easy confidence returned, 'I should be leading right now. But if the ball doesn't go in, you just have to be patient.'

Golf always has new lessons to teach, but patience is a virtue Ballesteros learned long ago. Just as well. He needed every ounce of it at Santa Ponsa. But even he, a player with hidden depths of stamina and resolve, was tested to breaking point by a six-hole marathon play-off with young Swede, Jesper Parnevik. And Ballesteros's mind was not always focused as sharply as it might have been on the task in hand. Even in the thick of battle his thoughts were sometimes elsewhere. 'I really had a very hard time to concentrate on the golf course today,' said Seve on Saturday. 'Sometimes you find it more difficult than on other days.' But, like a man

facing the hangman's noose, a play-off focuses the golfer's mind wonderfully.

Ballesteros and Parnevik were tied after 72 holes on 277, 11 under par. They retraced their steps up and down Santa Ponsa's demanding 460-yards, uphill par four 18th no fewer than six times before Ballesteros holed from four feet for par and victory. It was the first time in four days the Spaniard had led the tournament outright. 'I'm only playing for second place,' he said mischievously after each round.

Indeed, it took Ballesteros until the fourth hole on Sunday before he found himself part of a tie for the lead. But like the middle distance runner who is a master tactician, Ballesteros hovered a couple of shots off the pace all weekend, ready to step out of the leader's slipstream and sprint for the finishing line.

It was a lesson in staying power for the beaten Parnevik. The Swede played his way to 14 under par, three shots clear of the field – which by then amounted effectively only to Ballesteros – with four holes to play. A maiden Tour victory should have been a formality for the son of Swedish TV personality Bosse Parnevik who celebrated his 27th birthday on tournament Saturday.

But Parnevik senior, who followed his son's final group on Sunday, was on hand to witness, not Jesper's triumph, but three bogeys in four holes which wiped out his lead. It was then into match-play where Ballesteros, a five-times World Match-Play champion and Ryder Cup veteran, has no peer.

It was the third time in the tournament's five years that Ballesteros has triumphed. And the second time in three years that he has overcome a Swede in extra time – he beat Magnus Persson to the title in 1990. 'I am 35, but I feel 20 after this win.' said Ballesteros. 'It was my hardest victory for a long time, but the golfer who resists the most is the one who usually wins.'

Good advice for Parnevik and the

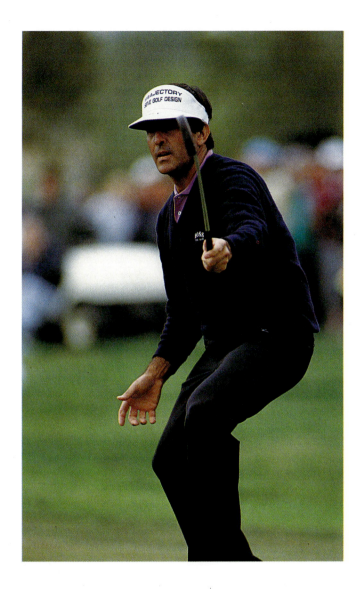

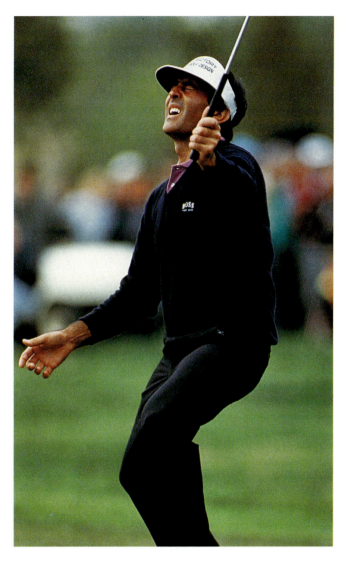

Inflated promotion over the

golf course.

score of pretenders who came in search of Ballesteros's scalp. None came with greater hope than Gordon Brand Junior. Partnered with Ballesteros for the first two days the Bristol-based Scot holed from 35 feet for a birdie on the first hole of his first round. After rounds of 68 and 66 he had crafted a four-stroke lead at the halfway stage.

But all Brand's early aggression eventually signified nothing after closing rounds of 74 and 73 left him four strokes behind Ballesteros and Parnevik. 'I started in a Rolls-Royce and ended up on a donkey,' was his memorable description of what, for him, turned into a highly forgettable final two days.

The most forgettable moment of all came with perhaps the sweetest shot Brand struck all week.

By the fourth hole on Saturday the twice Ryder Cup player had extended his halfway lead to six shots. He was still three clear as he stood on the 15th tee — a 190-yard par three. The perfectly-

Severiano Ballesteros agonises over

missed putt.

struck four iron sailed through the green into treacherous rough, from where the Scot was happy to escape with bogey. 'That was probably the best shot I hit all day and I nearly made double bogey from it,' he said. 'I seemed to lose my momentum from there on.' Brand finished bogey, bogey, par, bogey.

Tied at the end of Saturday with England's Barry Lane at eight-under — only a shot clear of a group of three, Ballesteros, Parnevik and Ireland's former Walker Cup player Eoghan O'Connell — Brand just slipped away.

The Open de Baleares continues to be good to Ballesteros. Apart from three wins, his company, Amen Corner, promoted it with Turespana as the welcome new sponsor.

The one-and-a-half hour play-off played havoc with Ballesteros's travelling arrangements and the new champion was forced to spend an extra night in Majorca. But then, as Seve had displayed all week, patience is a virtue he has in abundance.

Ballesteros finally ends the play-off.

Jesper Parnevik held the lead until the final few holes.

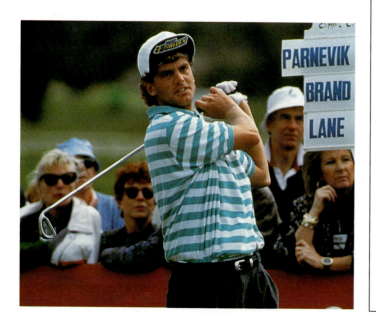

POS	NAME	CTY	1	2	3	4	TOTAL	PRIZE MONEY
	COURSE: SANTA PONSA		**DATE: 5-8.3**			**YARDAGE: 7158**		**PAR: 72**
1	Seve BALLESTEROS	Sp	70	70	69	68	277	£41660
2	Jesper PARNEVIK	Swe	70	72	67	68	277	27770
3	Vicente FERNANDEZ	Arg	69	70	71	69	279	15650
4	Santiago LUNA	Sp	69	70	71	70	280	11550
	Jose RIVERO	Sp	70	73	68	69	280	11550
6	Gordon BRAND Jnr	Scot	68	66	74	73	281	7500
	Eduardo ROMERO	Arg	70	71	70	70	281	7500
	Barry LANE	Eng	67	71	70	73	281	7500
9	Gary EVANS	Eng	73	71	68	70	282	4702
	Colin MONTGOMERIE	Scot	71	71	69	71	282	4702
	Mats LANNER	Swe	72	71	72	67	282	4702
	Phillip PRICE	Wal	71	72	68	71	282	4702
	Glen DAY	USA	67	72	73	70	282	4702
14	Eoghan O'CONNELL	Ire	71	70	68	74	283	3522
	Heinz P THUEL	Ger	70	72	70	71	283	3522
	Peter BAKER	Eng	70	71	70	72	283	3522
	Wayne RILEY	Aus	68	70	72	73	283	3522
	Howard CLARK	Eng	69	72	69	73	283	3522
19	Chris MOODY	Eng	69	74	71	70	284	2891
	Lucien TINKLER	Aus	71	70	69	74	284	2891
	Patrick HALL	Eng	68	72	70	74	284	2891
	Jose Maria CANIZARES	Sp	68	73	72	71	284	2891
	Philip WALTON	Ire	69	74	73	68	284	2891
	Mark ROE	Eng	70	73	72	69	284	2891
25	Joakim HAEGGMAN	Swe	71	70	71	73	285	2512
	Haydn SELBY-GREEN	Eng	72	72	70	71	285	2512
	Costantino ROCCA	It	74	70	71	70	285	2512
	Jose COCERES	Arg	73	71	72	69	285	2512
29	Peter SMITH	Scot	69	73	73	71	286	2180
	Mats HALLBERG	Swe	67	72	73	74	286	2180
	Chris WILLIAMS	Eng	71	72	72	71	286	2180
	Paul CURRY	Eng	70	71	75	70	286	2180
	Paul LAWRIE	Scot	71	74	70	71	286	2180
34	Thomas LEVET	Fr	71	72	73	71	287	1900
	John METCALFE	Eng	71	74	68	74	287	1900
	Peter TERAVAINEN	USA	71	73	74	69	287	1900
	Rick HARTMANN	USA	75	69	73	70	287	1900
	Robert LEE	Eng	67	73	75	72	287	1900
39	David R JONES	Eng	72	72	74	70	288	1625
	Paul BROADHURST	Eng	72	71	71	74	288	1625
	Brian MARCHBANK	Scot	69	73	75	71	288	1625
	James SPENCE	Eng	73	72	70	73	288	1625
	Giuseppe CALI	It	71	72	71	74	288	1625
	Stephen BENNETT	Eng	69	70	73	76	288	1625
45	Orrin VINCENT III	USA	75	69	72	73	289	1400
	Johan RYSTROM	Swe	71	73	72	73	289	1400
	Bill MALLEY	USA	72	70	73	74	289	1400
48	Philip PARKIN	Wal	75	69	75	71	290	1225
	Carl MASON	Eng	68	74	70	78	290	1225
	Jay TOWNSEND	USA	70	74	71	75	290	1225
	Silvio GRAPPASONNI	It	70	70	77	73	290	1225
52	Ross McFARLANE	Eng	68	70	77	76	291	1050
	Hugh BAIOCCHI	SA	70	74	73	74	291	1050
	Gavin LEVENSON	SA	71	71	74	75	291	1050
55	Jonathan SEWELL	Eng	72	71	71	78	292	875
	Jim PAYNE	Eng	75	70	74	73	292	875
	Des SMYTH	Ire	72	72	76	72	292	875
	Roger WINCHESTER	Eng	71	74	75	72	292	875
59	Tod POWER	Aus	73	71	72	77	293	725
	Ignacio FELIU	Sp	74	70	71	78	293	725
	Paul CARRIGILL	Eng	70	75	70	78	293	725
	Derrick COOPER	Eng	69	74	75	75	293	725
	Jose DAVILA	Sp	72	73	72	76	293	725
64	Olle NORDBERG	Swe	71	73	73	77	294	637
	Liam WHITE	Eng	72	73	72	77	294	637
66	Per-Ulrik JOHANSSON	Swe	72	73	72	78	295	398
	Dennis EDLUND	Swe	73	69	76	77	295	398
	Jimmy HEGGARTY	N.Ire	69	76	73	77	295	398
69	Martin GATES	Eng	73	71	74	79	297	394
70	Miguel Angel JIMENEZ	Sp	69	75	76	79	299	392
71	Chris VAN DER VELDE	Hol	72	71	82	W/D	225	390

RIVERO CONTINUES THE SPANISH ASSAULT

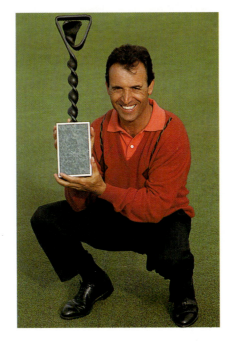

Jose Rivero took his European career earnings to over £1 million while recording a fourth consecutive victory for Spanish players on the 1992 Volvo Tour

Through the highlands and islands of his native land, Jose Rivero strode to all manner of heroics in the early weeks of the 1992 season. In the Tour-within-a-tour that was the Turespana series of tournaments he started his tenth season as a tournament professional by finishing third, second and fourth and putting millions of pesetas into the family coffers.

Then came the Open Catalonia, and with it the wiry little man from Madrid proved that what had passed before had been no more than the preliminary skirmishes in a larger and more glorious campaign as he produced some determined golf to take the title with a total of 280, eight under par. Thus Rivero won his first tournament since 1988, and if his victory was narrowly achieved, it was no less deserved for all that.

The facts, simply related, are that Rivero won by a stroke from Jose Maria Canizares, his veteran compatriot, Johan Rystrom of Sweden, and Haydn Selby-Green of England. The flesh on those bare bones made for more succulent fare by far.

The tournament, played out on the Mas Nou course that sits, visually stunning and physically testing, literally on the top of a dynamited mountain overlooking the resort of Platja d'Aro on the Costa Brava, produced more successes and failures, more triumphs and disasters, than you could shake a stick at. It was compelling stuff.

Of the many sub-plots that wove their way through the four days, none was more colourful than that provided by Selby-Green, a lofty and elegant Yorkshireman from Doncaster. He was just plain Haydn Green in the days when he was an England amateur international,

then, in 1990, he married his wife Jay, tacked her maiden name on to his – and became the only hyphenated golfer on the Volvo Tour.

But Selby-Green proved that he was more than just a name that sounded vaguely like a firm of solicitors. He had had, for a start, a strangely varied career in which he twice tried, and failed, to win a Tour card in the early 1980s, won one and lost it again in 1990, and finally finished 13th in the PGA European Tour Qualifying School in the autumn of 1991. In between he had tried his hand at sports promotion, and had owned a pool and snooker club in Poole for a time. In this one tournament, only his 25th in a ten-year career as a professional, he proved that, at 33, he was here to stay.

Selby-Green played some golf that was as gritty as his home town, and very nearly put himself into a play-off when, with Rivero in the clubhouse, having completed a closing 67, he birdied the 70th hole of the tournament from 15 feet to go six under par, then picked up another stroke at the next from eight feet. He missed the fairway on the last, played a magnificent six-iron to within eight feet of the pin. He had virtually a straight putt, which seemed to be going in until it ground to a halt no more than one roll from the hole. It was all over; but what a finish.

Rivero had been there or thereabouts throughout the tournament, but was still two off the pace when he started his final round. He had three birdies going to the turn in 34, but his big move was

undoubtedly an eagle three on the tenth, where he holed a nine-iron shot from fully 130 yards. He then birdied the next from no more than 18 inches. He was never again headed.

A 70 left Rivero two strokes behind a quintet of players after the first round, and by the end of day two the lead was being shared by Roger Winchester, Magnus Sunesson and David Gilford, who had a dream start by playing the first three holes in four under par, including two birdies and an eagle two on the second, achieved with a holed seven-iron from nearly 150 yards.

Sunesson's joy, unconfined at the end of the day, was more than a little muted 24 hours later when he went from six under par and leading the field to three under and nowhere in the course of one disastrous hole. He was unhappy enough with what he thought was a bogey six at the 17th, then found himself on the wrong end of a two-stroke penalty. Mike Stewart, the Tournament Director, used a

Spanish TV replay to prove to Sunesson that as he had attempted a recovery from thick undergrowth, the ball had popped straight up in the air and fallen to earth via his right thigh.

That put Selby-Green, who had a 66 that won him a £6,000 bonus from Johnnie Walker for a course record, in the lead along with Mats Lanner, and the scene was set for a grand finale.

Rivero, who had been quietly going about his business in the previous three days, timed things to perfection. He saved his best for last, and not even the manifold perils of Mas Nou, or a tall, powerful Yorkshireman by the name of Haydn Selby-Green, were about to stop him now.

Martin Poxon between the rock and

a hard place.

COURSE: MAS NOU, GIRONA		DATE: 11-14.3			YARDAGE: 6		PAR: 72	

POS	NAME	CTY	1	2	3	4	TOTAL	PRIZE MONEY
1	Jose RIVERO	Sp	70	71	72	67	280	£50000
2	Haydn SELBY-GREEN	Eng	72	73	66	70	281	22370
	Jose Maria CANIZARES	Sp	74	73	67	67	281	22370
	Johan RYSTROM	Swe	68	76	70	67	281	22370
5	Jose Maria OLAZABAL	Sp	74	69	69	71	283	10733
	Anders FORSBRAND	Swe	72	73	67	71	283	10733
	Mats LANNER	Swe	74	68	69	72	283	10733
8	Paul BROADHURST	Eng	76	69	71	68	284	6730
	Magnus SUNESSON	Swe	69	71	73	71	284	6730
	Darren CLARKE	N.Ire	68	75	72	69	284	6730
11	Jesper PARNEVIK	Swe	70	72	71	72	285	5170
	Mark MOULAND	Wal	74	73	69	69	285	5170
	Santiago LUNA	Sp	74	72	71	68	285	5170
14	Brian BARNES	Scot	74	74	70	68	286	4230
	Roger WINCHESTER	Eng	70	70	72	74	286	4230
	David GILFORD	Eng	73	67	74	72	286	4230
	Antonio GARRIDO	Sp	73	71	71	71	286	4230
	Philip WALTON	Ire	69	73	70	74	286	4230
19	Peter TERAVAINEN	USA	74	74	67	72	287	3660
	Juan QUIROS	Sp	72	71	72	72	287	3660
21	Peter LONARD	Aus	73	73	70	72	288	3285
	David WILLIAMS	Eng	73	75	72	68	288	3285
	Des SMYTH	Ire	73	71	69	75	288	3285
	Roger CHAPMAN	Eng	68	76	71	73	288	3285
	Richard BOXALL	Eng	75	73	72	68	288	3285
	Jean VAN DE VELDE	Fr	69	73	73	73	288	3285
27	Jose Manuel CARRILES	Sp	74	72	75	68	289	2704
	Gordon J BRAND	Eng	72	74	76	67	289	2704
	Eduardo ROMERO	Arg	72	73	70	74	289	2704
	Andrew MURRAY	Eng	68	73	76	72	289	2704
	David R JONES	Eng	76	71	71	71	289	2704
	Chris MOODY	Eng	70	72	73	74	289	2704
	Glen DAY	USA	72	73	72	72	289	2704
34	Justin HOBDAY	Eng	75	71	70	74	290	2340
	Alfonso PINERO	Sp	68	75	74	73	290	2340
	Philip PARKIN	Wal	73	74	74	69	290	2340
37	Wayne RILEY	Aus	76	72	74	69	291	1920
	Adam HUNTER	Scot	76	70	70	75	291	1920
	Paul WAY	Eng	77	71	73	70	291	1920
	Eric GIRAUD	Fr	74	72	73	72	291	1920
	Eoghan O'CONNELL	Ire	69	76	71	75	291	1920
	Miguel Angel JIMENEZ	Sp	71	77	73	70	291	1920
	Robert KARLSSON	Swe	73	73	72	73	291	1920
	Grant TURNER	Eng	75	73	72	71	291	1920
	Marc FARRY	Fr	73	70	74	74	291	1920
	Per-Ulrik JOHANSSON	Swe	73	73	78	67	291	1920
	John HAWKSWORTH	Eng	75	73	72	71	291	1920
48	Jon ROBSON	Eng	78	69	71	74	292	1350
	Steven BOWMAN	USA	73	75	73	71	292	1350
	Ignacio FELIU	Sp	74	73	74	71	292	1350
	Derrick COOPER	Eng	72	74	76	70	292	1350
	Bill MALLEY	USA	70	78	72	72	292	1350
	Andrew SHERBORNE	Eng	69	74	74	75	292	1350
	Jeremy ROBINSON	Eng	71	73	74	74	292	1350
	Jonathan SEWELL	Eng	73	73	74	72	292	1350
56	Russell CLAYDON	Eng	76	69	74	74	293	997
	Silvio GRAPPASONNI	It	71	74	72	76	293	997
	Mats HALLBERG	Swe	77	68	75	73	293	997
	Hugh BAIOCCHI	SA	71	77	73	72	293	997
60	Peter MITCHELL	Eng	73	75	71	75	294	855
	Rick HARTMANN	USA	73	74	73	74	294	855
	Jimmy HEGGARTY	N.Ire	75	71	74	74	294	855
	Stephen HAMILL	N.Ire	71	77	73	73	294	855
64	Wayne STEPHENS	Eng	74	74	71	77	296	660
	Ricardo GONZALEZ	Arg	73	75	69	79	296	660
	John METCALFE	Eng	73	73	71	79	296	660
67	Brian MARCHBANK	Scot	75	73	75	75	298	448
68	Orrin VINCENT III	USA	74	74	76	76	300	446
69	Alberto BINAGHI	It	74	73	76	78	301	444
70	Fredrik LINDGREN	Swe	75	73	79	75	302	442

RAFFERTY CLINCHES VICTORY IN DRAMATIC STYLE

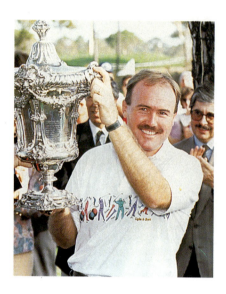

It was certainly a huge gamble, and almost a miracle. To stage the Portuguese Open on a course only eight months old was risky; to do so at only five weeks' notice, riskier still.

But it all came right on the night for Vila Sol, the Donald Steel-designed course on the outskirts of Quarteira that proved it belonged up there with all the other jewels of the Algarve, San Lorenzo, Quinta do Lago, Penina and Vilamoura. Four days of brilliant sunshine undoubtedly assisted, but the course still needed to produce the right champion and the approval of the players before it could truly claim to have arrived.

Victory for the favourite, 1989 Volvo Order of Merit winner Ronan Rafferty, in a finish where most of the cream, in the form of Anders Forsbrand, Peter Senior and Sam Torrance, rose to the top to challenge, was a script written in heaven. All that was missing from a Portuguese point of view was the presence of local hero Daniel Silva at the business end of the proceedings. After a second-day 66 hopes were high, but with so much expected of Portugal's first and only Tour player, he was a stroke a hole worse on day three and first man out with a marker on Sunday.

His turn will come, but this week belonged to Rafferty, the Ascot-based Ulsterman who, with his year but ten weeks old, brought his earnings just a few coppers short of a quarter of a million pounds. A six-figure cheque in the Palm Meadows Cup in Queensland had been

A final green putt of 35 feet by Ronan Rafferty enabled him to record his seventh European victory

followed by joint second place in Bangkok, a play-off defeat by Ballesteros in Dubai and the runner-up spot again, this time to the redoubtable Tom Watson, in Hong Kong.

Now came his first win in Europe since the Ebel European Masters - Swiss Open 18 months earlier and what a way to do it – with a downhill putt of 35 feet rammed home to deprive Forsbrand of what had looked like a certain play-off. It was as if

Ronan wanted a quick revenge on all those who were writing him off following a disastrous 1991 in which he slipped 30 places in the Volvo Order of Merit and lost his Ryder Cup place.

Rafferty's 15-under 273 simply carried on the 1992 fairytale. Starting with the win Down Under, that made him an extraordinary 67 under par for 20 rounds of the highest-quality golf. Not that he could in any way explain the transformation in his game.

'I'm just doing all the things I did last year,' said Rafferty. 'I did a bit of chipping in the back garden during the winter, which didn't please the missus too much – that's about the only difference. Now I'm getting the run of the ball, whereas last year I would be getting plugged under the face of a bunker.'

Of his four rounds at Vila Sol, Rafferty singled out the only one over 70 as being the key to victory. 'That second-day 71 was a disgraceful exhibition but I fought hard to make a score after driving out of bounds at the eighth and managed to keep myself in the tournament.'

Amazingly, Rafferty repeated the out of bounds in his closing 68 but again limited the damage by making a birdie with his second ball. The four penalty shots were all down to the driver, a club that most players used exceptionally sparingly on the ultra-tight 6,769-yards course with its insidious white out-of-bounds markers sneaking up on all sides.

Rafferty's straightness on such a claustrophobic course turned out to be the crucial factor. Forsbrand simply couldn't

veterans Jose-Maria Canizares and Juan Quiros, was raving about the place even after shooting 82 in the pro-am.

'It's a wonderful course, very enjoyable to play and very demanding in its shot-making. It's a course where you've got to hit the fairway, it makes you really think. Some pros are saying it takes the driver out of the game and that you get some unfair bounces, but for such a young course it's in amazing condition. I love it.' Torrance grew to admire it even more over the next four days because four excellent rounds signalled a welcome return to form for him after a very slow start to the year.

After Carl Mason had set the pace with a 66, the real scoring fireworks came from the spectacular Spaniards. On day two, Quiros snapped up 11 birdies and, unfortunately, four bogeys, to fall only one short of Fred Couples's 12-birdie European record set in the Scandinavian Masters the previous August. And the following day, Canizares, still a force at 45, blitzed nine birdies and an eagle in his 62, coming home in just 29 shots to earn the Johnnie Walker Tour Course Record Award of £2,000.

'I won't think of retiring until the day I stop making birdies,' said the ever-popular Canizares. For a man who once shot 27 for nine holes at Crans, that day could be a long, long way off.

And if you think Canizares was the

stay out of the trees when it mattered over the closing holes after overtaking the Irishman with a hat-trick of birdies.

'I didn't play at all well,' conceded the tall Swede, 'but it still needed two birdies from Ronan in the last three holes to beat me. I made an unbelieveable four out of the trees at the last, which I thought would be good enough to get me into a play-off. It was not to be, but I am proud of my competitiveness that forced him all the way.'

Peter Senior took third place in Portugal

after having a share of the lead at one stage in a tense final afternoon. It was the Australian's first tournament for a month and he was delighted to get so close. 'I planned to take seven weeks off after finishing fourth at the Australian Masters,' he said, 'but watching those Aussie cricketers perform so badly in the World Cup gave me itchy feet!'

Rafferty had every reason to speak well of Vila Sol (which he did) but Sam Torrance, who eventually shared fourth place with those two delightful Spanish

oldest competitor at Vila Sol, think again. When an invited Moroccan player failed to turn up at the last moment, they asked Christy O'Connor Senior, holidaying at a nearby country club, to fill the breach. Christy, now 67, got himself fitted up with some clubs and set to work with a will. 'If only I could putt, I could have had a half-decent score,' said 'Himself' after posting an opening 79, 'but it was a great bit of fun.' Though he failed to hand in his card after a second day 83, that marvellous wristy swing was still able to mesmerise a gallery that walked every step of the way with him. After all, it's not every day you get the chance to see a legend.

Peter Senior took third place on his first 1992 Volvo Tour appearance.

Juan Quiros in troublesome spot.

POS	NAME	CTY	1	2	3	4	TOTAL	PRIZE MONEY
1	Ronan RAFFERTY	N.Ire	67	71	67	68	273	£37500
2	Anders FORSBRAND	Swe	69	67	68	70	274	25000
3	Peter SENIOR	Aus	74	64	68	70	276	14070
4	Jose Maria CANIZARES	Sp	75	69	62	71	277	9533
	Juan QUIROS	Sp	69	65	74	69	277	9533
	Sam TORRANCE	Scot	70	67	71	69	277	9533
7	Barry LANE	Eng	71	68	72	67	278	6150
	Gordon J BRAND	Eng	68	73	71	66	278	6150
9	David GILFORD	Eng	73	69	70	67	279	5010
10	Paul WAY	Eng	73	70	71	66	280	3950
	Peter LONARD	Aus	69	72	67	72	280	3950
	Gordon BRAND Jnr	Scot	70	71	70	69	280	3950
	Vicente FERNANDEZ	Arg	70	69	71	70	280	3950
	Thomas LEVET	Fr	72	72	66	70	280	3950
15	Wayne STEPHENS	Eng	73	71	68	69	281	3263
	James SPENCE	Eng	74	70	66	71	281	3263
	Andrew SHERBORNE	Eng	72	70	73	66	281	3263
18	Jorge BERENDT	Arg	70	68	74	70	282	2610
	Johan RYSTROM	Swe	71	70	69	72	282	2610
	Peter MITCHELL	Eng	73	71	69	69	282	2610
	Miguel Angel MARTIN	Sp	75	67	70	70	282	2610
	Malcolm MACKENZIE	Eng	71	71	69	71	282	2610
	Haydn SELBY-GREEN	Eng	68	74	70	70	282	2610
	Miguel Angel JIMENEZ	Sp	68	71	73	70	282	2610
	Grant TURNER	Eng	68	71	73	70	282	2610
	Richard BOXALL	Eng	71	72	69	70	282	2610
27	Peter BAKER	Eng	71	74	68	70	283	2045
	Derrick COOPER	Eng	68	71	74	70	283	2045
	Rick HARTMANN	USA	73	71	67	72	283	2045
	Steven BOWMAN	USA	73	69	70	71	283	2045
	Eduardo ROMERO	Arg	72	72	68	71	283	2045
	Roger CHAPMAN	Eng	71	70	75	67	283	2045
33	Mike McLEAN	Eng	70	74	71	69	284	1736
	Russell CLAYDON	Eng	73	71	70	70	284	1736
	Jose DAVILA	Sp	69	74	66	75	284	1736
36	Christy O'CONNOR Jnr	Ire	68	68	74	75	285	1640
37	Martin POXON	Eng	69	75	68	74	286	1420
	Carl MASON	Eng	66	74	73	73	286	1420
	John METCALFE	Eng	71	67	75	73	286	1420
	Ross DRUMMOND	Scot	74	70	72	70	286	1420
	Hugh BAIOCCHI	SA	72	74	70	70	286	1420
	Darren CLARKE	N.Ire	72	71	71	72	286	1420
	Lucien TINKLER	Aus	73	70	69	74	286	1420
	Stuart LITTLE	Eng	73	72	68	73	286	1420
	Paul BROADHURST	Eng	71	71	74	70	286	1420
	Gavin LEVENSON	SA	71	73	71	71	286	1420
47	Desmond TERBLANCHE	SA	70	76	71	70	287	1160
	Manuel PINERO	Sp	73	71	70	73	287	1160
	Keith WATERS	Eng	72	72	75	68	287	1160
50	Paul LAWRIE	Scot	68	74	76	70	288	1000
	Martin GATES	Eng	70	72	74	72	288	1000
	Eric GIRAUD	Fr	69	77	74	68	288	1000
	Chris MOODY	Eng	72	67	74	75	288	1000
	Neal BRIGGS	Eng	74	72	72	70	288	1000
55	Glenn RALPH	Eng	69	77	73	70	289	840
	Paul McGINLEY	Ire	70	73	75	71	289	840
	Ricky WILLISON	Eng	70	72	72	75	289	840
58	Jean VAN DE VELDE	Fr	69	73	79	69	290	740
	David J RUSSELL	Eng	67	74	74	75	290	740
60	Jim PAYNE	Eng	77	69	73	72	291	675
	Jon ROBSON	Eng	70	72	73	76	291	675
62	German GARRIDO	Sp	71	74	72	75	292	630
63	Adam MEDNICK	Swe	72	72	72	77	293	570
	Stephen FIELD	Eng	75	68	76	74	293	570
	Stephen McALLISTER	Scot	73	71	76	73	293	570
66	Fredrik LINDGREN	Swe	70	76	72	76	294	399
	Garry HARVEY	Scot	74	69	74	77	294	399
68	Daniel SILVA	Port	74	66	84	72	296	395
	Anders SORENSEN	Den	70	75	77	74	296	395

COURSE: VILA SOL, VILAMOURA DATE: 19-22.3 YARDAGE: 6769 PAR: 72

FORSBRAND REMAINS THE RENAISSANCE MAN

Anders Forsbrand returned to Florence and successfully defended his title

Florence, the city that gave birth to the Renaissance, has also seen the career of Anders Forsbrand re-born.

When, in 1991, the Swede arrived in the beautiful Tuscan capital, his progress in recent years could not match the surroundings. He had not won on the Volvo Tour since 1987, nor matched his best finish in the rankings of eighth in 1986. He had even fallen as low as 114th in 1989, the year David Leadbetter persuaded him to undergo a Nick Faldo-like swing change.

Victory then in the 1991 Volvo Open di Firenze, by one shot from Barry Lane, convinced Forsbrand that the agony of the changes, like that of the foot-sore tourist ascending Giotto's Bell Tower of the city's cathedral, was worth it. He liked the view.

In fact, he liked it so much he came back and won the tournament again 12 months later, this time beating off the challenge of Australia's Peter Senior.

Victory at Ugolino, magnificently sited among the Chianti vines in the hills above Florence, was Forsbrand's first on Tour for a year, but in the previous six months he had hit a rich vein of form. If his hopes of becoming the first Swede to appear in a Ryder Cup match, rekindled with the 1991 win, had been ultimately extinguished, he showed what a team man he is by claiming three titles for his country – the Dunhill Cup (with Per-Ulrik Johansson and Mats Lanner), the World Cup of Golf by Philip Morris (also in the company of Johansson) and the Benson & Hedges Mixed Team event with Helen Alfredsson.

The week before, in Portugal, Forsbrand

had finished runner-up to Ronan Rafferty, who sunk a birdie putt of 35 feet on the final hole. Senior had been third. Now, with the Irishman absent, it was left to the Australian and the Swede to do battle.

Senior led by two strokes after the third

round, which was played on Sunday morning to put the tournament back on schedule after rain earlier in the week. Forsbrand made his move with a birdie at the third and then three in a row from the fifth to be out in four-under-par 31. 'For the first 12 holes I played as well as I can,' he said. It could have been even better. He lipped out four times, two of them horse-shoes. Senior held on for the time being with his own hat-trick of birdies on the front nine, but then round the turn his challenge collapsed quicker than an Italian government. 'I am disgusted at the way I finished,' he said after bogeying 12, 14 and 15. 'After the sixth hole I thought I just had to stand up to win.'

Another birdie at the last from Forsbrand brought him a five-under 66. Senior knew he had to birdie each of the remaining three holes to win but was defeated by the par three 17th. The Swede had not dropped a shot on any of the 36 holes played that day, collecting nine birdies. Senior's 69 matched his and Forsbrand's opening score, their worst of the week over the tight, tree-lined 6,229-yard, par-71 layout.

Even the sun came out to salute Forsbrand's final day performance. It was not always thus. Thursday was as perfect a day for art galleries as there is in this artists' city. Only 25 players completed their rounds and with more rain the following day, the first round was only just finished that night.

Robin Mann, from Suffolk, back in competition after a five-week lay off due to a wrist injury, led the way with a 66, thanks

The long putter carried Peter Senior to runner-up finish.

The 18th at Ugolino.

partly to holing a putt of 12 feet on the 13th green. It was the first stroke he faced on resuming his round. 'The night before it had been right lip,' he explained, 'but when I came back in the morning it was left lip.' He had so long to think about it, he got it right.

Aberdonian Paul Lawrie was positively relishing the conditions – bemoaning the lack of snow even – and joined Senior at the top of the leaderboard after Saturday's second round. But on the long Sunday, it was Surrey's Martin Gates who moved himself in behind Senior and Forsbrand, following a 65 on Saturday with a 66 on Sunday morning. Gates had his trousers tucked into his socks and it proved a wise precaution when he found a ditch with his second at the par-five 15th. He splashed around and a double-bogey seven was the result. But he hung on for third place, his best finish to date in his second year on Tour.

Ricky Willison achieved a similar feat. The 1991 English Amateur champion had failed to gain his Tour card at the PGA European Tour Qualifying School but, making the most of a rare outing, came in sixth, six behind Forsbrand. The only difference had come in the first round, the Englishman had matched the Swede stroke for stroke over the final 54 holes.

For Forsbrand there is no secret to his success: just work. 'I don't think anyone is ever satisfied,' he said. 'I still want to get better. There is still a lot to do if I am to compete with the absolute best.' Florence is as good a place to start as any.

POS	NAME	CTY	1	2	3	4	TOTAL	PRIZE MONEY
1	Anders FORSBRAND	Swe	69	69	67	66	271	£37500
2	Peter SENIOR	Aus	69	66	68	69	272	25000
3	Martin GATES	Eng	73	65	66	71	275	14070
4	David GILFORD	Eng	72	67	68	69	276	10375
	Jorge BERENDT	Arg	70	68	71	67	276	10375
6	Ricky WILLISON	Eng	75	67	67	68	277	6716
	Eduardo ROMERO	Arg	73	70	69	65	277	6716
	Peter MITCHELL	Eng	68	68	69	72	277	6716
9	Des SMYTH	Ire	73	68	68	69	278	4530
	Steven RICHARDSON	Eng	70	67	72	69	278	4530
	Paul LAWRIE	Scot	68	67	76	67	278	4530
12	Andrew SHERBORNE	Eng	73	71	68	67	279	3890
13	Vicente FERNANDEZ	Arg	70	71	68	71	280	3414
	Jonathan SEWELL	Eng	71	70	68	71	280	3414
	Peter BAKER	Eng	71	68	71	70	280	3414
	Ross DRUMMOND	Scot	72	65	70	73	280	3414
	James SPENCE	Eng	68	69	69	74	280	3414
18	David CURRY	Eng	73	69	71	69	282	2820
	Paul CURRY	Eng	73	67	71	71	282	2820
	John McHENRY	Ire	71	68	69	74	282	2820
	Nick GODIN	Eng	70	69	71	72	282	2820
22	Miguel Angel MARTIN	Sp	71	72	72	68	283	2480
	Mathias GRONBERG	Swe	69	72	68	74	283	2480
	Mark ROE	Eng	71	69	72	71	283	2480
	Wayne STEPHENS	Eng	68	68	71	76	283	2480
26	Brian MARCHBANK	Scot	71	67	77	69	284	2290
27	Silvano LOCATELLI	It	71	71	73	70	285	2080
	Roger WINCHESTER	Eng	76	66	72	71	285	2080
	Robin MANN	Eng	66	74	72	73	285	2080
	Gordon BRAND Jnr	Scot	71	69	71	74	285	2080
	Fredrik LARSSON	Swe	72	68	74	71	285	2080
32	Jon ROBSON	Eng	74	70	72	70	286	1835
	Paul BROADHURST	Eng	70	71	73	72	286	1835
34	Malcolm MACKENZIE	Eng	75	68	73	71	287	1621
	David R JONES	Eng	70	70	75	72	287	1621
	Daniel SILVA	Port	74	69	72	72	287	1621
	Robert LEE	Eng	71	72	71	73	287	1621
	Adam MEDNICK	Swe	73	71	70	73	287	1621
	David WILLIAMS	Eng	70	73	70	74	287	1621
40	Thomas LEVET	Fr	74	68	70	76	288	1360
	Jim RUTLEDGE	Can	73	69	74	72	288	1360
	Bill LONGMUIR	Scot	74	69	71	74	288	1360
	Sam TORRANCE	Scot	73	71	71	73	288	1360
	Orrin VINCENT III	USA	72	72	72	72	288	1360
	Jose COCERES	Arg	72	72	73	71	288	1360
	Luca FLORI (AM)	It	72	70	76	71	289	1360
	Emanuele CANONICA	It	74	70	75	69	288	1360
47	Eoghan O'CONNELL	Ire	74	69	74	73	290	1180
	Desmond TERBLANCHE	SA	73	71	75	71	290	1180
49	Lee VANNET	Scot	69	73	71	78	291	1080
	Andrew HARE	Eng	75	69	70	77	291	1080
	Per HAUGSRUD	Nor	72	70	77	72	291	1080
52	Dennis EDLUND	Swe	73	70	71	78	292	980
	Jeff MATHEWS	Eng	76	68	74	74	292	980

COURSE: GOLF DEL'UGOLINO   DATE: 26-29.3   YARDAGE: 6229   PAR: 71

Anders Forsbrand

studies action replay.

CANIZARES IS LATEST MILLIONAIRE

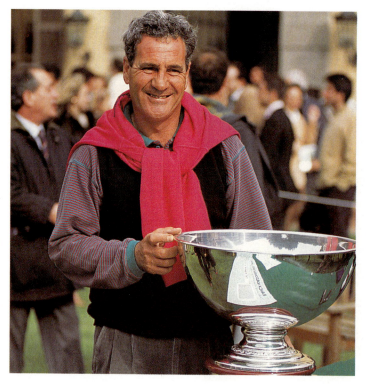

It had been nearly ten years since Jose Maria Canizares had been asked to make a winner's speech. When the 45-year old Spaniard had last stood on the rostrum, Europe had never won the Ryder Cup, Nick Faldo hadn't won a major title, and it was still possible to play municipal courses at weekends.

In between Canizares's 1983 Bob Hope British Classic triumph and his 1992 Roma Masters win, many putts have fallen into the cup – not least the one the Spaniard looks set to be remembered for: a slippery putt of four feet to beat America's Ken Green in the final day singles at The Belfry to gain the point that ensured Europe retained the Ryder Cup in 1989.

After the crucible of the last hole at The Belfry, two-putting for victory from 20 feet at the final hole of the 1992 Roma Masters should have been a formality. The Castelgandolfo greens may well have been among the trickiest all season, but a regulation two putts should not have been beyond the powers of one of the Volvo Tour's silkiest putters.

England's Barry Lane, still in the midst of his own win drought since he won the 1988 Bell's Scottish Open, could not entertain the Spaniard missing. Lane, the clubhouse leader, having thundered out of the pack with a closing six-under-par 66 – the lowest round of the week on a treacherous Robert Trent Jones Junior

Jose Maria Canizares's victory in the first Roma Masters took his European earnings past the million pound mark

layout – watched his older rival.

Eight shots behind Canizares at the start of the day Lane was now one shot adrift preparing to concede defeat. 'I really can't see him three putting from there,' said Lane, peering down from his

clubhouse perch to the kidney-shaped 18th green below. 'Canizares is such a good putter, I can only see him holing it.'

The fates had duly been tempted. Canizares rolled his first putt two-and-a half feet past, missed the return, and before he had time to feel shocked he and Lane were off back to the 166-yard, par three 17th, the first play-off hole.

The Spanish veteran of 21 Tour campaigns and four Ryder Cups was soon ballooning his tee shot high and right into heavy rough. With his ball deep in clover, Canizares most definitely wasn't. With Lane, after a tee shot that shadowed the flagstick all the way, at the back of the green in one, Canizares, who had gone into Sunday with a five-shot lead, looked as buried as his ball.

After Canizares had chipped to 15 feet and rolled his putt dead for bogey, it was then Lane's turn to hole 'one of those putts' for victory. His first putt had drifted five feet past and Lane, whose 66 had included four birdies and an eagle, failed with the return, and recorded his first bogey of the day.

With both players on the fourth extra hole, the 385-yard, par four 18th, in regulation, but with neither threatening a birdie, a trip back to the 17th looked inevitable. That was before Canizares's

Italian architecture overlooks the Castelgandolfo course.

First victory for nine years for Jose Maria Canizares.

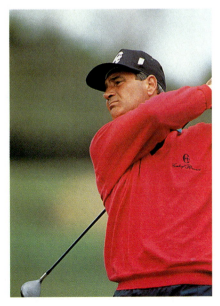

rolled home his ball from 20 feet. Now Lane needed to repeat the heroics of his birdie putt from the back of the 18th green minutes earlier which had forced the play-off in the first place. The attempt from 15 feet was not short, but it was not on line either, and carried on rolling.

The Roma Masters at Castelgandolfo, as it had promised to do, had been decided on the greens. They had driven all but the most courageous to despair. Bill Longmuir, who went into the final day in second place some five shots behind

Canizares, suffered more than most. 'Tell me how many players only missed one green today, and had 38 putts?' said the Scot, whose closing 75 included successive three putts at the second and third.

The difficulty of the Castelgandolfo layout was increased by the persistent and inconsistent wind. Built into the centre of a long-since extinct volcano, Castelgandolfo lies exposed in a natural bowl, easy prey to the whims of the Roman weather.

The scoring paid testimony to the severity of the course. Canizares and severity of the course. Canizares and Lane, tied at two under, were the only players to finish under par after four rounds. At eight over, the cut was the highest so far in the season. It is unusual that players can shoot 81 on Thursday and not be taking the early flight home on Friday.

On such a demanding course Lane's final round 66 was a fine achievement. Although not as low, Canizares's third round 69 – on a day when only one other player managed to break par, Alfonso Pinero with a 71 – was perhaps even more remarkable. Five birdies in seven holes from the fifth saw the Spaniard defying gravity by moving up the leaderboard when everyone else was moving down.

Castelgandolfo's main claim to fame, apart from the fact it now has a golf course, is that the Pope has his summer villa there. But for one weekend at least, miracle-making in this corner of Italy was not the work of the Pontif. Defying the ageing process and the Latin weather was left to one Jose Maria Canizares, whose first prize of £37,500 took his European career earnings to £1 million.

Play-off victim
Barry Lane.

COURSE: CASTELGANDOLFO			DATE:2-5.4		YARDAGE: 6742		PAR: 72	
POS	NAME	CTY	1	2	3	4	TOTAL	PRIZE MONEY
1	Jose Maria CANIZARES	Sp	72	71	69	74	286	£37500
2	Barry LANE	Eng	72	72	76	66	286	25000
3	Jim PAYNE	Eng	70	73	77	69	289	14070
4	Mark ROE	Eng	68	76	75	72	291	9533
	Paul CURRY	Eng	72	71	75	73	291	9533
	Eduardo ROMERO	Arg	71	75	72	73	291	9533
7	Anders FORSBRAND	Swe	73	75	77	67	292	6150
	Bill LONGMUIR	Scot	70	72	75	75	292	6150
9	Mark JAMES	Eng	70	73	76	74	293	4745
	David WILLIAMS	Eng	71	74	75	73	293	4745
11	Jose RIVERO	Sp	75	77	73	69	294	3903
	Costantino ROCCA	It	81	70	73	70	294	3903
	David CURRY	Eng	74	75	72	73	294	3903
14	Mark DAVIS	Eng	72	72	78	73	295	3485
	Glenn RALPH	Eng	74	72	76	73	295	3485
16	Malcolm MACKENZIE	Eng	71	73	77	75	296	3190
	Tony JOHNSTONE	Zim	77	70	73	76	296	3190
18	Alfonso PINERO	Sp	77	72	71	77	297	2920
	Des SMYTH	Ire	76	72	74	75	297	2920
20	Jim RUTLEDGE	Can	74	76	72	76	298	2521
	John McHENRY	Ire	72	75	76	75	298	2521
	Chris MOODY	Eng	72	77	74	75	298	2521
	Jon ROBSON	Eng	72	76	74	76	298	2521
	Jarmo SANDELIN	Swe	76	73	73	76	298	2521
	Silvio GRAPPASONNI	It	74	77	73	74	298	2521
	Jorge BERENDT	Arg	71	76	78	73	298	2521
27	Michael ARCHER	Eng	77	72	78	72	299	2185
	Marco DURANTE	It	72	77	77	73	299	2185
29	Paul LAWRIE	Scot	74	77	76	73	300	2010
	Giuseppe CALI	It	80	72	75	73	300	2010
	Garry HARVEY	Scot	70	71	81	78	300	2010
32	Jonathan CHEETHAM	Eng	73	74	77	77	301	1800
	Haydn SELBY-GREEN	Eng	73	72	82	74	301	1800
	Stephen HAMILL	N.Ire	75	77	77	72	301	1800
35	Juan QUIROS	Sp	75	73	78	76	302	1580
	Alexander CEJKA	Ger	76	76	74	76	302	1580
	Eoghan O'CONNELL	Ire	75	74	74	79	302	1580
	Charles RAULERSON	USA	73	74	77	78	302	1580
	Neal BRIGGS	Eng	74	78	73	77	302	1580
	Santiago LUNA	Sp	71	76	78	77	302	1580
41	Miguel Angel JIMENEZ	Sp	71	81	74	77	303	1380
	Jeremy ROBINSON	Eng	72	76	78	77	303	1380
	Mats HALLBERG	Swe	76	76	76	75	303	1380
	Frederic REGARD	Fr	73	76	76	78	303	1380
45	Johan TUMBA	Swe	75	77	77	75	304	1200
	Stuart LITTLE	Eng	72	78	77	77	304	1200
	Thomas LEVET	Fr	76	74	77	77	304	1200
	Tony CHARNLEY	Eng	76	73	80	75	304	1200
	Massimo MANNELLI	It	76	74	73	81	304	1200
50	Torsten GIEDEON	Ger	76	76	80	73	305	1040
	Patrick HALL	Eng	74	75	78	78	305	1040
	Alberto BINAGHI	It	75	77	75	78	305	1040
53	Adam MEDNICK	Swe	75	76	78	77	306	940
	Glyn KRAUSE	Eng	73	75	80	78	306	940
55	Mathias GRONBERG	Swe	77	73	78	79	307	820
	Olle NORDBERG	Swe	75	77	73	82	307	820
	Daniel WESTERMARK	Swe	75	75	78	79	307	820
	Paul CARRIGILL	Eng	71	79	80	77	307	820
59	Roger WINCHESTER	Eng	72	75	80	81	308	660
	Steen TINNING	Den	74	73	80	81	308	660
	Alessandro ROGATO	It	75	76	81	76	308	660
	Peter SMITH	Scot	75	75	83	75	308	660
	Peter HEDBLOM	Swe	73	77	85	73	308	660
64	Tim PLANCHIN	Fr	73	77	80	79	309	570
65	Gordon J BRAND	Eng	81	71	78	80	310	540
66	David JAMES	Scot	76	74	79	82	311	400
67	Neil RODERICK	Wal	76	73	82	81	312	397
	William GUY	Scot	78	74	79	81	312	397
69	David R JONES	Eng	76	76	81	81	314	393

EVERY CROWD HAD A SILVA LINING

Urged on by his countrymen, Portugal's Daniel Silva became the first man from that country to win in Europe

The eyes streamed uncontrollably onto anaesthetised cheeks, the wind howled, and the flags billowed starch-stiff from their masts. It was not nice, traipsing round the clifftop links of La Moye that Sunday afternoon in early April. But to one Daniel Silva, raised in sunnier climes by far, it was no more than a stroll in the park as he helped himself to the Jersey European Airways Open title with a total of 277, 11 under par, and gratefully stuffed £37,500 into his pocket.

The chunkily-built Silva, aged 25, was born to Portuguese parents in Johannesburg, and spent his formative years there before returning to his native land in 1986. He might speak his mother tongue with a South African accent you could cut with a knife, but there was no mistaking where his patriotic fervour lay as he became the first Portuguese to win a Volvo Tour event.

He would have had little chance of escaping his birthright in Jersey, in any case. The beautiful little Channel Island positively groans with Portuguese accents in the summer months, relying as it does on the good folk of Madeira to staff its hotel and restaurant trade.

Silva had only been on the island a few hours before the grapevine was carrying the message: come to La Moye, we have a potential hero on our hands. And thus it was that the waiters and kitchen porters, the chefs and sommeliers dogged Silva's footsteps throughout the tournament, most of them not knowing a tee peg from a toothpick but happy that they were supporting one of their own.

What they saw as the weather turned spiteful after three gentle days, mostly in the sun, was a performance of some style from their man. As those vastly more experienced in the ways of seaside golf fell off the back of the lorry, Silva stayed firmly aboard with a closing 73 to take the winner's cheque by a couple of strokes from the charging Chris Moody,

with Robert Karlsson, Peter Mitchell and Mark Roe, the overnight leader, two further behind.

The motoring analogy is for once not such a bad one actually, since Silva is attached to Pine Cliffs Golf and Country Club in the Algarve, the president of which is Nigel Mansell.

Silva was supported, both financially and morally, by Mansell when he was trying to earn himself a place on the Tour in the late 1980s, and he was quick to give thanks to the fastest driver in the world. 'Nigel is such a positive person, and his attitude has flowed through me,' he said. 'I can't thank him enough for what he's done for me.'

Small sentimental wallowings duly disposed of, it was time for Silva to reflect upon a final round in which he played with a maturity far beyond his comparatively tender years in a round containing 15 pars, one birdie and two bogeys.

Meanwhile, Roe, so impressive on the first three days, could make nothing of the conditions, seven bogeys in a round of 79 scuppering his chances. The two players lying second with Silva overnight, Mitchell and Derrick Cooper, fared no better, and the only real threat at the last came from Moody.

Playing 13 groups from the end, he returned an impressive 69 including four birdies and a bogey, equalling the best round of the day. As he sat back in the warmth of the clubhouse, Moody saw name after name subside from the leaderboard and watched his own keep on climbing. In the end it was not quite

enough, but it still added up to the biggest pay day he had had since winning the Ebel European Masters-Swiss Open in 1988.

Moody was nowhere after the first round, when Cooper shared the lead with Barry Lane and Keith Waters, and nowhere after the second, by which time Roe and Silva had taken a one-stroke advantage. At that moment Moody must have wished he'd got a slice of the action the previous day, when a local book-maker took a total of £1,000 on Roe at 40-1.

Andrew Chandler, Roe's manager, denied the allegations from certain quarters that he had laid down a thousand of the best, but did confess to having made a modest speculation each way on his client. It was enough, anyway, for the odds to be cut with unseemly haste to a more reasonable 20-1.

Roe claimed to have calmed down a good deal since the days early in his career when he was given to careering hyperactively round the golf course like an ant on speed. He admitted, however, to being a martyr to the devil chocolate: 'I'm

a four Twixes and a Crunchie man,' he said with a hint of defiance. At any rate, he still managed to keep up a pretty rapid clip in a round of 65, which was matched by Silva.

Roe's new-found powers of forbearance were tested to the limit on the third day, when sea mists shrouded the course in their clammy embrace and caused several interruptions of play. He was stranded for half an hour on the tenth tee before he could see enough to join Silva, his partner, on the fairway, having already waited for 45 minutes to play his second shot on the hole before. His patience was rewarded with a 68, which put him in the lead by two.

So the scene was set. Would Roe claim the second victory of his career, or Silva his first? In the end the personable young man from Portugal prevailed to become the 50th first-time winner since the advent of the all-exempt Tour in 1984. And Andrew Chandler, golfer, golfer's manager and all-round good egg, went home happy. He didn't pick the winner, but he still knew a good each-way bet when he saw one.

Mark James
drives on the final hole.

Daniel Silva salutes
first Volvo Tour victory, left.

Silva makes friends
with the trophy.

Defending champion
Sam Torrance.

								PRIZE
COURSE: LA MOYE		**DATE: 9-12.4**			**YARDAGE: 6817**			**PAR: 72**
POS	**NAME**	**CTY**	**1**	**2**	**3**	**4**	**TOTAL**	**PRIZE MONEY**
1	Daniel SILVA	Port	69	65	70	73	277	£37500
2	Chris MOODY	Eng	69	71	70	69	279	25000
3	Peter MITCHELL	Eng	72	67	65	77	281	11606
	Robert KARLSSON	Swe	70	67	70	74	281	11606
	Mark ROE	Eng	69	65	68	79	281	11606
6	David J RUSSELL	Eng	69	71	70	72	282	5375
	David GILFORD	Eng	69	67	69	77	282	5375
	Paul BROADHURST	Eng	70	72	68	72	282	5375
	Barry LANE	Eng	66	71	71	74	282	5375
	Mark JAMES	Eng	67	69	70	76	282	5375
	Heinz P THUEL	Ger	70	69	70	73	282	5375
	Martin GATES	Eng	70	70	69	73	282	5375
13	Peter BAKER	Eng	69	71	72	71	283	3341
	Thomas LEVET	Fr	71	72	70	70	283	3341
	Des SMYTH	Ire	69	72	69	73	283	3341
	Andrew SHERBORNE	Eng	72	67	70	74	283	3341
	Neal BRIGGS	Eng	69	73	71	70	283	3341
	Richard BOXALL	Eng	70	73	69	71	283	3341
19	Bernard GALLACHER	Scot	69	70	70	75	284	2563
	Anders SORENSEN	Den	68	74	71	71	284	2563
	Stephen FIELD	Eng	71	73	71	69	284	2563
	Derrick COOPER	Eng	66	70	68	80	284	2563
	Kevin DICKENS	Eng	72	70	72	70	284	2563
	Steen TINNING	Den	73	68	69	74	284	2563
	Carl MASON	Eng	71	71	67	75	284	2563
	Chris PLATTS	Eng	70	70	74	70	284	2563
27	Brian MARCHBANK	Scot	73	70	70	72	285	1883
	Wayne RILEY	Aus	69	70	73	73	285	1883
	Patrick HALL	Eng	71	72	71	71	285	1883
	Gordon BRAND Jnr	Scot	68	69	71	77	285	1883
	Bill LONGMUIR	Scot	68	68	74	75	285	1883
	Jimmy HEGGARTY	N.Ire	70	71	71	73	285	1883
	Philip WALTON	Ire	74	69	71	71	285	1883
	Russell CLAYDON	Eng	71	67	73	74	285	1883
	Andrew HARE	Eng	70	70	71	74	285	1883
	Peter FOWLER	Aus	77	67	69	72	285	1883
	David WILLIAMS	Eng	70	70	69	76	285	1883
38	Martin POXON	Eng	71	69	72	74	286	1400
	Mats LANNER	Swe	72	71	66	77	286	1400
	Christy O'CONNOR Jnr	Ire	70	73	71	72	286	1400
	Roger CHAPMAN	Eng	69	71	71	75	286	1400
	David A RUSSELL	Eng	70	73	71	72	286	1400
	Glenn RALPH	Eng	71	68	68	79	286	1400
	Sam TORRANCE	Scot	69	68	70	79	286	1400
	Jim RUTLEDGE	Can	70	73	69	74	286	1400
	David CURRY	Eng	70	67	75	74	286	1400
47	Paul LAWRIE	Scot	71	70	71	75	287	1140
	Peter SMITH	Scot	67	70	77	73	287	1140
	Darren CLARKE	N.Ire	71	69	72	75	287	1140
	Roger WINCHESTER	Eng	70	71	68	78	287	1140
51	Andrew MURRAY	Eng	72	72	71	73	288	920
	Mark DAVIS	Eng	69	75	69	75	288	920
	Phillip PRICE	Wal	69	75	69	75	288	920
	Denis DURNIAN	Eng	69	74	73	72	288	920
	Malcolm MACKENZIE	Eng	67	72	72	77	288	920
	Robert LEE	Eng	70	70	72	76	288	920
	Keith WATERS	Eng	66	74	72	76	288	920
58	Jeremy ROBINSON	Eng	70	70	68	81	289	740
	Adam HUNTER	Scot	71	72	71	75	289	740
60	Eamonn DARCY	Ire	68	73	70	79	290	675
	Gary EVANS	Eng	71	71	74	74	290	675
62	Magnus SUNESSON	Swe	73	67	73	79	292	615
	Michael KING	Eng	72	71	74	75	292	615
64	Jon ROBSON	Eng	70	70	79	74	293	570
65	Darren PROSSER	Eng	69	74	72	79	294	540
66	Kenneth TRIMBLE	Aus	74	69	73	81	297	400

GILFORD KEEPS COOL IN THE HEAT

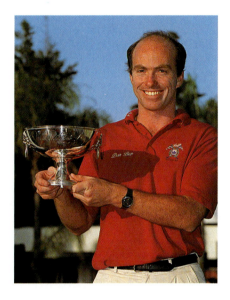

Amid soaring temperatures, David Gilford remained cool and calm to win his second Volvo Tour title

A week after laid-back Freddie Couples had won the US Masters at Augusta, an Englishman by the name of David Gilford showed a similar sort of temperament to win the £250,000 Moroccan Open.

Gilford and Couples are out of the same school; one that teaches composure amid a crisis. And so, when Gilford knew he had to hole a curly birdie putt of eight feet on the last green to get into a play-off with the young Swede Robert Karlsson, there was never much doubt about him finding the centre of the hole. That he holed two more putts of a similar length during the three holes of the play-off was hardly less surprising.

David Gilford's lack of hair makes him look older than his 26 years. His golf has a mature edge to it as well, and his second professional victory established him as one of the senior campaigners on the Volvo Tour even though he has only been a professional for five years. An old head on young shoulders in every sense.

It was an extraordinary exhibition of patience because Gilford did not exactly get off to a flying start in the first round. He bogeyed the first hole, in fact he bogeyed three of the first four holes, and his 76 put him eight shots off the lead held by another Swede, Fredrik Lindgren.

Gilford was, however, not the only player finding the Robert Trent Jones layout too hot to handle as temperatures soared into the 90s. Bernhard Langer, flying straight in from Augusta, had a pair of 76s and declared: 'This is the toughest course on Tour, tougher even

than Valderrama.' And another pre-tournament favourite, Paul Broadhurst, was flying home early after a second round 80, describing it as 'one of the most difficult courses I've ever played on'.

The course may have been tough but it was a magnificent test of golf and received unanimous praise from the players. Par was always going to be difficult to beat though, and a blustery wind for the first two days meant the cut came at a record ten over par.

Lindgren still led at the halfway stage, despite being confronted by a snake as he made his way from the ninth green to the tenth tee. His caddie, apparently well-practised in the art of dealing with such things, stamped on it and heroically saved his master from distraction.

The happy knack which Sweden seems to have had over the last decade of producing top tennis players seems to have turned its attentions to golf, and there are a whole host of golfers itching to break through. Lindgren and Karlsson were just two. Indeed, of the 11 Swedes in the field, ten of them made the cut and four finished in the top ten. In contrast, of the 11 Moroccans in the field, not one of them made the cut, and they finished a combined 211 over par.

Gilford was lying 25th after two rounds, moving steadily up the field despite wrapping his two iron round a tree and being unable to use it for the remainder of the tournament. His patience was rewarded in the third round however, when he birdied four of the first five holes on his way to a 68. He shared in a tie for the lead at one-over-par after 54 holes with Karlsson.

Karlsson has spent two years on the Volvo Tour, and his best finish before this week was third in the Scandinavian Masters in 1991. He has a lot of golf in front of him, and is still only 22. A shot further back was the Englishman Ricky Willison, the 34-year old former printer who played in the Walker Cup last September at Portmarnock, and was enjoying his first season as a professional.

'I was playing so well that at times I thought I could walk on water,' said Willison.

He eventually finished a very creditable third, a miraculous performance for someone who failed to get his card at the PGA European Tour Qualifying School, and had to rely on a sponsor's invitation just to play. His performances this season almost certainly ensured his card for next year and he was just two shots from making the play-off.

In the play-off, Karlsson could not match Gilford's birdie at the third play-off hole (the 18th), the second time he had birdied this par five in half an hour. The Moroccan crowd watched and admired the Englishman who had virtually come back from the dead.

Moroccans are taking to golf as they do to couscous. They are lapping it up, and the enthusiasm from the youngsters is unbelievable. They have a king – Hassan II – who is fanatical about the game, and

Second Volvo Tour title for
David Gilford.

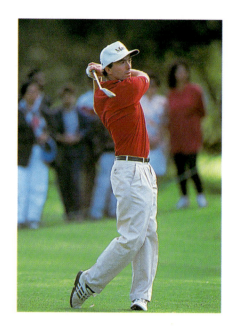

has put a substantial amount of his own money into promoting the sport. What they need now is a star of their own to follow. But for the time being they had to be content with cheering a Midlander who has a reputation for being quiet.

Gilford is also living proof that Crewe has more to it than a train station. He is Mr Consistency himself, the man who played in 26 tournaments in 1991 and finished in the money in 25 of them. This triumph was proof, if proof were needed, that he has not only put the disappointments of Kiawah Island behind him, but that his victory in the NM English Open in 1991 was no fluke. What Morocco would give for someone like him.

Tranquil setting at Royal
Dar-Es-Salaam.

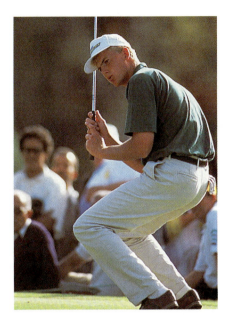

Runner-up

Robert Karlsson.

COURSE: ROYAL DAR-ES-SALAM DATE:16-19.4 YARDAGE: 7222 PAR: 72

POS	NAME	CTY	1	2	3	4	TOTAL	PRIZE MONEY
1	David GILFORD	Eng	76	73	68	70	287	£41660
2	Robert KARLSSON	Swe	70	75	72	70	287	27770
3	Ricky WILLISON	Eng	70	75	73	71	289	15650
4	Mats HALLBERG	Swe	71	75	73	71	290	11550
	Darren CLARKE	N.Ire	74	75	70	71	290	11550
6	Steven BOWMAN	USA	71	73	74	73	291	7025
	Fredrik LINDGREN	Swe	68	74	76	73	291	7025
	Anders FORSBRAND	Swe	70	78	71	72	291	7025
	Gordon MANSON	Scot	74	72	73	72	291	7025
10	Phillip PRICE	Wal	74	75	73	70	292	4800
	Vijay SINGH	Fij	74	71	78	69	292	4800
12	Brian MARCHBANK	Scot	78	73	71	71	293	4155
	Andre BOSSERT	Swi	76	73	74	70	293	4155
14	Bill LONGMUIR	Scot	71	78	71	74	294	3387
	Jeremy ROBINSON	Eng	74	77	72	71	294	3387
	Ross DRUMMOND	Scot	75	77	71	71	294	3387
	Magnus SUNESSON	Swe	74	74	74	72	294	3387
	Alfonso PINERO	Sp	77	73	73	71	294	3387
	Jim PAYNE	Eng	76	70	73	75	294	3387
	Mark JAMES	Eng	72	75	74	73	294	3387
21	Gordon J BRAND	Eng	70	76	74	75	295	2700
	Tony JOHNSTONE	Zim	74	78	75	68	295	2700
	Adam HUNTER	Scot	73	76	75	71	295	2700
	Philip WALTON	Ire	76	75	72	72	295	2700
	Peter FOWLER	Aus	76	75	75	69	295	2700
	Mike CLAYTON	Aus	72	75	73	75	295	2700
	Philip PARKIN	Wal	77	73	70	75	295	2700
28	Alexander CEJKA	Ger	69	77	78	72	296	2287
	Jean VAN DE VELDE	Fr	75	72	75	74	296	2287
	John MORSE	USA	75	72	72	77	296	2287
	Michel BESANCENEY	Fr	77	70	75	74	296	2287
32	Glenn RALPH	Eng	72	75	77	73	297	1950
	Anders SORENSEN	Den	76	75	71	75	297	1950
	Kevin DICKENS	Eng	76	76	73	72	297	1950
	Christian POST	Den	69	76	77	75	297	1950
	Bernhard LANGER	Ger	76	76	71	74	297	1950
	Derrick COOPER	Eng	75	73	73	76	297	1950
	Stephen FIELD	Eng	78	70	76	73	297	1950
39	John METCALFE	Eng	74	79	76	69	298	1700
	Jon ROBSON	Eng	77	74	71	76	298	1700
	Tod POWER	Aus	74	78	74	72	298	1700
42	Jay TOWNSEND	USA	78	75	71	75	299	1550
	Nick JOB	Eng	74	77	77	71	299	1550
	Roger CHAPMAN	Eng	74	75	74	76	299	1550
45	Keith WATERS	Eng	75	77	75	73	300	1400
	David WILLIAMS	Eng	74	76	76	74	300	1400
	Mark MOULAND	Wal	77	75	70	78	300	1400
48	Dennis EDLUND	Swe	78	73	80	70	301	1225
	Karl ABLEIDINGER	Aut	78	78	77	70	301	1225
	Jose COCERES	Arg	70	79	75	77	301	1225
	Paolo QUIRICI	Swi	74	74	78	75	301	1225
52	Grant TURNER	Eng	76	73	80	73	302	1050
	Stuart LITTLE	Eng	77	75	77	73	302	1050
	Wraith GRANT	Eng	74	74	79	75	302	1050
55	Ole ESKILDSEN	Den	78	69	77	79	303	925
	Stephen BENNETT	Eng	77	76	75	75	303	925
57	Fredrik LARSSON	Swe	74	80	80	70	304	780
	Justin HOBDAY	Eng	72	79	78	75	304	780
	Alberto BINAGHI	It	71	81	77	75	304	780
	Michael ARCHER	Eng	74	78	82	70	304	780
	Peter SMITH	Scot	77	77	74	76	304	780
62	Olle NORDBERG	Swe	76	78	80	71	305	700
63	Garry HARVEY	Scot	76	78	78	74	306	650
	Chris PLATTS	Eng	79	75	78	74	306	650
	Mike MILLER	Scot	73	77	82	74	306	650
66	Adam MEDNICK	Swe	76	77	74	80	307	399
	Jose Manuel CARRILES	Sp	76	77	77	77	307	399
68	John MCHENRY	Ire	76	78	82	72	308	396
69	Orrin VINCENT III	USA	71	79	80	79	309	394
70	Anssi KANKKONEN	Fin	76	78	81	77	312	392

FORSBRAND GOES TO THE TOP

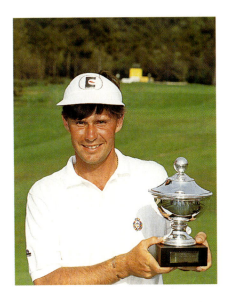

With his second win in five weeks Anders Forsbrand became the first Swede to top the Volvo Order of Merit

The Credit Lyonnais Cannes Open closed with a grand finale. In this international resort in southern France, two Swedish golfers strode on to the last green on Sunday separated by a single stroke after 71 holes of keen competition under invariably azure skies.

First to putt was Per-Ulrik Johansson, who lay 30 feet from the cup in two and who trailed Anders Forsbrand, his team-mate in Sweden's victorious Dunhill and World Cup teams the previous autumn, by a stroke. Johansson studied his putt carefully, hit it perfectly, and then launched a spontaneous attempt on the world high jump record as his ball disappeared into the hole.

His jubilation was understandable – after all, it was a heck of a putt to make in the circumstances – but it was also optimistic. Forsbrand's ball had finished a mere 18 inches from the flag after a beautifully judged pitch to the 72nd green.

Professionals don't often miss putts of that length, and Forsbrand wasn't about to now. After all, he had not finished worse than seventh in his last five tournaments, one of which – the Volvo Open in Florence in March – he had won, so his confidence was hardly shaken by Johansson's last-gasp heroics. He tapped the ball in to secure his fourth PGA European Tour title and become the first Swede to go top of the Volvo Order of Merit. And he was where he had been when the tournament had started over the pine-lined Mougins course four days earlier – at the top of the leaderboard.

Forsbrand had opened up with a seven-under-par 65 that enabled him to take a one-shot lead on the pack which was led by Johansson. 'My confidence is higher than it has ever been,' said Forsbrand that evening after a bogey-free display. 'And my mental attitude is getting better.'

But the two most celebrated names in the field at Cannes were less than ecstatic about their form. Ian Woosnam, fresh – or rather stale – from his ultimately lacklustre defence of the US Masters title – had a 74 and complained: 'I'm getting worse if anything.' By the end of the week, when a concluding 66 had lifted him into a tie for fifth, he was happier, 'I know what I want to work on; it's improving', if by no means content.

The defending champion, David Feherty, wasn't around at the weekend. As if he didn't have enough on his mind with his wife about to bear their second child, the airline had temporarily lost his clubs and he had broken a tooth on the flight to Nice. After a 76 on Thursday he said: 'I played more like Jacques Tati than Jack Nicklaus.' After a 79 the next day had ensured he would miss the cut, he quipped: 'The lights were on but there was no-one at home.'

By Friday night, Johansson had caught Forsbrand but the Swedish monopoly bid had been frustrated by Scotland's Mike Miller. His second-round 68 had earned him a share of the lead – one that lasted until he played the first hole of his third round. A hooked drive into an unplayable lie and a fluffed chip cost him a six, whereas Johansson struck a gorgeous three-iron to four feet and made the putt for a birdie three. Since Forsbrand had just bogeyed the hole by three-putting from ten yards, Johansson had established a clear advantage over his rivals before proceedings had hardly begun.

Although Forsbrand continued to be occasionally shaky on the greens, three-putting twice more in the hot afternoon, he hit every one in regulation figures and got his somewhat untrusty blade under sufficient control towards the end of his round to birdie four successive holes from the 14th. The result was a 68 for him, while Johansson had only managed to gain two further shots on par after that first hole. On 204, he trailed Forsbrand by a shot. David Jones from Essex had recorded a 66 to be on 206 and Ryder Cup player Colin Montgomerie was on 207. Jones, with sad predictability, was to fade quickly away on Sunday, but Montgomerie was not.

That Forsbrand prevailed might have come as no surprise to anyone who heard Johansson say on Saturday night, 'He is the best player in Europe at the moment', but it was not the obvious denouement with six holes to play. Bogeys at the ninth and tenth, both sturdy but by no means intimidating par-fours, had left Forsbrand two shots behind Johansson. They were level after the 13th, where Johansson should have hit the nine-iron he thought rather than the eight-iron

his caddie suggested. He overshot the green and took a bogey five while Forsbrand hit a preposterously long drive followed by a sand wedge to ten feet for a birdie.

At 12 under par, the two Swedes had been caught by Colin Montgomerie, who had survived an indifferent start to birdie four consecutive holes from the tenth. With five holes to play, it was a three-man race.

The 14th proved pivotal. 'Monty' hit his second shot into the creek that sinuously protects the front right of the green and wound up with a bogey six. Forsbrand chipped and putted for his birdie four at the same hole; Johansson chipped and two-putted for a par. Johansson then birdied the par-three 15th but Forsbrand birdied the long 16th to restore his lead. The 17th was, in match-play terms, halved in fours, and the 18th you already know about.

The only blemish on a perfect day for Forsbrand was the performance of Zimbabwe's Tony Johnstone. A closing 62 not only elevated him alongside Woosnam into fifth place and earned him £10,000 from the Johnnie Walker Tour Course Record Award, it bagged him a Rolex watch for shooting the lowest round of the week. Until Johnstone's magnificent ten-under-par effort, Forsbrand's 65 on Thursday had looked set to reward him with the handsome timepiece.

Not that the Swede had too much too grouse about, of course. His winner's cheque granted him entry to the PGA European Tour 's 'Millionaires' Club', with career winnings of £1,044,407. In that respect at least, his time had come.

The 15th tee was well signposted, right.

Colin Montgomerie challenged strongly for the title.

Exultant leap from Per-Ulrik Johansson as he holes his putt on the 72nd.

The winner and mascot.

POS	NAME	CTY	1	2	3	4	TOTAL	PRIZE MONEY

COURSE: CANNES MOUGINS   DATE:23-26.4   YARDAGE: 6849   PAR: 72

POS	NAME	CTY	1	2	3	4	TOTAL	PRIZE MONEY
1	Anders FORSBRAND	Swe	65	70	68	70	273	£58330
2	Per-Ulrik JOHANSSON	Swe	66	69	69	70	274	38880
3	Colin MONTGOMERIE	Scot	70	69	68	69	276	21910
4	Vijay SINGH	Fij	67	75	70	66	278	17500
5	Peter TERAVAINEN	USA	69	69	71	71	280	12526
	Ian WOOSNAM	Wal	74	68	72	66	280	12526
	Tony JOHNSTONE	Zim	69	72	77	62	280	12526
8	Robert KARLSSON	Swe	71	69	70	72	282	8750
9	Chris VAN DER VELDE	Hol	71	69	71	72	283	6200
	Carl MASON	Eng	72	67	73	71	283	6200
	David GILFORD	Eng	73	65	74	71	283	6200
	Paul CURRY	Eng	74	67	69	73	283	6200
	Russell CLAYDON	Eng	73	69	73	68	283	6200
	Sam TORRANCE	Scot	71	74	68	70	283	6200
	Barry LANE	Eng	72	70	68	73	283	6200
16	Glen DAY	USA	72	70	68	74	284	4399
	Des SMYTH	Ire	74	71	68	71	284	4399
	Ricky WILLISON	Eng	75	67	71	71	284	4399
	Joakim HAEGGMAN	Swe	71	71	71	71	284	4399
	Rick HARTMANN	USA	71	69	72	72	284	4399
	Mike CLAYTON	Aus	72	69	70	73	284	4399
	Fredrik LINDGREN	Swe	71	71	72	70	284	4399
23	Silvio GRAPPASONNI	It	70	71	74	70	285	3727
	Gordon J BRAND	Eng	72	68	76	69	285	3727
	Eamonn DARCY	Ire	74	68	73	70	285	3727
	David R JONES	Eng	71	69	66	79	285	3727
27	Jay TOWNSEND	USA	70	70	72	74	286	3155
	Frank NOBILO	NZ	71	70	77	68	286	3155
	Phillip PRICE	Wal	68	74	75	69	286	3155
	Andrew MURRAY	Eng	74	70	72	70	286	3155
	Derrick COOPER	Eng	68	70	76	72	286	3155
	Jim RUTLEDGE	Can	74	66	76	70	286	3155
	Peter O'MALLEY	Aus	72	71	72	71	286	3155
34	Bill MALLEY	USA	70	71	73	73	287	2660
	Mike MILLER	Scot	67	68	76	76	287	2660
	Malcolm MACKENZIE	Eng	71	73	71	72	287	2660
	Anders SORENSEN	Den	70	72	75	70	287	2660
	Steven RICHARDSON	Eng	69	75	71	72	287	2660
39	Stephen FIELD	Eng	74	71	72	71	288	2310
	Robert LEE	Eng	69	75	76	68	288	2310
	Mark McNULTY	Zim	70	74	72	72	288	2310
	Paul McGINLEY	Ire	73	70	73	72	288	2310
	Jose DAVILA	Sp	73	70	67	78	288	2310
44	Jesper PARNEVIK	Swe	73	71	71	74	289	2030
	Philip WALTON	Ire	71	68	75	75	289	2030
	Miguel Angel JIMENEZ	Sp	71	72	74	72	289	2030
47	David WILLIAMS	Eng	74	71	72	73	290	1890
48	Jeremy ROBINSON	Eng	71	72	71	77	291	1680
	Mats LANNER	Swe	73	72	73	73	291	1680
	Ove SELLBERG	Swe	73	70	78	70	291	1680
	Ian PALMER	SA	70	74	74	73	291	1680
	Grant TURNER	Eng	71	73	74	73	291	1680
53	Jose Maria CANIZARES	Sp	69	71	76	76	292	1330
	Ross McFARLANE	Eng	70	72	75	75	292	1330
	Quentin DABSON	Fr	70	68	75	79	292	1330
	Steven BOWMAN	USA	71	74	76	71	292	1330
	Santiago LUNA	Sp	70	74	71	77	292	1330
(AM)	Nicolas KALOUGUINE	Fr	70	73	71	78	292	–
58	Haydn SELBY-GREEN	Eng	74	71	72	76	293	1102
	Ken BROWN	Scot	71	74	72	76	293	1102
60	Gavin LEVENSON	SA	71	73	74	76	294	997
	Jose COCERES	Arg	68	77	75	74	294	997
	Mike McLEAN	Eng	73	71	75	75	294	997
	David A RUSSELL	Eng	71	71	78	74	294	997
64	Jonathan SEWELL	Eng	72	70	78	75	295	770
	Jean Francois REMESY	Fr	69	74	77	75	295	770
	Daniel SILVA	Port	69	72	78	76	295	770
67	Kenneth TRIMBLE	Aus	70	73	78	75	296	521
	Glenn RALPH	Eng	71	73	75	77	296	521
	Christophe MUNIESA	Fr	69	71	77	79	296	521
70	Stephen HAMILL	N.Ire	75	70	73	79	297	516

LYLE IS BACK
WITH A VENGEANCE

In his first appearance on the 1992 Volvo Tour, Sandy Lyle showed that his past frustrations were all behind him

S andy Lyle, that likeable competitor who had emerged from what for someone else might have been a mind-blowing three-year slump with a victory in the BMW International in the late autumn of 1991, knew he had to win again quickly to prove that Munich had not been a fluke.

Unlike his colleagues on the Volvo Tour Lyle, who has always enjoyed early year golf in America, took himself off there to work on his game and managed a creditable sixth place finish behind Fred Couples at the Los Angeles Open with wife Jolande as his caddie. She had caddied for her husband before in Japan, planned to do the first three tournaments in America with him in 1992 but had decided after Los Angeles to take the job on a more permanent basis. She caddied at all his early US appearances including the Masters at Augusta and the Lancia Martini Italian Open marked the family team's 1992 European debut.

The slump had had a serious effect on Lyle's popularity as a 'must' for any tournament. His 1985 Open and 1988 Masters wins had been quickly forgotten. but Lyle had no intention of waiting to be wooed by the men sponsoring tournaments. When he arrived, unheralded and unsung, at Monticello where big-hitting John Daly, the USPGA champion and Mark O'Meara, the US Ryder Cup player, were top-billed along with Jose Maria Olazabal, he told reporters: 'What's the point of frittering away all the good early season work in America by sitting at home.'

It was a commendable attitude and it proved that after all his troubles, Sandy was eager and enthusastic to play.

The pro-am was cut to nine holes because of heavy rain – a problem encountered before at earlier Italian Opens at Monticello which lies close to the snow-capped Alps. It is early in the year to be so far north in Italy, but the weather forecast for the four days of the Championship was positive enough –

sunshine and little wind – for the fans to hope for low scores, not least from Daly who flies the ball 290 yards and who impressed the remarkable Italian pro Aldo Casera, the 1948 winner and pre-Second World war entrant who was once again in the field. Daly, back happily with his fiancee Bettye Fulford after a much-publicised and apparently unpleasant break-up, took some of the bigger galleries. He thrilled the fans but he dropped too many shots a round and finish down the field in his first Volvo Tour appearance. Yet, enjoying lashings of spaghetti, he gave Italy, Monticello, the fans and officials a massive thumbs up.

It was Mark O'Meara who fired a second round 65, bettered only by Malcolm Mackenzie on the week, who was the main American threat despite back spasms which did not affect him when he was swinging but did when he stood still. With Olazabal finding his new irons not to his liking, missing too many greens and putting too much pressure on his short game to be a factor over the weekend and Anders Forsbrand, at that point topping the Volvo Order of Merit slipping away after two fine opening rounds, it was left to O'Meara, a re-vitalised Paul Way, Colin Montgomerie and Vijay Singh to emerge as Lyle's main challengers in the third and fourth rounds.

Montgomerie, third a week earlier in Cannes and on a ten successive weeks tournament run, had promised himself a win in one of the first four events he was playing since returning home from a month on the US Tour. Despite missing

Team Lyle
en route to victory.

Paul Way was
on the comeback trail.

three out of four halfway cuts, he had come back a tougher and wiser competitor. He was ready to win, but in the end had to make do with second spot to fellow countryman Lyle, missing by just two inches the putt across the last green that woiuld have forced an all-Scottish play-off.

Way, inspired by close friend Nigel Mansell who on the final day at Monticello won his fourth straight Grand Prix of the year at Jerez in Spain, holed from 20 feet on the last green to get the third place tie he deserved with O'Meara but it was Lyle who played and putted best to deservedly win his second Italian title in nine years. He was the first repeat winner since Belgian Flory Van Donck scored his fourth success in 1955 and Lyle won with a performance which justified all the hard work he had put in during those long hard months when little was going right for him.

In fact, the secret of his success was a gamble he made on the first day. He made a crucial change to his game plan

minutes after starting the round. He changed his putting style, moving to a left-hand-below-right method which he had practised with but never, he confessed. had the courage to try in a tournament. He putted not too successfully in the traditional way on the first but, encouraged by wife Jolande he took the plunge, changed grips and ended the week without having a single three putt.

'The change has helped me line up my shoulders and hips better,' said Lyle, whom Way felt had not played with such confidence in a long time. Of course, it was not easy for him over the last two days after breaking clear of the five-way halfway log jam with Montgomerie, O'Meara, Olazabal and Anders Forsbrand who stayed in top spot in the money-list despite slipping over the weekend.

Lyle moved to 13th on the rankings as he swept through to score one of the most joyous wins of the year and one which silenced those critics who considered he needed to do more than win one event to

signal the end of his slump. Way's slump, broken only by his 1987 win in the European Open, had been even longer than Lyle's but there was every prospect of his breakthrough soon to the winners' ranks after his performance at Monticello.

Yet Lyle was hero of the week, modest as always, looking as usual delighted for himself but just a little sorry for those he beaten. Of course that is his nature. He is a gentle killer on the links but he is such a superb competitor when fully concentrating that he, Jolande and his fans left Monticello hoping that the Lancia Martini Italian Open would be the springboard to more 1992 successes.

Despite finding the rough off the tee more often than he would have wished, his had been an almost flawless performance in an event which had produced its fair number of surprises and trick shots. Daly twice walked into the water at the 16th to play shots on the second day without bothering to take off his shoes or socks and Jose Rivero, at the same hole on the same day, clambered onto the tin

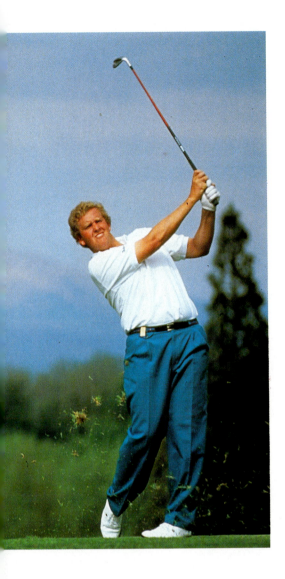

Blue backdrop for Colin

Montgomerie.

roof of a small hut to play his ball which had finished there.

No such excessive waywardness came from Lyle during the week as he handed in rounds of 70, 66, 65 and 69, the score he had predicted he needed to hold off all challengers, to take the first prize by a shot.

There was, it seems, perhaps one further reason why Sandy won. Midway through the event wife Jolande decided their Como-centre hotel was far too noisy and insisted on a move up into the mountains to the quietness and stillness of Villa d'Este to ensure Sandy got two good nights' rest. That proved an off-course masterstroke in the Lyle triumph. 'Now the caddie fees will be going up,' said Sandy who pocketed £61,038. Jolande simply smiled.

COURSE: MONTICELLO	DATE: 30.4-3.5	YARDAGE: 6973	PAR: 72					
POS	NAME	CTY	1	2	3	4	TOTAL	PRIZE MONEY
1	Sandy LYLE	Scot	66	71	65	68	270	£61038
2	Colin MONTGOMERIE	Scot	67	70	68	66	271	40652
3	Mark O'MEARA	USA	72	65	68	67	272	20621
	Paul WAY	Eng	69	69	66	68	272	20621
5	Vijay SINGH	Fij	71	68	69	68	276	15525
6	Jose RIVERO	Sp	71	70	69	68	278	10988
	Frank NOBILO	NZ	73	68	69	68	278	10988
	Eduardo ROMERO	Arg	70	72	71	65	278	10988
9	Per-Ulrik JOHANSSON	Swe	69	73	70	67	279	7420
	Barry LANE	Eng	69	71	71	68	279	7420
	Mats LANNER	Swe	69	71	68	71	279	7420
12	Glen DAY	USA	68	71	70	71	280	5669
	Jay TOWNSEND	USA	71	69	70	70	280	5669
	Paul LAWRIE	Scot	73	69	70	68	280	5669
	Steven BOWMAN	USA	69	70	68	73	280	5669
	Steven RICHARDSON	Eng	72	71	69	68	280	5669
17	Malcolm MACKENZIE	Eng	76	64	73	68	281	4447
	Richard BOXALL	Eng	69	70	72	70	281	4447
	Jose Maria OLAZABAL	Sp	65	72	71	73	281	4447
	Jose Maria CANIZARES	Sp	70	70	69	72	281	4447
	Justin HOBDAY	SA	70	72	71	68	281	4447
	Vicente FERNANDEZ	Arg	69	72	72	68	281	4447
	John DALY	USA	72	69	69	71	281	4447
24	Craig PARRY	Aus	73	71	71	67	282	3845
	Tony JOHNSTONE	Zim	70	71	68	73	282	3845
	Carl MASON	Eng	72	71	71	68	282	3845
27	Jonathan SEWELL	Eng	73	71	72	67	283	3351
	Santiago LUNA	Sp	71	71	72	69	283	3351
	Roger CHAPMAN	Eng	75	69	68	71	283	3351
	Jim PAYNE	Eng	68	72	72	71	283	3351
	Ricardo GONZALEZ	Arg	71	71	68	73	283	3351
	Anders FORSBRAND	Swe	68	69	72	74	283	3351
33	Andrew SHERBORNE	Eng	72	71	69	72	284	2966
	Rick HARTMANN	USA	71	71	71	71	284	2966
35	Mark MOULAND	Wal	74	71	68	72	285	2637
	Thomas LEVET	Fr	71	71	70	73	285	2637
	Jesper PARNEVIK	Swe	70	72	72	71	285	2637
	Fredrik LINDGREN	Swe	71	73	70	71	285	2637
	Paul CURRY	Eng	72	72	68	73	285	2637
	Magnus SUNESSON	Swe	74	69	72	70	285	2637
	Jon ROBSON	Eng	71	72	68	74	285	2637
42	Mike McLEAN	Eng	69	74	72	71	286	2161
	Jose COCERES	Arg	69	71	69	77	286	2161
	Jim RUTLEDGE	Can	71	72	71	72	286	2161
	Brett OGLE	Aus	71	71	71	73	286	2161
	Jean VAN DE VELDE	Fr	73	70	76	67	286	2161
	Kenneth TRIMBLE	Aus	72	73	67	74	286	2161
48	Peter TERAVAINEN	USA	71	72	71	73	287	1758
	Baldovino DASSU	It	73	69	75	70	287	1758
	Giuseppe CALI	It	73	71	72	71	287	1758
	Peter O'MALLEY	Aus	70	73	73	71	287	1758
	Mike CLAYTON	Aus	75	68	74	70	287	1758
53	Marco DURANTE	It	74	71	70	73	288	1391
	Juan QUIROS	Sp	71	72	71	74	288	1391
	Gary EVANS	Eng	71	73	74	70	288	1391
	Denis DURNIAN	Eng	70	72	74	72	288	1391
	Marc FARRY	Fr	74	71	72	71	288	1391
58	Gordon BRAND Jnr	Scot	71	72	74	72	289	1153
	Patrick HALL	Eng	71	73	73	72	289	1153
60	David CURRY	Eng	72	72	70	76	290	1080
	Peter BAKER	Eng	72	73	72	73	290	1080
62	Stephen FIELD	Eng	71	74	73	73	291	886
	Mikael PILTZ	Fin	70	72	76	73	291	886
	Kevin DICKENS	Eng	70	73	74	74	291	886
	Silvio GRAPPASONNI	It	72	72	74	73	291	886
	Miguel Angel JIMENEZ	Sp	72	71	75	73	291	886
67	David J RUSSELL	Eng	73	72	77	70	292	547
68	Tony CHARNLEY	Eng	72	70	79	72	293	542
	John HAWKSWORTH	Eng	71	72	77	73	293	542
	Tod POWER	Aus	71	74	72	76	293	542
	Brian MARCHBANK	Scot	73	71	75	74	293	542

SENIOR WHIPS THE CREAM IN CORNWALL

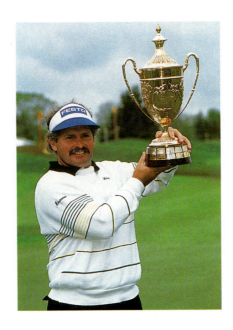

*Peter Senior snatched
the Benson and Hedges
title at St Mellion
from one of
the best fields assembled
on the Volvo Tour*

Few people gave Peter Senior a second glance when he arrived for the Benson and Hedges International Open at St Mellion. The small Australian who caught the eye was Craig Parry who had led after 54 holes of the US Masters.

Senior only arrived on Monday. Although he had finished second in the Chunichi Crowns event the previous day (and had won, in all, nearly £300,000 already for the year) he would surely be too tired to perform at his best on one of Europe's most difficult courses. Or so we thought. Besides, there seemed to be so many other players with outstanding credentials for winning the first Volvo Tour event of the season to be held in Britain.

One was Anders Forsbrand, the first Swede to lead the Volvo Order of Merit and the first to become a millionaire from it. Another was Nick Faldo, who was trying to end a run of 11 months without a victory. A third was Sandy Lyle, anxious to demonstrate his new left-hand-below-his-right putting style and that his victory the previous Sunday, his second on the Volvo Tour since last summer, was not a fluke.

Parry's 67 was the best of the opening day. It contained six birdies and only one bogey and was good enough to take a one-stroke lead over Colin Montgomerie and Forsbrand.

Montgomerie, a talented golfer, was in a rare vein of good form. He had not been over 70 for ten rounds and in that time he was 28 under par. 'He has a safe game, hits a high soft fade and has a wonderful touch,' said Lyle, who played

with him. 'There is no reason why Monty should not go all the way to the top.'

Set on top of a Cornish headland, St Mellion is rarely without wind and it got up for Friday's second round. Even so the cut fell at eight over, four fewer than in 1991. Montgomerie's bulk was useful in helping him keep his feet on the ground and he had a 72 for a total of 140, two

strokes better than Jim Payne, another hefty man, Peter Mitchell and Mats Lanner. Parry was blown to a 76 and was on 143, one over par, as were Lyle and Faldo.

Bad as the weather was on Friday, it was much worse on Saturday, the worst since the first day of the 1986 Open some said. Near gale-force winds and monsoon-like rain storms made conditions so difficult that one quarter of the field scored in the 80s. Eights were not uncommon, nines not unheard of and there was even a ten. After 54 holes not one player was under par. Parry and Lanner, joint leaders, were on level par.

Faldo and Montgomerie were two who said it was too early in the year to stage a tournament in Britain. Right course, wrong time, said Faldo, seeming to forget that midsummer's day was only six weeks away. Even on a calm day St Mellion is a rigorous test with its narrow fairways and small, undulating greens. It is one of the most unremitting courses in Europe. On a day such as that, some found it too difficult.

Mitchell took an 80, Lyle an 82. 'It's no fun out there,' said Lyle, wet and disconsolate. 'It will take me three weeks to get my game back. It was ridiculous.'

Montgomerie ballooned to a 13-over par 85, running up a three-over-par seven on the first hole and a five-over-par nine on the 13th. Jesper Parnevik three-putted the 18th for an 86 and then jumped in the greenside lake. 'I deserved it,' he said, ' It was warmer in than out.'

It was significant to discover who

Buggy convoy takes Tony Johnstone and Peter Senior to the play-off on the 18th.

Below, Johnstone chips to the 18th in the play-off.

Peter Senior pitches to the 72nd hole.

Jim Payne attempts a gorse record on the third.

played well on such a foul day. Parry, who comes from Sunshine in Australia, had a 73; Forsbrand, who has become so consistent since he changed his swing, had a 72 and Senior leaped up the field after a 70. Parry just got on with the job of playing good golf in trying circumstances. 'I am right on track at the moment,' he said. 'I have a better attitude than some of the guys out there.'

Odd, then, that on the calm and over-cast last day Parry took 75. Lanner fared even worse – a 77. At one point five men were tied for the lead, the most menacing of which was Faldo. He birdied the ninth, tenth, 11th and 16th for a 69. Good, but not quite good enough. Payne, a rookie, held on resolutely for a 71, his best finish as a professional, to tie with Faldo.

Birdies at the 14th and 15th took Tony Johnstone to the head of the field. He played the last five holes in two under par and just as he secured his par on the 18th, Senior holed a 15-foot putt on the 17th to draw level.

The play-off on the 18th was quick. Johnstone fluffed a chip from the fringe and took two more to get down. Senior, on the green in two, two-putted from 40 feet with his broomhandle putter and won by one stroke. It was his fifth play-off and his fifth victory at the first extra hole.

Senior gives hope to small men and yippers the world over. Four years ago he couldn't putt at all – until Sam Torrance gave him a putter with a 50-inch handle. That worked. Two years ago while playing the the Bell's Scottish Open he froze on the backswing, unable to bring the club down. Hard work enabled him to beat that frailty, too.

He was playing so well that this was his fourth tournament victory since December and in his past six events he had always finished among the first three. Not much attention was paid to him at the start of the week, but it certainly was at the end.

*Cornish panorama showing
the 18th at St Mellion.*

*John Hawksworth with the
ones that didn't get away.*

COURSE: ST MELLION G. & C. C. DATE: 7-10.5 YARDAGE: 7054 PAR: 72

POS	NAME	CTY	1	2	3	4	TOTAL	PRIZE MONEY
1	Peter SENIOR	Aus	74	73	70	70	287	£83330
2	Tony JOHNSTONE	Zim	71	73	74	69	287	55550
3	Jim PAYNE	Eng	72	70	75	71	288	28150
	Nick FALDO	Eng	71	72	76	69	288	28150
5	Anders FORSBRAND	Swe	68	77	72	72	289	21200
6	Paul CURRY	Eng	72	73	75	70	290	17500
7	Craig PARRY	Aus	67	76	73	75	291	15000
8	Philip WALTON	Ire	71	76	75	70	292	11825
	Santiago LUNA	Sp	71	78	72	71	292	11825
10	Mats LANNER	Swe	69	73	74	77	293	9595
	Bernhard LANGER	Ger	71	74	73	75	293	9595
12	Vicente FERNANDEZ	Arg	75	75	75	69	294	7907
	Costantino ROCCA	It	72	74	77	71	294	7907
	Colin MONTGOMERIE	Scot	68	72	85	69	294	7907
	Eduardo ROMERO	Arg	71	77	73	73	294	7907
16	Per-Ulrik JOHANSSON	Swe	73	78	68	76	295	6285
	Jose RIVERO	Sp	72	75	74	74	295	6285
	Anders SORENSEN	Den	71	75	78	71	295	6285
	Peter TERAVAINEN	USA	75	72	75	73	295	6285
	David GILFORD	Eng	72	74	79	70	295	6285
	Gary EVANS	Eng	73	76	72	74	295	6285
	Daniel SILVA	Port	71	77	76	71	295	6285
23	Des SMYTH	Ire	74	76	77	69	296	5325
	Vijay SINGH	Fij	74	74	76	72	296	5325
	Mats HALLBERG	Swe	72	74	80	70	296	5325
	Peter MITCHELL	Eng	74	68	80	74	296	5325
27	Wayne RILEY	Aus	69	76	78	74	297	4800
	Jose Maria OLAZABAL	Sp	70	78	74	75	297	4800
	Roger CHAPMAN	Eng	74	78	74	71	297	4800
30	Sandy LYLE	Scot	72	71	82	73	298	4350
	Frank NOBILO	NZ	76	76	77	69	298	4350
	Jay TOWNSEND	USA	70	74	79	75	298	4350
33	Richard BOXALL	Eng	73	75	76	75	299	3900
	Miguel Angel JIMENEZ	Sp	76	76	72	75	299	3900
	Gordon BRAND Jnr	Scot	76	73	77	73	299	3900
	Glen DAY	USA	69	77	81	72	299	3900
	Keith WATERS	Eng	75	74	74	76	299	3900
38	Jon ROBSON	Eng	73	75	75	77	300	3350
	Patrick HALL	Eng	72	75	79	74	300	3350
	Mark MOULAND	Wal	72	76	78	74	300	3350
	Peter O'MALLEY	Aus	76	76	71	77	300	3350
	Adam HUNTER	Scot	72	76	79	73	300	3350
	Steven RICHARDSON	Eng	73	79	71	77	300	3350
44	Jeff HAWKES	SA	71	77	76	77	301	2650
	Ernie ELS	SA	76	76	70	79	301	2650
	Andrew HARE	Eng	77	75	73	76	301	2650
	Eamonn DARCY	Ire	75	73	77	76	301	2650
	Mark JAMES	Eng	73	75	82	71	301	2650
	Danny MIJOVIC	Can	74	78	78	71	301	2650
	Mike CLAYTON	Aus	76	75	77	73	301	2650
	Mark DAVIS	Eng	80	72	75	74	301	2650
52	David J RUSSELL	Eng	73	72	79	78	302	1900
	Paul BROADHURST	Eng	80	72	74	76	302	1900
	Carl MASON	Eng	76	70	78	78	302	1900
	Manuel PINERO	Sp	76	75	78	73	302	1900
	Joakim HAEGGMAN	Swe	71	76	79	76	302	1900
	John BLAND	SA	78	74	75	75	302	1900
	Martin GATES	Eng	73	74	81	74	302	1900
59	Mike HARWOOD	Aus	69	78	80	76	303	1500
	Stephen FIELD	Eng	74	78	76	75	303	1500
	Johan RYSTROM	Swe	75	73	82	73	303	1500
62	Jesper PARNEVIK	Swe	69	76	86	73	304	1325
	Gavin LEVENSON	SA	77	73	80	74	304	1325
	Malcolm MACKENZIE	Eng	71	75	84	74	304	1325
	Chris PLATTS	Eng	72	78	79	75	304	1325
66	Paul WAY	Eng	76	74	75	80	305	750
67	Russell CLAYDON	Eng	70	77	83	76	306	746
	Glyn DAVIES	Wal	75	77	78	76	306	746
	Gordon J BRAND	Eng	72	77	83	74	306	746
70	John McHENRY	Ire	78	74	79	76	307	740

30A

13mg TAR 1·1mg NICOTINE
SMOKING CAUSES CANCER
Health Departments' Chief Medical Officers

SHERBORNE IS MADRID SPECIALIST

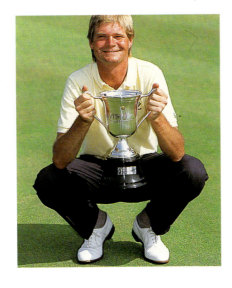

Following his maiden Volvo Tour victory in last year's Madrid Open, Andrew Sherborne made it a Madrid double in the Peugeot Spanish Open

You've got two thirtysomething Englishmen, who both happen to be 6'3", slugging it out down the stretch on a Sunday afternoon in a Volvo Tour event.

One is every inch an athlete; the other looks like one of those sixth-formers who has grown too quickly. One has got a silky-smooth swing and is playing beautiful golf; the other is having a few problems. One's got four major championships to his name; the other's only claim to fame is a single, solitary Tour win. Now, of course, you know which one wins.

But far more miraculous than Andrew Sherborne holding off a concerted challenge from Nick Faldo for the Peugeot Spanish Open title was that the tournament took place at all.

Just 11 days before the off, the venue, Club de Campo, notified the promotion company, Severiano Ballesteros's Amen Corner, that there was likely to be a workers' strike during the week of the tournament. Unlike those in the upper reaches of the Volvo Order of Merit, the workers at the city-owned Club de Campo felt they weren't being paid enough.

'The strike was against the mayor of Madrid, who has a policy of not giving way,' said former Walker Cup player Roddy Carr, who now runs the tournament through Amen Corner company. 'A bus strike here lasted ten weeks.'

So rather than face a severely disrupted tournament, the Volvo Tour circus simply decided to set up its big-top marquee elsewhere. After an emergency meeting, the Real Automovil Club de

Espana (RACE), which had once before held the Spanish Open, in 1969, was chosen as the most likely alternative. The club welcomed the event with open arms, the course was approved, and then commenced the monumental task of moving the whole shebang from one side of Madrid to the other.

'We – my company – had to start it all from zero,' said Seve. In the space of 48

hours, 2,000 square metres of tentage had been removed, and incredibly, come May 14, the RACE had been won. With the fairways having been narrowed, and the course stretching to 7,150 yards, this was sure to be a tough test. But on day one, Steven Richardson showed the course contempt, knocking it round in 65, a new course record, then announced: 'Someone is bound to beat it.' Sure enough, just over 24 hours later, someone did. A man who has toiled in the shadows of Seve and Jose Maria Olazabal, Santiago Luna, clipped a shot off Richardson's record, then, less than 24 hours after that, Jose Rivero put in his bid to be low Spaniard (Seve and Ollie seemed to be having a permanent siesta), shooting an even more sensational 63, birdieing all four par-threes, by far the hardest holes on the course. Then an hour-and-a-half later, as the temperatures soared close to 100 degrees, along came Sherborne, throwing a 63 of his own into the melting pot. That took him to 16 under par, four clear of Rivero and five ahead of Luna and defending champion Eduardo Romero. Sherborne and Rivero shared £6,000 for the Johnnie Walker Tour Course Record Award.

Faldo meanwhile had been grinding along for the first two days, opening with a couple of rounds of 70. Then on Saturday, after three lacklustre opening holes, he had a quick putting pit stop beside the third green, checking his ball position with the tried and tested method of dropping a ball from your left eye (to check the eye is directly over the ball). A

*Nick Faldo ran
Sherborne close.*

*No sign of victory for Ian Woosnam
and Jose Maria Olazabal.*

minor adjustment there brought immediate results: Faldo birdied seven of the next 15 holes for a 66, and suddenly he was back on familiar territory – the leaderboard, albeit six adrift of Sherborne.

When Faldo opened up his account on Sunday with birdies at the first two holes, he must have fancied his chances. But Sherborne, who never before had held a halfway lead, birdied the first and the fourth, and with playing partner Rivero four-putting the short third, he led the tournament by six shots.

But then Sherborne's lanky frame was put through the mangle. A pulled drive at the fifth, a pushed approach at the sixth. Suddenly Faldo and Romero were closing fast. Suddenly it wasn't quite so easy any more. Sherborne's lead was down to just one, and he was facing a plugged lie in a bunker at the long ninth. But he saved his par there, thanks to a long putt, and he got a par at the next, too, despite a spectator who pocketed his ball after his tee shot came to rest just off the fairway (he was allowed to drop another one).

Having come through all that with his one-shot lead still intact, and with Romero now fading fast, Sherborne coasted home, playing the back nine in one under par. In the end, he needed a par at the last to beat Faldo by a shot, which he managed with apparent nonchalant ease.

As Faldo watched from the refuge of the scorer's tent behind the green as

*Third place for
Justin Hobday.*

*Stony silence from
Eduardo Romero.*

Sherborne two-putted from 10 feet for his par, a spectator came up to him. 'You know where you blew it, don't you?' said the man peremptorily. 'You lost it at the 14th. I watched you.'

'Thank you very much,' said Faldo. 'All I need now is a know-all.' Faldo didn't need telling, but in fact the know-all was right. Faldo had hit a crisp second shot at the 522-yard par-five, which ranked as the second easiest hole over the week, to within 35 feet, just off the back of the green. Two putts there for his sixth birdie of the day would bring him abreast of Sherborne. But instead he took three, missing the second one from four feet.

Sherborne came along 20 minutes later, duly got his regulation birdie, and with it a two-shot lead. In the end Faldo's last-gasp birdie at the 72nd wasn't enough.

But Faldo wasn't too disappointed. In fact, he seemed as pleased for Sherborne as Sherborne was, and he was delighted with his pair of clickety-clicks over the weekend. 'Fred Couples got hot for three months,' said Faldo earlier, 'maybe I'll get hot for the summer. If I can maintain this I'll be very happy.'

Sherborne was pretty happy too. Last year's Madrid Open champion was this year's Spanish Open champion. Time for a party back home at his Long Ashton club in Bristol. Perhaps paella was on the menu?

POS	NAME	CTY	1	2	3	4	TOTAL	PRIZE MONEY
1	Andrew SHERBORNE	Eng	71	66	63	71	271	£66660
2	Nick FALDO	Eng	70	70	66	66	272	44440
3	Justin HOBDAY	SA	72	66	71	66	275	25040
4	Jose RIVERO	Sp	74	67	63	72	276	16980
	Santiago LUNA	Sp	69	64	72	71	276	16980
	Eduardo ROMERO	Arg	67	68	70	71	276	16980
7	Miguel Angel JIMENEZ	Sp	66	69	72	70	277	12000
8	Eamonn DARCY	Ire	71	68	72	67	278	9460
	Steven RICHARDSON	Eng	65	74	71	68	278	9460
10	Steven BOWMAN	USA	71	70	71	67	279	7680
	Jose Maria OLAZABAL	Sp	70	69	69	71	279	7680
12	Costantino ROCCA	It	73	68	67	72	280	6480
	Peter FOWLER	Aus	73	70	73	64	280	6480
	Jean VAN DE VELDE	Fr	72	71	69	68	280	6480
15	Jose ROZADILLA	Sp	71	66	74	70	281	5306
	Paul LAWRIE	Scot	72	69	68	72	281	5306
	Jon ROBSON	Eng	72	71	68	70	281	5306
	David GILFORD	Eng	70	70	69	72	281	5306
	Stephen McALLISTER	Scot	72	69	71	69	281	5306
	Colin MONTGOMERIE	Scot	73	70	68	70	281	5306
21	Mats HALLBERG	Swe	72	71	66	73	282	4500
	Peter TERAVAINEN	USA	72	71	68	71	282	4500
	Peter LONARD	Aus	72	70	71	69	282	4500
	John BLAND	SA	70	70	68	74	282	4500
25	Gordon BRAND Jnr	Scot	68	71	69	75	283	4020
	Dennis EDLUND	Swe	69	71	67	76	283	4020
	Joakim HAEGGMAN	Swe	74	69	68	72	283	4020
	Ricky WILLISON	Eng	67	71	73	72	283	4020
29	David FEHERTY	N.Ire	73	69	73	69	284	3488
	Vijay SINGH	Fij	73	68	70	73	284	3488
	Steen TINNING	Den	71	73	71	69	284	3488
	Giuseppe CALI	It	72	72	66	74	284	3488
	Johan RYSTROM	Swe	68	72	69	75	284	3488
34	Silvio GRAPPASONNI	It	69	73	71	72	285	3000
	Sandy LYLE	Scot	70	69	77	69	285	3000
	Seve BALLESTEROS	Sp	70	71	70	74	285	3000
	Andrew HARE	Eng	74	70	72	69	285	3000
	John McHENRY	Ire	68	73	70	74	285	3000
	Mike McLEAN	Eng	72	72	69	72	285	3000
40	Jim PAYNE	Eng	71	73	73	69	286	2520
	Thomas LEVET	Fr	71	71	71	73	286	2520
	Ricardo GONZALEZ	Arg	67	77	69	73	286	2520
	Miguel Angel MARTIN	Sp	68	72	72	74	286	2520
	Juan QUIROS	Sp	70	70	73	73	286	2520
	Ross DRUMMOND	Scot	74	70	72	70	286	2520
46	Gary EVANS	Eng	70	73	70	74	287	1920
	Jose COCERES	Arg	73	70	67	77	287	1920
	Gavin LEVENSON	SA	74	70	73	70	287	1920
	Danny MIJOVIC	Can	68	70	74	75	287	1920
	Wayne RILEY	Aus	70	73	72	72	287	1920
	Philip PARKIN	Wal	69	72	71	75	287	1920
	Marc FARRY	Fr	68	70	72	77	287	1920
	Jonathan SEWELL	Eng	72	69	74	72	287	1920
	Robin MANN	Eng	78	66	75	68	287	1920
55	Bill MALLEY	USA	72	71	71	74	288	1480
	John METCALFE	Eng	73	70	75	70	288	1480
57	Ian PALMER	SA	72	69	72	76	289	1293
	Jose DAVILA	Sp	72	69	72	76	289	1293
	Daniel WESTERMARK	Swe	73	71	72	73	289	1293
60	Derrick COOPER	Eng	69	73	76	72	290	1160
	Neil HANSEN	Eng	72	72	74	72	290	1160
	Per HAUGSRUD	Nor	72	70	75	73	290	1160
63	Alfonso PINERO	Sp	72	71	74	74	291	1040
	Vicente FERNANDEZ	Arg	71	73	76	71	291	1040
	Ross McFARLANE	Eng	71	73	75	72	291	1040
66	Jose Manuel CARRILES	Sp	71	71	78	74	294	600
67	Mark MOULAND	Wal	71	71	76	77	295	597
	Robert KARLSSON	Swe	71	72	74	78	295	597
69	Adam HUNTER	Scot	69	74	74	W/D	217	594

COURSE: REAL AUTOMOVIL CLUB DE ESPANA, MADRID
DATE: 14-17.5   YARDAGE: 7111   PAR: 72

JOHNSTONE
SEIZES THE MOMENT

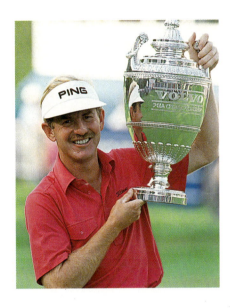

With a stunning final round Tony Johnstone captured the most important title of his career

When the PGA European Tour was born 21 years ago, its objectives were made unmistakeably clear. The first priority was to raise playing standards to world-class heights through increasing levels of opportunity and incentive. Today, nothing better measures the progress made than the global stature enjoyed by the Volvo PGA Championship. In a comparatively short space of time it has taken a position of importance and respect close behind golf's oldest championship, the Open.

And rightly so. This year, the Volvo PGA Championship field was rivalled only by the Open for its international strength. It comprised players from 20 nations, including five of the six currently-ranked best in the world, and the winners of 13 major titles. Who wants to argue about the rising standards of European golf? Or the increasing opportunity and incentive behind it? In 1972 Tony Jacklin earned £2,193 by winning the PGA Championship at Wentworth. Now, 20 years later, £100,000 awaited the winner of the same title, sponsored by Volvo, on the same course.

There is never any shortage of news both on and off the course at a Volvo PGA. First PGA European Tour Enterprises unveiled its mobile physio-therapy unit, a massive, lavishly-equipped bus part-sponsored by Gatorade, the sports drink. It would follow the Tour around Europe, attending to the players. Then to bring a fine championship to a rousing conclusion came the announcement that Volvo was to extend its sponsorship of this championship for another three years – and was planning to increase the prize money by £100,000 to £700,000 next year.

All in all, it was more like the annual general meeting of a highly successful company, one at which record profits are announced and a record dividend is promised. All this and days of endless sunshine, too.

In fact, all that was needed was for Seve Ballesteros to wow the crowds with his golf. When he is on song he remains an enthralling golfer, a man you simply cannot ignore. At his best, he raises the level of a 72-hole tournament and turns it into a four-day festival of golf.

Alas, it was not to be this time. Ballesteros arrived at Wentworth, pronounced the course in fantastic condition, the best he had ever seen it, and then explained that he had little chance of winning. He was tired, he said. He had been on the go since March the previous year and he was finding it hard to raise any enthusiasm for golf. He wasn't even cheered up by the realisation that he had won every fourth event he had entered at Wentworth. 'Not bad, eh?' he asked rhetorically with a wan smile but the way he said it suggested he knew in his heart that he wouldn't improve on it this week. 'I am not playing well and I don't know whether I am not playing well because I have no desire or whether I have no desire because I am not playing well.'

Not only did he mean it, but he soon demonstrated it. After rounds of 76 and 73 he was out of the tournament, the first cut he had ever missed at Wentworth. Ian Woosnam went close to missing it, too. 'There's no spark,' said Woosnam after two rounds of 72. 'There are no signs of improvement. In fact, it's getting worse.'

Sandy Lyle teetered on the brink of failing. At one point in the second round he became so frustrated he broke the shaft of his one iron over his knee. 'As long as it was in the bag I was tempted to use it,' he said after birdieing the 16th and 17th to beat the cut by two strokes. 'I

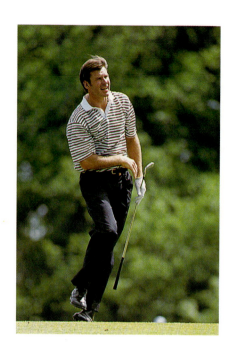

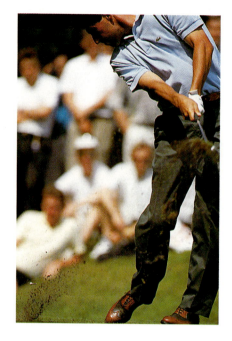

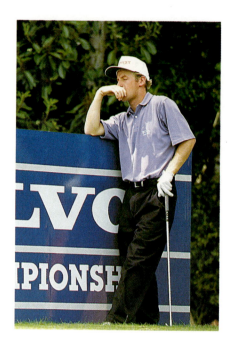

*Soft shoe shuffle
from Nick Faldo.*

*Head down from
Jose Maria Olazabal.*

*Gary Evans in
contemplative mood.*

didn't want that to happen so I took it out of play.'

Even Jose Maria Olazabal found it hard to sparkle. Even when he chipped in from 35 yards on the third green, a curling, deft shot, he seemed underwhelmed. His rounds of 71 and 70 left him eight strokes off the pace.

The top of the leaderboard, then, was not crammed with the biggest names. Jamie Spence, who has yet to win a tournament in Europe, was in front. Andrew Sherborne, still riding his confidence after victory in Madrid one week earlier, was second. Peter Senior, who had won at St

Mellion at the beginning of the month, was in third place and Gordon Brand Junior, David Gilford and Tony Johnstone were one stroke behind him.

Nick Faldo, after rounds of 70 and 68, appeared to be in pole position, ready to overtake the younger, less experienced players as the tournament reached its climax. 'I really expect to come through in the second half of the event,' said Faldo. 'It is very different for players who are leading from now on. There are going to be photographers taking pictures of everything they do, peeling a banana, having a drink, going to the lavatory. All those irritations add up to the twitch factor.'

Nothing affected Magnus Sunesson, the 28-year-old Swede, in the third round. Sunesson reads books like *The Quantum Game* and *The Inner Game of Golf* to help his mental approach. 'It's all in here,' he said, tapping his forehead. 'They help me believe in myself a lot more, to see things more clearly.' He could hardly have seen things any more clearly than he did on his way to a 64. He had nine birdies in all. His putting was remarkable, perhaps as a result of a consultation with Harold Swash and his flexible-shafted putter. 'I regard this championship as a small major. It has been on my mind for months.'

The same could probably have been said about Gary Evans, the fair-haired former amateur from Worthing, who got the last place in the tournament after a good performance in Spain. While Sunesson read books to improve his mental attitude, Evans visited a Buddhist temple in Sussex. He had another reason for wanting to do well. His father had cancer.

'He's had the full works,' said Evans. 'Two heart attacks, 11 operations. The more I play well, the better he feels. It's good to see him smile. I love to be part and parcel of the finish to a tournament. It proves I have got the bottle.'

Faldo had been in danger of losing touch with the leaders after three bogeys in his outward half. He had a birdie on the 12th and hoped to pick up at least two more on the 17th and 18th. He did better than that by getting his four on the 17th and then eagling the last, hitting a three-iron to eight feet for a round of 69. 'I like to think that if I play well I can shoot a 66 in the final round. This is a big pressure event. We are playing for a lot of bucks. I am in a good position and I have a good chance.'

Indeed he had. Four-times the PGA champion, he lay three strokes behind Sunesson, perfectly placed to strike for victory and the £100,000 first prize that went with it. On his home course, where he had become an honorary life member a few days earlier, and playing well, Faldo was ready to move to the front.

Climax to a magnificent

championship.

Instead, Tony Johnstone, his playing companion, caught the others by surprise with a nearly perfect round of 65.

Johnstone, as they say in athletics, got a flier. He was out in 30, three birdies and an eagle. Alongside him Faldo was spluttering, unable to get going. Johnstone came to the 15th tee with a four-stroke lead and though he fluffed chip shots on the 17th and 18th he still had a winning margin of two strokes.

Brand's hopes were to all intents and purposes finished on the tenth when he took five. Sunesson (71) and Evans (69) will both have been happy to better par under the greatest pressure of their professional lives and showed themselves capable of winning tournaments from the front in the future.

Johnstone, who had lost a play-off at St Mellion two weeks earlier, was understandably delighted at his success. 'I feel fabulous,' said the 36-year old Zimbabwean. 'In fact if I felt any better it would probably be illegal.' He said he cherished the ten-year exemption he got as a result of the win and was delighted at the thought of all the bonuses that would accrue as well as invitations to the World Series in the US and the Johnnie Walker World Championship in Jamaica in December.

He was a man totally at peace with himself. 'Winning this event is worth a lot more than the top prize itself,' he said as he toyed with his visor. 'It's the most important event after the Open.'

To the victor,
the spoils.

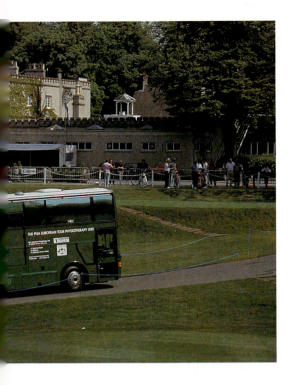

*PGA European Tour Physio
Unit arrives at Wentworth*

*Rain-soaked window into the mind
of Nick Faldo.*

*Severiano Ballesteros
drives off the first.*

*Andrew Sherborne approaches
the fourth.*

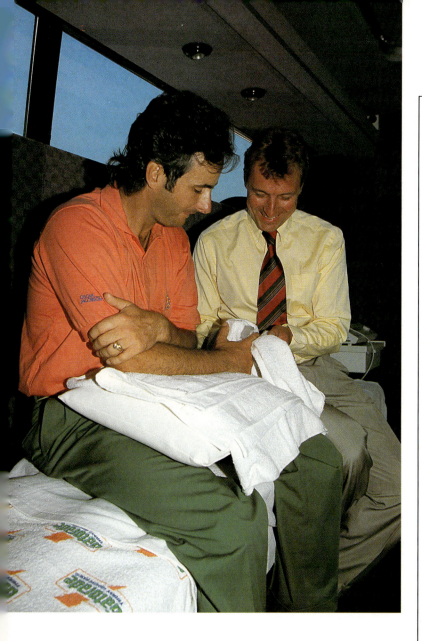

The winner faces

the cameras.

David Feherty receives

attention for snakebite.

POS	NAME	CTY	1	2	3	4	TOTAL	PRIZE MONEY
1	Tony JOHNSTONE	Zim	67	70	70	65	272	£100000
2	Gordon BRAND Jnr	Scot	67	70	68	69	274	52110
	Jose Maria OLAZABAL	Sp	71	70	67	66	274	52110
4	Magnus SUNESSON	Swe	72	68	64	71	275	27700
	Gary EVANS	Eng	74	66	66	69	275	27700
6	Jose Maria CANIZARES	Sp	70	72	66	68	276	19500
	David GILFORD	Eng	64	73	71	68	276	19500
8	Nick FALDO	Eng	70	68	69	70	277	15000
9	Johan RYSTROM	Swe	69	69	72	68	278	13440
10	Peter SENIOR	Aus	67	69	74	69	279	10428
	Eduardo ROMERO	Arg	70	70	69	70	279	10428
	James SPENCE	Eng	67	66	75	71	279	10428
	Paul WAY	Eng	71	69	68	71	279	10428
	Colin MONTGOMERIE	Scot	70	72	67	70	279	10428
15	David WILLIAMS	Eng	69	69	70	72	280	7586
	Eoghan O'CONNELL	Ire	69	70	68	73	280	7586
	Andrew SHERBORNE	Eng	70	65	71	74	280	7586
	Eamonn DARCY	Ire	72	68	70	70	280	7586
	Barry LANE	Eng	69	70	70	71	280	7586
	John BLAND	SA	72	68	72	68	280	7586
	Peter MITCHELL	Eng	65	73	69	73	280	7586
	Bernhard LANGER	Ger	70	70	72	68	280	7586
	Jeff HAWKES	SA	73	68	69	70	280	7586
24	Steven RICHARDSON	Eng	71	70	72	68	281	6210
	Mike HARWOOD	Aus	69	71	70	71	281	6210
	Sandy LYLE	Scot	70	73	70	68	281	6210
	Costantino ROCCA	It	69	72	71	69	281	6210
28	Paul LAWRIE	Scot	70	70	71	71	282	5580
	Mark MOULAND	Wal	65	75	72	70	282	5580
	Gavin LEVENSON	SA	70	70	74	68	282	5580
31	Rodger DAVIS	Aus	67	73	73	70	283	4808
	Peter TERAVAINEN	USA	71	68	74	70	283	4808
	Jean VAN DE VELDE	Fr	71	70	72	70	283	4808
	Ian WOOSNAM	Wal	72	72	69	70	283	4808
	Giuseppe CALI	It	70	71	72	70	283	4808
	Paul McGINLEY	Ire	68	72	74	69	283	4808
	Brett OGLE	Aus	69	71	71	72	283	4808
38	Chris MOODY	Eng	70	72	70	72	284	4020
	Robert ALLENBY	Aus	70	73	67	74	284	4020
	Vijay SINGH	Fij	72	69	71	72	284	4020
	Paul BROADHURST	Eng	69	72	71	72	284	4020
	Miguel Angel MARTIN	(Sp	73	69	73	69	284	4020
	John HAWKSWORTH	(Eng	71	70	73	70	284	4020
44	Richard BOXALL	(Eng	67	74	72	72	285	3420
	Stephen FIELD	(Eng	71	71	71	72	285	3420
	Mark ROE	(Eng	73	69	72	71	285	3420
	Santiago LUNA	(Sp	71	69	77	68	285	3420
48	Jose DAVILA	(Sp	73	68	72	73	286	3060
	Mark McNULTY	(Zim	72	67	75	72	286	3060
50	Andrew OLDCORN	(Eng	71	70	74	72	287	2700
	Antonio GARRIDO	(Sp	70	72	72	73	287	2700
	Miguel Angel JIMENEZ	(Sp	74	67	72	74	287	2700
	Justin HOBDAY	(SA	72	72	76	67	287	2700
54	Per-Ulrik JOHANSSON	(Swe	73	66	75	74	288	2280
	Malcolm MACKENZIE	Eng	73	67	72	76	288	2280
	Darren CLARKE	N.Ire	70	72	71	75	288	2280
57	Nick JOB	Eng	69	73	76	71	289	1940
	Bill McCOLL	Scot	69	74	71	75	289	1940
	Steven BOWMAN	USA	70	71	76	72	289	1940
60	Andrew MURRAY	Eng	74	70	73	73	290	1710
	Ross McFARLANE	Eng	73	70	77	70	290	1710
	Roger CHAPMAN	Eng	73	71	75	71	290	1710
	John CHILLAS	Scot	67	73	74	76	290	1710
64	Mats LANNER	Swe	71	73	74	73	291	1560
65	Jose RIVERO	Sp	72	72	74	74	292	1500
66	Ken BROWN	Scot	71	69	81	72	293	900
67	Patrick HALL	Eng	73	68	80	73	294	898
68	Christy O'CONNOR Jnr	Ire	71	72	81	RETD	224	896

COURSE: WENTWORTH CLUB, WEST COURSE
DATE: 22-25.5   YARDAGE: 6945   PAR: 72

O'CONNOR IS MASTER SURVIVOR

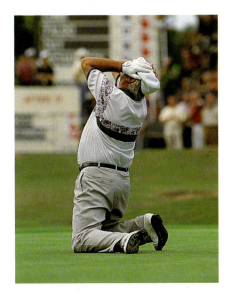

Christy O'Connor Junior survived a helicopter crash and a sudden-death play-off to win the Dunhill British Masters

Traumatic events are commonplace amid the intense competition of the Volvo Tour, but few professionals can point to one 200 feet above a golf course yet to be built as the moment that changed their career.

Such a distinction belonged to Christy O'Connor Junior when he fell out of the sky one day in May 1992, then gained a new lease of life as a European tournament star. Salvation for the genial Irishman may have been the work of the Beatitudes: the golf he subsequently played to win the Dunhill British Masters certainly bore a divine influence.

The fright of Christy's life came after an inspection of one of his new course projects near Dublin, while he was on his way to visit another course at Athlone. Shortly after take-off his helicopter pilot reported a loss of engine power. The machine plunged, slewed sideways on to the roof of a barn, cannoned off a wall and finished upside down in a yard with O'Connor and the pilot trapped in their seats, unable to release their safety belts. Rescuers were rapidly on the scene and both escaped unharmed, but not before moments of panic when the all-pervading smell of kerosene brought fear of fire.

Christy was, however, a victim of delayed shock which struck him during the subsequent Volvo PGA Championship at Wentworth where he was forced to withdraw after the third round. 'I suddenly got very jittery and just did not want to be on a golf course,' he said.

Next morning the Irishman arrived at Woburn and met Seve Ballesteros, whose interest in the PGA title he had won the previous year had ended through failure to survive the halfway cut. A few practice holes and a reassuring chat over a glass of beer left Christy with his feet firmly back on the ground. 'I came to realise that after my scare the sight of a putt missing the hole was no big deal,' he said. 'Missing putts was no longer the most important thing.'

Christy was therefore in carefree mood for his joust at Woburn where Ballesteros was again defending against a quality field that contained Nick Faldo, Ian Woosnam, Sandy Lyle and the fifth European to win at Augusta, the German Bernhard Langer. New Volvo PGA champion Tony Johnstone was attempting to emulate the Spaniard's PGA-Masters double of the previous year, and American Ryder Cup player Paul Azinger was also a candidate for the £100,000 first prize. Azinger's decision to make his debut in a British-based Volvo Tour event had been prompted by his desire to be recognised as a world class performer. 'In that context an American has to play regularly in Europe,' said the Florida golfer who had won the BMW International Open in Munich in 1990.

Ove Sellberg, a Swede who had spent most of the previous six months in the Sunshine State trying to get his game into shape, shot 66 to be the surprise pacemaker after a first round in which Langer and England's Steven Richardson established impressive marks with 67.

Langer had not played in any of the three previous Dunhill promotions because of his dislike of the hard and bouncy fairways of the Duke's course. But the installations of a new irrigation system and excellent maintenance had Woburn with its rhododendrons in full bloom, looking as pretty as a picture...until the deluge arrived on the second day. Over two inches of rain caused a six hour delay and left the second round still unfinished when darkness arrived.

Luck, though, was still with O'Connor who had managed to complete his second passage through the pines in 67, and was drying out in the clubhouse at six under par with the more fancied players scattered all over the course. Christy had been up at the crack of dawn and had seen his start heavily delayed, but that gave him the opportunity to consider the merits of a putting tip he had received from Ian Woosnam who had noticed that O'Connor was aiming the blade of his club left of the hole. As soon as the Irishman squared up, the putts began to go straight into the middle.

More rain on Saturday caused further disruption to the schedules as three-quarters of the players struggled to get through their second outing. Langer, who started his round at 6.40pm on Friday, sank his final putt on the 18th some 23 hours later to be the halfway leader with a 65 for a 12-under-par total of 132. 'I liked the way I played,' he remarked, 'but I cannot remember ever taking so long to get round a golf course.' The German had seven birdies to lead American Glen Day (65) and Richardson (66) by a stroke.

Tournament Director Michael Tate was left with little alternative but to schedule the final two rounds for Sunday and reduce the field from the customary 65 to the leading 50 and ties. The decision eliminated all those on level par after 36 holes and ruled out Woosnam, Peugeot Spanish Open champion Andrew Sherborne and Fijian Vijay Singh who had won the Turespana Masters in Malaga in March.

The survivors numbered 54 and were allotted a maximum of 45 minutes between the third and fourth rounds, in order to facilitate a finish within the allotted television times. Langer and Richardson completed their 54th hole only eight minutes before they were due to start again.

O'Connor's total of putts, which had been a commendable 33 and 32 in his opening round, was reduced to a startling 27 in his third of 66. He birdied six holes of the inward half, including the last three, to get home in 32 and the longest putt he sank in that spell was from eight feet. Yet he was still three behind Johnstone whose 65 for 201 had given him the lead over Langer, Day and Richardson with Faldo

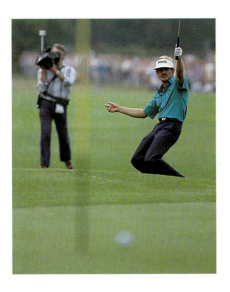

*Left, Christy O'Connor Junior
recovers on the 72nd.*

looming on the horizon, level with Spain's Santiago Luna who had 65 for 205.

Christy had just 12 minutes' rest before going back to work on a egg sandwich and surely 36 holes in one day, and the strain of being in contention would be too much for a 43 year old?

It might have seemed so as Johnstone, with two early birdies to reach 15 under, reached the halfway stage of the final round with a one-shot lead. Faldo loomed as his chief threat by going out in 31 to join Richardson and Day in second place.

O'Connor reached the turn in 34, making up for a wayward drive into trees at the sixth with a birdie from ten feet at the seventh. Then, after a par at the tenth which left him four stokes off the lead, Christy produced the most remarkable eight-hole finale in this Masters history.

He single-putted each of the last eight greens, six of them for birdies as he had done in the morning, and signed for

another 66 to tie with Johnstone on 270. The fairytale was complete when the inspired O'Connor returned to the 16th where he had achieved a miraculous three some 40 minutes earlier, and was conceded his greatest victory without taking his putter from his bag.

The 16th, a dog-leg par four of 425 yards was where Christy cut his drive into the woods in the final round and found his ball on a bare pathway from which his only option appeared to be a recovery chip to the fairway. But he had spotted a gap no more than eight feet wide which might get him to the green, and he elected to go for it. The man whose two-iron had helped to ensure the 1989 Ryder Cup tie at The Belfry, then hit another of outstanding merit. Christy's 'banana' from 190 yards out bisected the gap in the foliage and curled to within 12 feet of the flag.

After that the putt just had to go in, and

*Severiano Ballesteros
approaches the 16th.*

there was a similar inevitability about the birdie chance he created from an eight-iron stroke from behind a tree at the 17th.

The cheers echoing through the pines carried Christy to further glory at the 18th where they reached a crescendo as his birdie from 25 feet toppled into the cup at its last gasp. It was only his 25th putt of the round.

Johnstone also made a birdie four there to close with 69 and finish level, while Richardson's 35 foot eagle putt to make it a three-way play-off brushed the hole without dropping.

So it was back to the 16th where O'Connor had twice made a birdie on his longest golf day. This time he boomed

Fifth placed Bernhard Langer birdies

the third in the last round.

a perfect drive round the sentinel trees guarding the dog-leg, leaving himself a pitch of little more than 100 yards. From the moment it was struck the gallery knew it was close to perfection. The ball landed a foot from the hole and spun back to some 18 inches from its target.

Johnstone did not wait for the formalities after failing with his birdie chance from 30 feet, striding across the green to concede the Irishman's 'tiddler'. Beaten by a Senior, Australia's Peter, in the Benson and Hedges International Open at St Mellion, the Zimbabwean had succumbed to Junior in his second sudden-death decider in the space of four weeks.

'It was like Christy was on a crusade,' he said. 'His shot to the 16th was world class. I don't think God himself could have hit that shot as well.'

As O'Connor and his wife, Ann, celebrated, he was left to reflect on golf's never ending catalogue of surprises, and the strength of friendships. Ballesteros had helped to give him peace of mind, and Woosnam had supplied the technical aid with his putting tip. He also had to thank his uncle Christy Senior for unwittingly supplying extra motivation with his pre-Masters prediction that Nick Faldo would win the coveted title which the 67-year old Irish legend had twice won under the Dunlop banner.

O'Connor Senior had given Junior a pitching tip on his visit the previous week to Woburn but his Faldo forecast ultimately proved more valuable. 'He made me mad and I was determined to prove him wrong,' said the new British master golfer, 'Now I am so happy, and not just for being alive.'

Victor and vanquished share the moment.

POS	NAME	CTY	1	2	3	4	TOTAL	PRIZE MONEY
1	Christy O'CONNOR Jnr	Ire	71	67	66	66	270	£100000
2	Tony JOHNSTONE	Zim	69	67	65	69	270	66660
3	Steven RICHARDSON	Eng	67	66	69	69	271	37560
4	Nick FALDO	Eng	68	68	69	67	272	30000
5	Glen DAY	USA	68	65	69	71	273	21466
	Bernhard LANGER	Ger	67	65	70	71	273	21466
	Santiago LUNA	Sp	70	70	65	68	273	21466
8	Sandy LYLE	Scot	71	66	69	68	274	15000
9	David GILFORD	Eng	73	65	69	68	275	13440
10	Eduardo ROMERO	Arg	71	71	68	66	276	12000
11	Ernie ELS	SA	69	70	71	67	277	10660
	Paul BROADHURST	Eng	72	67	69	69	277	10660
13	Sam TORRANCE	Scot	72	70	69	67	278	9025
	Gary EVANS	Eng	69	71	68	70	278	9025
	Mark McNULTY	Zim	73	68	67	70	278	9025
	Derrick COOPER	Eng	72	69	71	66	278	9025
17	Seve BALLESTEROS	Sp	72	69	68	70	279	7285
	Costantino ROCCA	It	72	66	70	71	279	7285
	Giuseppe CALI	It	70	71	68	70	279	7285
	Jeff HAWKES	SA	72	68	69	70	279	7285
	Danny MIJOVIC	Can	68	72	71	68	279	7285
	Philip WALTON	Ire	70	69	73	67	279	7285
	Peter SENIOR	Aus	68	72	70	69	279	7285
24	Mike McLEAN	Eng	72	71	71	66	280	6300
	John MORSE	USA	68	71	66	75	280	6300
	Colin MONTGOMERIE	Scot	73	68	70	69	280	6300
27	Jose RIVERO	Sp	67	72	70	72	281	5850
	Chris MOODY	Eng	77	66	72	66	281	5850
29	Paul CURRY	Eng	73	68	72	69	282	5490
	James SPENCE	Eng	67	72	68	75	282	5490
31	Ove SELLBERG	Swe	66	75	66	76	283	5060
	Martin POXON	Eng	69	74	70	70	283	5060
	Des SMYTH	Ire	70	71	72	70	283	5060
34	Joakim HAEGGMAN	Swe	70	72	67	75	284	4620
	Eamonn DARCY	Ire	70	73	73	68	284	4620
	Mark JAMES	Eng	70	73	71	70	284	4620
	Michael ALLEN	USA	70	71	75	68	284	4620
38	Mike HARWOOD	Aus	71	72	71	71	285	4320
39	Howard CLARK	Eng	69	72	72	73	286	4020
	Peter FOWLER	Aus	69	72	70	75	286	4020
	Russell CLAYDON	Eng	69	70	75	72	286	4020
	Andrew OLDCORN	Eng	69	70	73	74	286	4020
43	Grant TURNER	Eng	70	72	74	71	287	3660
	Malcolm MACKENZIE	Eng	72	70	75	70	287	3660
45	Jesper PARNEVIK	Swe	70	72	72	74	288	3420
	Wayne WESTNER	SA	71	72	73	72	288	3420
47	Miguel Angel MARTIN	Sp	74	69	77	69	289	3060
	Rick HARTMANN	USA	72	69	74	74	289	3060
	Paul AZINGER	USA	71	72	73	73	289	3060
	Andrew MURRAY	Eng	67	74	76	72	289	3060
51	Mats LANNER	Swe	73	70	75	72	290	2700
	Mark ROE	Eng	68	73	77	72	290	2700
53	Magnus SUNESSON	Swe	68	75	72	76	291	2520
54	David R JONES	Eng	73	70	74	75	292	2400
55	Paul WAY	Eng	72	72			144	1832
	Ian WOOSNAM	Wal	75	69			144	1832
	Brett OGLE	Aus	71	73			144	1832
	Richard BOXALL	Eng	72	72			144	1832
	Greg J TURNER	NZ	72	72			144	1832
	Vijay SINGH	Fij	73	71			144	1832
	Peter O'MALLEY	Aus	69	75			144	1832
	John BLAND	SA	73	71			144	1832
	Marc FARRY	Fr	74	70			144	1832
	Andrew SHERBORNE	Eng	72	72			144	1832
	Jimmy HEGGARTY	N.Ire	68	76			144	1832

COURSE: WOBURN G. & C. C. DATE: 28-31.5 YARDAGE: 6940 PAR: 72

FALDO SURVIVES FOR REPEAT VICTORY

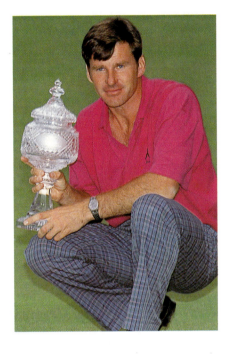

Nick Faldo squandered a four-stroke lead before winning a play-off to retain the Carrolls Irish Open

On the Volvo Tour, no championship better reflects the rising stature and world-class standards of European golf than the Carrolls Irish Open. A roll-call of its winners through 18 years would ideally serve for the opening pages of a first edition Debrett's Fairway Peerage. Among them, Severiano Ballesteros, Bernhard Langer and Ian Woosnam have won the title more than once. And when Nick Faldo, the defending champion, went into the final round of the 1992 action at Killarney with a lead of four shots, his path to join them seemed as simple as his recent run of performance had been awesome.

In only one round out of 23 all season had he scored over par for an aggregate 83 under par. Irish bookies have a famed sense of humour, but it didn't stretch to Faldo's golf. They labelled his victory a formality with odds of 2-5 on which some of his challengers didn't think so ridiculous. 'We are all playing for second place,' said one. 'I'm surprised they are making him play,' joked another. But, of course, there is no such thing as a certainty in golf. The game thrives on unpredictability. Which explains the warning words heard from Langer at the halfway point when Faldo stood 13 under par and five shots clear. 'You never know,' he cautioned. 'Strange things can happen in golf. Nick may look a winner now, but the game is never that simple.' Just 18 hours later Faldo was embroiled in desperate sudden-death combat with South Africa's Wayne Westner.

Indeed, the only constant element in

the 18th staging of Ireland's premier golfing event was the majestic scenery of Killarney's legendary scenery. The lakes and fells can rarely have looked lovelier as the bright sunshine glistened on the waters of Lough Leane at the start. Barry Lane set a splendid standard early with an opening six-under-par 66. When Faldo equalled that mark in the afternoon

he declared that the Killeen course was 'very close to becoming one of the best parkland stretches on the Tour.' It was a verdict based on punishing rough, menacingly narrow fairways and the constant demand for a high level of concentration.

By the end of the first day's play, Faldo and Lane were joint leaders ahead of Mats Hallberg, Langer and Carl Mason, all on 67.

In the light of later events, it was richly ironic that Westner should have claimed attention on the Friday, simply because of a hole-in-one at the short third. The fact was that the South African, an absentee from regular competition on the Volvo Tour since 1987 because of a ban imposed by certain countries, was no more than a supporting player; Faldo, with a second round of 65, had taken a vice-like grip on the proceedings. The champion described an inward journey of 31 strokes as 'officially awesome.' It characterised everything that is admirable in Faldo's game when at full flow. There were beautifully-shaped drives, sparkling iron shots and, from his standpoint, the most important feature of all, irresistible putting. He had 30 putts for the round, seven of them singles, ranging in length from only a foot at the short tenth to 35 feet for an eagle three at the next. So delighted was he with the quality of his play that he was somewhat disappointed at being denied a course record, given that the length and par of the fifth and seventh holes had been changed from the previous year.

By then, Faldo's closest challenger, on

Lakeside chip from runner-up Wayne Westner.

Nick Faldo in reflective mood.

136, was Ryder Cup colleague Paul Broadhurst, who was prepared to concede victory with 36 holes still to be played: 'All we are doing now is playing for second place and if I finish third I'll be delighted.' Broadhurst did finish third but had little cause for delight, given the way the tournament developed.

The supporting players at the halfway stage, two strokes behind Broadhurst and seven behind Faldo, were Colin Montgomerie, Malcolm Mackenzie and Westner. Meanwhile, Faldo had equalled the 36-hole score for the Irish Open, set by Magnus Persson at Royal Dublin in 1984.

Little had changed at the top of the leaderboard by Saturday evening. Faldo was visibly upset at failing to get up and down to save par on the 18th but his 68 left him still with a four-strokes cushion

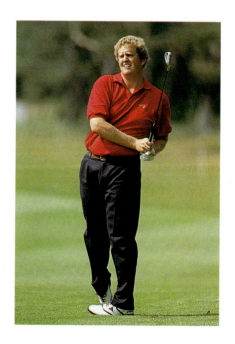

Colin Montgomerie leans into an iron shot.

over Broadhurst; Montgomerie and Westner were three strokes further back. As an interesting aside, Faldo was, in fact, nine strokes clear of Westner after they had completed 53 holes.

So to the final round and the makings of potentially one of the most dramatic upsets in the history of the Tour. As the wind began to rise, the champion pushed his wedge shot wide of the target at the first for a bogey. The lead over his playing companion was cut to three. Just when a surge was anticipated from Broadhurst, however, he lost his chance with bogeys at the third and fourth.

Westner, meanwhile, in the match ahead, covered the opening five holes in one over, apparently strengthening his chances of finishing runner-up. But the entire complexion of things changed dramatically over the sixth, seventh and eighth holes. Westner covered them in birdie, eagle, par while Faldo, almost unbelievably, carded double-bogey, birdie, double-bogey. Suddenly, the pair were level on 12 under par at the top of the leaderboard.

In trying to draw the ball onto the island green at the short sixth, Faldo had finished in the water. And his approach at the par four eighth had been blocked into a horrible lie in a bunker. To his eternal credit, the champion held his nerve so successfully as to cover the remaining 10 holes in two under par.

While Faldo played the 18th, needing a birdie three to tie, Westner was on the telephone to his wife in Johannesburg. About an hour later, he was on the phone to her again, this time with tears in his eyes. Against the odds, Faldo sank a putt of nine feet for the necessary birdie on the 72nd hole.

Westner had two splendid chances of capturing the title. The first came at the opening play-off hole, the 18th where, after Faldo had hooked his drive into water, the South African squandered a winning chance by over-hitting his approach iron into a greenside bunker, from which he took two to escape. His next chance was at the third play-off hole, again the 18th, where he left a birdie putt from eight feet short of the target.

When the end came, it was anti-

Paul Broadhurst pitched

into third place.

Wayne Westner's charge forced a
play-off with Faldo

climatic. Killarney's infamous 17th hole had caused Westner problems throughout the tournament. When it really mattered, with Faldo safely on the green in two, the South African hit a series of duff approaches, was eventually on the putting surface in four and duly conceded victory.

In his moment of triumph, Faldo thanked the Irish for loving him. And in celebrating his first victory since the same event a year previously, he commented: 'I was very lucky – it's an amazing game.' Those who had heard Langer's words of the previous Friday, permitted themselves a knowing smile.

Faldo's hopes were almost ditched in the final round.

POS	NAME	CTY	1	2	3	4	TOTAL	PRIZE MONEY
1	Nick FALDO	Eng	66	65	68	75	274	£76274
2	Wayne WESTNER	SA	68	70	68	68	274	50846
3	Paul BROADHURST	Eng	68	68	67	73	276	28649
4	Colin MONTGOMERIE	Scot	72	66	68	72	278	21144
	Anders FORSBRAND	Swe	71	68	70	69	278	21144
6	Paul LAWRIE	Scot	69	74	66	70	279	14874
	Bernhard LANGER	Ger	67	72	70	70	279	14874
8	Sam TORRANCE	Scot	74	72	67	67	280	11441
9	Jeff HAWKES	SA	74	72	67	68	281	10205
10	Malcolm MACKENZIE	Eng	72	66	72	74	284	9153
11	Glen DAY	USA	71	70	73	71	285	7472
	Carl MASON	Eng	67	72	70	76	285	7472
	Brian MARCHBANK	Scot	70	74	70	71	285	7472
	Peter O'MALLEY	Aus	77	70	70	68	285	7472
	Greg J TURNER	NZ	72	69	70	74	285	7472
16	Stephen FIELD	Eng	72	74	70	70	286	5842
	James SPENCE	Eng	69	71	73	73	286	5842
	Peter SENIOR	Aus	73	69	73	71	286	5842
	Brian BARNES	Scot	68	72	69	77	286	5842
	David J RUSSELL	Eng	68	72	73	73	286	5842
	Jon ROBSON	Eng	71	75	69	71	286	5842
22	Mats HALLBERG	Swe	67	72	75	73	287	5011
	Andrew SHERBORNE	Eng	74	67	71	75	287	5011
	Rodger DAVIS	Aus	71	69	73	74	287	5011
	Tony JOHNSTONE	Zim	71	74	75	67	287	5011
26	Frank NOBILO	NZ	73	68	72	75	288	4530
	Paul MCGINLEY	Ire	72	74	72	70	288	4530
	Chris VAN DER VELDE	Hol	73	72	70	73	288	4530
29	Stuart LITTLE	Eng	70	74	70	75	289	4050
	Gary NICKLAUS	USA	73	72	70	74	289	4050
	Eamonn DARCY	Ire	74	71	72	72	289	4050
	Paul WAY	Eng	74	71	71	73	289	4050
33	Manuel PINERO	Sp	71	76	69	74	290	3478
	Jay TOWNSEND	USA	73	72	73	72	290	3478
	Bill MALLEY	USA	71	74	74	71	290	3478
	Robert ALLENBY	Aus	70	74	71	75	290	3478
	Bill LONGMUIR	Scot	72	74	71	73	290	3478
	Ian WOOSNAM	Wal	71	75	70	74	290	3478
	John McHENRY	Ire	74	73	73	70	290	3478
40	Roger WINCHESTER	Eng	75	69	77	70	291	2929
	Barry LANE	Eng	66	74	74	77	291	2929
	Steen TINNING	Den	77	68	74	72	291	2929
	David R JONES	Eng	69	75	74	73	291	2929
	Peter MITCHELL	Eng	71	74	72	74	291	2929
45	Jim RUTLEDGE	Can	74	72	76	70	292	2242
	Adam HUNTER	Scot	74	73	76	69	292	2242
	Liam HIGGINS	Ire	71	69	76	76	292	2242
	John METCALFE	Eng	73	73	75	71	292	2242
	Jeremy ROBINSON	Eng	73	73	72	74	292	2242
	Mike McLEAN	Eng	74	72	74	72	292	2242
	Gordon J BRAND	Eng	72	73	72	75	292	2242
	Peter BAKER	Eng	70	73	79	70	292	2242
	Christy O'CONNOR Jnr	Ire	72	72	75	73	292	2242
	Jonathan SEWELL	Eng	69	74	77	72	292	2242
55	Jim PAYNE	Eng	69	75	78	71	293	1533
	Michael ALLEN	USA	75	72	71	75	293	1533
	Patrick HALL	Eng	68	76	76	73	293	1533
	Paul CURRY	Eng	72	73	78	70	293	1533
	Peter SMITH	Scot	74	73	74	72	293	1533
	Stephen McALLISTER	Scot	72	72	75	74	293	1533
61	Magnus SUNESSON	Swe	74	72	72	76	294	1258
	Mike SPOSA	USA	74	73	72	75	294	1258
	Martin GATES	Eng	73	69	72	80	294	1258
	Gary EVANS	Eng	70	75	74	75	294	1258
65	Jody FANAGAN (AM)	Ire	71	74	75	75	295	—
	Ernie ELS	SA	70	74	74	77	295	1144
66	Wayne STEPHENS	Eng	72	75	72	77	296	684
	Chris WILLIAMS	Eng	72	74	72	78	296	684
	Patrick GRIBBEN	N.Ire	75	72	74	75	296	684
69	Derrick COOPER	Eng	75	72	76	74	297	678

COURSE: KILLARNEY GOLF AND FISHING CLUB
DATE: 4-7.6   **YARDAGE: 7073**   **PAR: 72**

MITCHELL SOARS WITH THE EAGLES

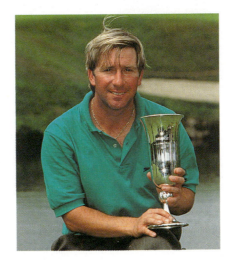

A final round of 62 including three eagles secured Peter Mitchell's first Volvo Tour title

There is not much *schlagobers* down the Old Kent Road. Little demand for it. Eels, cockles and winkles more like. But an unfamiliarity with one of Austria's national dishes – thick whipped cream for ladling onto tea-time chocolate cake in big dollops – did nothing to prevent Peter Mitchell from winning that country's Open, sponsored by Mitsubishi.

Mitchell is one of life's triers. Born in the Old Kent Road in 1958, he had been a professional for 18 years and his best finish prior to this was a third in Monte Carlo in 1991 and in Jersey in April. Having won by chipping in from eight yards, Mitchell shrugged it all off and questioned the merit of his win because he didn't have to hole a putt to win. 'A chip-in is not like holing a five-footer, is it?' he asked. 'I feel like I won by default.'

The Gut Altentann course on which Mitchell was to triumph won plaudits for its condition, not to mention its site in the midst of *Sound of Music* country outside Salzburg, but it acquired a notoriety of a different sort in the opening round. Orrin Vincent III, a 23-year-old rookie from Las Vegas, twice entered the record books. First he took a 14, ten over par, on the opening hole, the highest score at any hole in Europe this season. It took him five drives before he got one to stay on the fairway. Then his 20-over-par 92 was the biggest total for a complete round. After 18 holes he lay 27 strokes behind the leader, Patrick Hall who had managed

If Mitchell was an also-ran on the first day, he metamorphosed on the second day when he equalled the course record with a 62. It rained incessantly but not, perhaps, on Mitchell's parade. He had eight birdies and only 26 putts. After 36 holes he found himself trailing Jean Van de Velde and Per-Ulrik Johansson by two strokes.

After Vincent's ventures, it was the turn of Mark James to bring in the day's highest score on a single hole. The 16th hole cost James a 13 and he went from six under par to three over and out of the tournament. Not so Gary Nicklaus, the

second youngest of Jack's four sons. He birdied his last two holes to beat the cut for the second week in succession.

Overnight rain rendered the course waterlogged and the start of the third round was delayed by four hours. Because of this, Tour officials permitted players to tee up both on fairways and in the rough in order to beat the puddles. 'The fairways don't drain quickly and there was a prospect of not being able to play today or tomorrow,' explained Michael Tate, the Tournament Director. 'Some players didn't like the decision but I believe it was the right one.'

Play was suspended twice because of lightning and finally abandoned when a downpour drove the remaining competitors to seek shelter before the entire field had completed their round.

Mitchell needed all his south London cheerfulness as he tramped in to the clubhouse after completing 15 of his 18 holes. He and Van de Velde retained their share of the lead at 11 under par. Peter Fowler had seven birdies and was ten under.

Victory for Mitchell could hardly have been further from his mind the next morning when he returned to complete his third round. He bogied the 16th and 17th and then ran up a double bogey at the last. Three holes played, four strokes lost. He was four strokes behind Johansson.

He wiped that out with an inspired start, as inspired as his previous three holes had been bad. He birdied the first, eagled the second and the eighth and

Gary Nicklaus in placing mode.

First round leader Patrick Hall.

was out in 31. Three birdies in five holes after the turn took him to within one stroke of the clubhouse leaders, Jamie Spence, who had finished with a 63, and David J Russell.

Still, the shot that won Mitchell his first title in 13 years on Tour was a three-wood 250-yards over a ravine on the 18th. Mitchell will remember it for the rest of his life. He knew that a birdie would only be good enough to tie with Spence and Russell. There was nothing for it. He had to go for it. The ball ended just off the putting surface, 25 feet from the flag, and Mitchell chipped in from there. This eagle, his third of the day, gave him a 62, his second of the tournament, which was one stroke better than Spence, Russell and Peter Fowler.

Until then, Mitchell's best cheque didn't compare with the £58,330 he won. 'I can't believe it' said Mitchell. 'I have been in the last group four times this season. I must have learned something.'

POS	NAME	CTY	1	2	3	4	TOTAL	PRIZE MONEY
1	Peter MITCHELL	Eng	74	62	73	62	271	£58330
2	David J RUSSELL	Eng	66	72	69	65	272	26096
	Peter FOWLER	Aus	70	69	67	66	272	26096
	James SPENCE	Eng	68	71	70	63	272	26096
5	Ole ESKILDSEN	Den	69	68	71	68	276	13540
	Barry LANE	Eng	67	74	68	67	276	13540
7	Per-Ulrik JOHANSSON	Swe	66	68	71	72	277	9625
	Jean VAN DE VELDE	Fr	68	66	72	71	277	9625
9	Jose Manuel CARRILES	Sp	70	69	72	67	278	7820
10	Ross DRUMMOND	Scot	68	69	73	69	279	6486
	Richard BOXALL	Eng	70	70	69	70	279	6486
	Patrick HALL	Eng	65	75	69	70	279	6486
13	Paul BROADHURST	Eng	72	70	72	66	280	5373
	Malcolm MACKENZIE	Eng	72	72	68	68	280	5373
	Andrew SHERBORNE	Eng	68	70	70	72	280	5373
16	Carl MASON	Eng	70	71	72	68	281	4627
	Jay TOWNSEND	USA	66	74	72	69	281	4627
	Brian MARCHBANK	Scot	72	72	68	69	281	4627
	Anders SORENSEN	Den	71	69	68	73	281	4627
20	Thomas LEVET	Fr	72	71	71	68	282	3885
	Joakim HAEGGMAN	Swe	71	68	73	70	282	3885
	Martin GATES	Eng	71	69	72	70	282	3885
	Robert ALLENBY	Aus	67	73	72	70	282	3885
	Darren CLARKE	N.Ire	71	73	68	70	282	3885
	Costantino ROCCA	It	69	74	69	70	282	3885
	David R JONES	Eng	72	66	69	75	282	3885
27	Adam MEDNICK	Swe	70	68	76	69	283	3202
	Juan QUIROS	Sp	72	72	72	67	283	3202
	Gordon MANSON	Scot	68	75	69	71	283	3202
	Derrick COOPER	Eng	69	73	70	71	283	3202
	Jose Maria CANIZARES	Sp	68	72	70	73	283	3202
	Roger CHAPMAN	Eng	68	74	68	73	283	3202
33	Jim PAYNE	Eng	71	70	73	70	284	2765
	Eoghan O'CONNELL	Ire	71	72	70	71	284	2765
	John HAWKSWORTH	Eng	72	69	69	74	284	2765
	Gordon BRAND Jnr	Scot	73	69	68	74	284	2765
37	John METCALFE	Eng	70	69	76	70	285	2275
	Glenn RALPH	Eng	70	72	71	72	285	2275
	Mark DAVIS	Eng	71	67	75	72	285	2275
	Peter O'MALLEY	Aus	69	74	71	71	285	2275
	Bill LONGMUIR	Scot	66	77	71	71	285	2275
	Paul HURRING	Eng	71	71	72	71	285	2275
	Ove SELLBERG	Swe	70	71	72	72	285	2275
	Jim RUTLEDGE	Can	67	74	71	73	285	2275
	Russell CLAYDON	Eng	70	74	70	71	285	2275
	Mark MOULAND	Wal	73	69	74	69	285	2275
47	Ross McFARLANE	Eng	68	74	72	72	286	1680
	Fredrik LINDGREN	Swe	73	70	71	72	286	1680
	Alfonso PINERO	Sp	71	73	70	72	286	1680
	Gary NICKLAUS	USA	71	72	72	71	286	1680
	Andrew MURRAY	Eng	70	71	74	71	286	1680
	Robert LEE	Eng	73	70	73	70	286	1680
	Claude GRENIER	Can	73	71	72	70	286	1680
54	Neal BRIGGS	Eng	67	72	74	74	287	1230
	Mike CLAYTON	Aus	71	72	71	73	287	1230
	Desmond TERBLANCHE	SA	67	73	74	73	287	1230
	Ricardo GONZALEZ	Arg	67	75	73	72	287	1230
	Peter BAKER	Eng	72	71	73	71	287	1230
	Alberto BINAGHI	It	70	74	73	70	287	1230
60	Adam HUNTER	Scot	70	74	71	73	288	980
	Lucien TINKLER	Aus	72	69	75	72	288	980
	Grant TURNER	Eng	69	71	76	72	288	980
	Robert KARLSSON	Swe	68	76	73	71	288	980
	Kenneth TRIMBLE	Aus	73	71	75	69	288	980
65	Sven STRÖVER	Ger	73	71	71	74	289	875
66	Eric GIRAUD	Fr	72	71	76	71	290	525
67	Stephen BENNETT	Eng	70	73	75	73	291	523
68	Wraith GRANT	Eng	70	74	77	76	297	521

COURSE: GUT ALTENTANN GOLF AND COUNTRY CLUB, SALTZBURG
DATE: 11-14.6   YARDAGE: 8805   PAR: 72

RUSSELL
IS FLAWLESS

Four flawless rounds took David J. Russell to an emphatic victory in Lyon.

David J. Russell did not take long to recover from the disappointment of his near miss in Austria after discovering there is more than one route to victory. The Derbyshire professional claimed the Volvo Tour's newest title, the Open de Lyon Trophée V33 at Villette d'Anthon, by playing from his heart, not just his head.

Russell's second PGA European Tour win in 18 seasons came seven years after his first, and it was by the convincing margin of six strokes over Australia's Brett Ogle. What is more it was achieved after a display of precision strokeplay of which Nick Faldo would have been envious.

On a testing course where the rough resembled paddocks of prairie, Russell did not record a single bogey in the 72 holes. A total of 19 birdies, one eagle and 52 pars was a magnificent tribute to his accuracy, and the Volvo Tour witnessed a near perfect performance. 'Throughout my career I have always believed that the only way to win was to play with the head and always think about money,' he said. 'But things happen in life that can change a player's entire attitude and in my case it was the death of my wife's mother. It devastated our family, and particularly my children.'

Russell considered withdrawal on the eve of the new French event, but decided to stay, and as he put it: 'Play from the heart'. His renewed determination, coupled with the reproduction of the form he showed in taking joint second place in Salzburg led him on an irresistible crusade. For Russell 'playing from the heart' also meant from the middle of the

fairways and the centre of the greens where he holed out with commendable confidence to return a 21-under par aggregate. 'I don't think I had a negative thought all week,' he said after returning scores of 68, 66, 67, then holding off the charging Ogle with a closing 66. Only in the last few holes when the destiny of the Trophée V33 was no longer in doubt, did he adopt par as his yardstick.

By then Ogle's belligerent 64, the best score of the week, had been trumped by Russell's eagle at the tenth where he was home with a one-iron that never left the flag and deposited his ball just six feet away. The putt sent Russell back into a

four-stroke lead and he cruised to the £37,500 winner's cheque after Ogle had set the clubhouse target of 15 under par to take second place.

Predictions of a spate of low scoring were plentiful after Denmark's Steen Tinning had shot 58 in a practice round and Robert Karlsson, one of the most talented young Swedish players had a first round 64. When Janerick Dahlstrom, an amateur invitee, who turned out to be French and not Scandinavian, breezed to a 66 it looked odds on that the tournament would swiftly become a putting competition.

But the north wind that blew down the Rhone Valley on the second day permitted only a handful to break 70 as the waiting rough gobbled up every wayward shot. Russell's 66 established his command, his only serious problem being an attack of hay fever brought on by the pollen carried in the wind.

The challenge in round three came from an unexpected quarter. Grant Waite has been a golfer in limbo ever since he failed to gain his US Tour card for 1992. A New Zealander born in Australia, he won the New Zealand Open in February and then led his country to victory in the Alfred Dunhill Cup qualifying round in Hong Kong. He had managed to secure a sponsor's invitation and made a bold attempt to secure a place on the 1993 Volvo Tour on his first European appearance.

Waite's 65 took him to an 11-under-par 205 after 54 holes but Russell responded with yet another perfect

performance, although he had to thank his caddie Jimmy Finch of Southport for staying out in front. Finch has the eyes of a hawk and he averted potential penalty at the par-five third after his employer had for once driven into the rough. Russell was about to play what he thought was his ball until Finch spotted the authentic Russell missile a foot away in the thick grass. The golfer went on to make the first of his five birdies, and the caddie got a pat on the back.

Waite managed only a final 71 to drop to seventh place and the last day challenges were mounted by Ogle, American Jay Townsend with a 65, and Paul Broadhurst with 67. Broadhurst had decided not to try and qualify for the US Open because of disappointing form, but could not shake it off to justify his pre-event favouritism. A spate of back nine birdies elevated him to a share of third place with Townsend.

Russell's two early birdie strikes to turn in 34 put him 17 below, but Ogle who had begun the last day eight shots in arrears, launched a vigorous attack. He gathered six birdies in the first 11 holes then eagled the long 15th and birdied the 16th to be only one behind. It was then that Russell turned to his one-iron, and after that had performed its task, Ogle's three putts at the 18th meant the Midlander had only to avoid serious trouble. That he did with ease, and ended in champion style with birdies at the 17th and 18th.

'Somehow I knew I would win,' he said. 'It never crossed my mind that I would lose. I have had to suffer a lot of knocks in golf, but this was one week when I was convinced everything would go my way.'

Performance par excellence from
David J. Russell.

The 18th green
at Lyon.

Gavin Levenson and caddie check the yardage.

Brett Ogle was gobsmacked by Russell's scoring.

								PRIZE
POS	NAME	CTY	1	2	3	4	TOTAL	MONEY
1	David J RUSSELL	Eng	68	66	67	66	267	37500
2	Brett OGLE	Aus	69	72	68	64	273	25000
3	Jay TOWNSEND	USA	67	74	68	65	274	12660
	Paul BROADHURST	Eng	66	72	69	67	274	12660
5	Carl MASON	Eng	70	70	68	67	275	8675
	Robert KARLSSON	Swe	64	71	72	68	275	8675
7	Gavin LEVENSON	SA	71	69	66	70	276	6150
	Grant WAITE	NZ	69	71	65	71	276	6150
9	Rick HARTMANN	USA	68	74	67	68	277	4240
	Mike CLAYTON	Aus	67	74	68	68	277	4240
	Robin MANN	Eng	70	70	67	70	277	4240
	Wayne WESTNER	SA	69	69	70	69	277	4240
	Miguel Angel JIMENEZ	Sp	72	70	70	65	277	4240
14	Jose COCERES	Arg	72	70	67	69	278	3485
	Jonathan SEWELL	Eng	71	71	68	68	278	3485
16	Paul McGINLEY	Ire	70	71	68	70	279	3260
17	Jim PAYNE	Eng	68	73	73	66	280	3050
	Miguel Angel MARTIN	Sp	72	70	71	67	280	3050
19	Roger WINCHESTER	Eng	70	72	71	68	281	2684
	Ole ESKILDSEN	Den	70	75	70	66	281	2684
	Glenn RALPH	Eng	67	72	72	70	281	2684
	Mike McLEAN	Eng	69	70	73	69	281	2684
	Derrick COOPER	Eng	69	69	70	73	281	2684
24	Jan Erik DAHLSTROM (AM)	Fr	66	74	70	72	282	-
	Andrew HARE	Eng	71	68	69	74	282	2256
	Michael ARCHER	Eng	69	71	68	74	282	2256
	Jim RUTLEDGE	Can	69	74	68	71	282	2256
	Frank NOBILO	NZ	70	71	73	68	282	2256
	Stephen BENNETT	Eng	70	71	70	71	282	2256
	Peter SMITH	Scot	67	70	73	72	282	2256
30	Gordon BRAND Jnr	Scot	69	75	70	69	283	1870
	Martin POXON	Eng	70	74	70	69	283	1870
	David CURRY	Eng	72	70	73	68	283	1870
	Peter McWHINNEY	Aus	69	73	72	69	283	1870
	Ricky WILLISON	Eng	70	76	71	66	283	1870
35	Jorge BERENDT	Arg	70	71	71	72	284	1620
	Ian SPENCER	Eng	70	72	71	71	284	1620
	Jarmo SANDELIN	Swe	68	74	72	70	284	1620
	De Wet BASSON	SA	69	75	68	72	284	1620
39	Gary NICKLAUS	USA	67	71	72	75	285	1420
	Stephane DE MARBOEUF	Fr	70	72	72	71	285	1420
	Costantino ROCCA	It	67	73	71	74	285	1420
	Philip WALTON	Ire	72	74	69	70	285	1420
	Peter LONARD	Aus	69	71	73	72	285	1420
	Tod POWER	Aus	70	69	70	76	285	1420
45	Stuart LITTLE	Eng	72	71	72	71	286	1120
	Wraith GRANT	Eng	72	73	69	72	286	1120
	Peter BAKER	Eng	72	70	74	70	286	1120
	Jean Ignace MOUHICA	Fr	71	73	73	69	286	1120
	Greg J TURNER	NZ	67	75	76	68	286	1120
	Keith WATERS	Eng	70	75	70	71	286	1120
	Tim PLANCHIN	Fr	74	71	69	72	286	1120
	Jamie SPENCE	Eng	69	74	72	71	286	1120
	Steen TINNING	Den	71	71	71	73	286	1120
54	Desmond TERBLANCHE	SA	69	75	70	73	287	900
	Grant TURNER	Eng	72	71	72	72	287	900
56	Neal BRIGGS	Eng	72	73	75	68	288	800
	Lucien TINKLER	Aus	73	72	69	74	288	800
	Thomas LEVET	Fr	69	75	74	70	288	800
59	Darren PROSSER	Eng	73	69	73	74	289	690
	Tony CHARNLEY	Eng	69	74	74	72	289	690
	John HAWKSWORTH	Eng	71	71	73	74	289	690
62	Alfonso PINERO	Sp	70	75	71	74	290	615
	Gery WATINE	Fr	70	76	74	70	290	615
64	Per HAUGSRUD	Nor	76	70	76	69	291	570
65	Daniel WESTERMARK	Swe	74	69	74	76	293	540
66	Jon ROBSON	Eng	70	75	74	75	294	399
	Heinz P THUEL	Ger	69	77	71	77	294	399
68	Gordon MANSON	Scot	71	74	75	75	295	396

COURSE: LYON G.C. VILLETTE-D'ANTHON
DATE: 18-21.6   YARDAGE: 6763   PAR: 72

MARTIN BREAKS THROUGH AT LAST

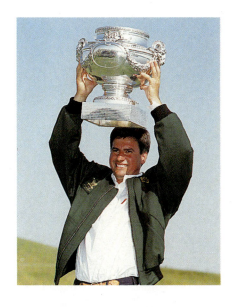

Miguel Angel Martin took advantage of a lapse by Nick Faldo to record his first victory in the Volvo Tour.

Nick Faldo was waiting for his moment. In the Peugeot French Open the Faldo machine, technically superior to all the other models on the starting grid, had cruised round three laps in seven under par. The circuit was the French Golf Federation's tough but highly praised Le Golf National, Europe's first stadium course, which, incidentally, is about as typically French as EuroDisney – a sort of Sawgrass meets Birkdale.

By Saturday night, Faldo was sharing the lead, just waiting for that chicane where he could put his foot down and leave the rest in a trail of smoke. He was in pole position to bury the field down the home straight. Sunday, surely, would be nothing more than a lap of honour.

Look at the opposition. A Frenchman by the name of Eric Giraud was tied with Faldo, winless Spaniard Miguel Martin was a shot back, and behind him, in the main, were no big names.

The enthusiastic French gallery – *c'est normal* – were briefly prepared to let their optimism over Giraud overcome common sense. After all, it had been 22 long years since a Frenchman – Jean Garaialde – had won on the Tour, and not since 1969 had a Frenchman – Garaialde again – won their national Open. So not surprisingly, Giraud registered a little higher on the clapometer as the last group stepped onto the first tee on Sunday morning for the final round showdown.

Claude-Roger Cartier, the President of the French Golf Federation, was beside himself with nervous anticipation.

'I don't even want to think about it,' he said before the final pair teed off. 'We've been working for so long with all those boys. I hope we will have a winner soon, but for it to be today, in Paris, well...'

But the facts were: Faldo was 34, with 27 worldwide wins to his name, including four major titles, while Giraud, a 22-year-old rookie, the son of the professional at Paris's St Cloud club, only had a French Amateur title as his claim to fame. Faldo hadn't finished outside the top eight in his previous six starts in Europe, and the week before he had finished joint fourth in the US Open, Giraud on the other hand, had missed seven of his previous eight cuts. Quite clearly, Faldo was going to be first past the chequered flag.

And true enough, Giraud soon succumbed to the enormity of the situation, as expected (he would only just manage to break 80), and with just five holes remaining, Faldo was on cruise control for victory, his second of the season, just in time to give himself a boost for the Open. He had a two-shot lead, despite having hardly holed a thing all day.

But then, inexplicably, he had a high-speed blow-out. All of a sudden, he put on his Sunday worst. Faldo dropped a shot at the long 14th (a six at a par five is the cardinal sin for a professional), then he pulled his drive into deep rough at the 15th for another bogey. He missed a birdie chance from eight feet at the next, and by the time he reached the 17th green, he wasn't leading the tournament any more.

Up ahead, that winless Spanish professional Miguel Martin was doing all the right things. He'd had ten single putts in his round before he got to the 468-yard 18th, and there, sensing he needed a birdie to win (he didn't), unleashed a massive drive, flighted a perfect nine-iron shot to within five feet, then slotted in the putt for a birdie. Now Faldo's birdie putt from 30 feet on the 17th was to tie, rather than retake, the lead. Faldo left the putt six feet short. Then he missed the

Nick Faldo congratulates
Miguel Angel Martin

Gordon Brand Junior indicates the
one that got away.

Runner-up Martin Poxon
approaches the 15th

Left, crowds gather round the
leaderboard.

Right, pensive moment
from Faldo.

Home hope Eric Giraud on the 18th.

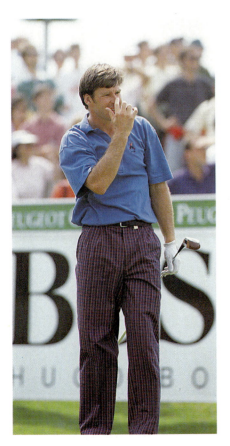

next one too. Martin was no longer a winless Spanish pro.

'I've been waiting ten years for my first win,' said the 30 year-old Madrileno. 'Today I am lucky, because one of the best players in the world makes so many mistakes.' Martin, by contrast, hardly made any, despite being 'absolutely paralysed by nerves' all day.

As for Faldo, he stumbled his way home with an awful, clumsy double-bogey at the last for good measure, and eventually found himself sharing third place with Italy's Costantino Rocca. 'I was brain-dead on 17,' said Faldo. 'Totally switched off.' He blamed his poor finish on the marshalling and, particularly, the number of press and photographers inside the ropes. That brings to mind the story of Joyce Wethered putting out at

Sheringham as a train hurtled by. 'Didn't the train put you off?' she was asked. 'What train?' she replied. In other words, Faldo perhaps wasn't concentrating like the Faldo of old. The Faldo of new was showing his weariness, his battle scars, and a new-found vulnerability – he'd looked shaky when he was in with a chance at the Volvo PGA Championship in May, he'd looked in pain as putt after putt missed coming down the stretch in the Dunhill British Masters, he had almost lost the Carrolls Irish Open when everyone else thought they were playing for second, and at the US Open at Pebble Beach, in admittedly tough conditions, he'd closed with a 77. All this from the official world number two, who unofficially everyone knows is the best player the world. But let's face it, even the best can have moments occasionally when they show that they are, after all, human.

Faldo's loss was very much the gain of Englishman Martin Poxon. In second place, he was almost as happy as Martin – he had completed his round some two hours before the Spaniard, and was astonished to find his closing 65 would be good enough for his highest ever finish and his biggest ever cheque in 15 years on the Tour: 'Christmas has come in June,' he said, £44,440 richer.

Poxon's week was a rare island of pleasure in a career of frustration. Professionals have to devour many a disappointment between breakfast and dinner, and for Faldo, blowing a two-shot lead with five to play by dropping five shots must be one of the hardest things to swallow. But Faldo, ever striving for perfection, positive come what may, took it all in his stride. 'I'm still playing well,' he said. 'I'm really pleased with my golf. Everything is as good as I could wish.'

Faldo: 'Come back, all is forgiven.'

Happy winning family group.

POS	NAME	CTY	1	2	3	4	TOTAL	PRIZE MONEY
1	Miguel Angel MARTIN	Sp	70	71	66	69	276	£66660
2	Martin POXON	Eng	72	68	73	65	278	44440
3	Costantino ROCCA	It	69	73	72	66	280	22520
	Nick FALDO	Eng	71	70	65	74	280	22520
5	Peter BAKER	Eng	70	69	70	72	281	16940
6	John McHENRY	Ire	67	71	72	72	282	10584
	Sandy LYLE	Scot	71	74	66	71	282	10584
	Peter SMITH	Scot	71	70	70	71	282	10584
	Anders FORSBRAND	Swe	73	72	67	70	282	10584
	Vicente FERNANDEZ	Arg	68	73	72	69	282	10584
11	Glen DAY	USA	74	68	66	75	283	7360
12	Stephen FIELD	Eng	70	74	72	68	284	5810
	Robert ALLENBY	Aus	71	69	75	69	284	5810
	Carl MASON	Eng	70	73	69	72	284	5810
	Paul McGINLEY	Ire	72	71	71	70	284	5810
	Jose COCERES	Arg	76	68	65	75	284	5810
	Frank NOBILO	NZ	72	71	69	72	284	5810
	Greg J TURNER	NZ	68	73	71	72	284	5810
	David GILFORD	Eng	72	70	66	76	284	5810
20	Mark ROE	Eng	73	70	71	71	285	4380
	Russell CLAYDON	Eng	71	70	75	69	285	4380
	Peter LONARD	Aus	72	69	73	71	285	4380
	Gary EVANS	Eng	68	70	74	73	285	4380
	Marc PENDARIES	Fr	75	66	71	73	285	4380
	Gordon BRAND Jnr	Scot	71	68	71	75	285	4380
	Joakim HAEGGMAN	Swe	72	68	74	71	285	4380
	Eric GIRAUD	Fr	68	65	73	79	285	4380
28	Howard CLARK	Eng	72	71	75	68	286	3497
	Barry LANE	Eng	74	70	70	72	286	3497
	Mark JAMES	Eng	72	71	69	74	286	3497
	Colin MONTGOMERIE	Scot	75	67	71	73	286	3497
	Martin GATES	Eng	69	74	70	73	286	3497
	Paul WAY	Eng	74	71	70	71	286	3497
	Johan RYSTROM	Swe	68	66	79	73	286	3497
35	Grant WAITE	NZ	71	72	70	74	287	3000
	David R JONES	Eng	71	72	72	72	287	3000
	Philip WALTON	Ire	75	69	75	68	287	3000
	Mike McLEAN	Eng	75	68	77	67	287	3000
39	David WILLIAMS	Eng	74	68	74	72	288	2440
	Vijay SINGH	Fij	71	74	71	72	288	2440
	John BLAND	SA	74	71	70	73	288	2440
	Mark MOULAND	Wal	73	71	71	73	288	2440
	Andrew MURRAY	Eng	73	68	75	72	288	2440
	Glenn RALPH	Eng	74	68	69	77	288	2440
	Patrick HALL	Eng	73	72	74	69	288	2440
	Roger WINCHESTER	Eng	72	70	74	72	288	2440
	Peter SENIOR	Aus	70	69	74	75	288	2440
	Jean VAN DE VELDE	Fr	72	73	68	75	288	2440
49	Heinz P THUEL	Ger	73	70	72	74	289	1880
	Andrew HARE	Eng	69	74	78	68	289	1880
	Christy O'CONNOR Jnr	Ire	67	69	76	77	289	1880
	Giuseppe CALI	It	74	71	71	73	289	1880
53	Phillip PRICE	Wal	72	71	76	71	290	1445
	Jon ROBSON	Eng	74	71	70	75	290	1445
	Steven RICHARDSON	Eng	74	70	72	74	290	1445
	Marc FARRY	Fr	71	72	78	69	290	1445
	Lucien TINKLER	Aus	70	75	73	72	290	1445
	Derrick COOPER	Eng	72	72	76	70	290	1445
	Santiago LUNA	Sp	72	71	72	75	290	1445
60	Paul LAWRIE	Scot	74	67	77	73	291	1180
	Miguel Angel JIMENEZ	Sp	72	70	74	75	291	1180
62	Paul BROADHURST	Eng	72	70	69	81	292	1100
	Darren CLARKE	N.Ire	72	73	74	73	292	1100
64	Ross McFARLANE	Eng	71	74	73	75	293	1020
	Eamonn DARCY	Ire	75	69	73	76	293	1020
66	Jay TOWNSEND	USA	73	71	81	69	294	599
	Steven BOWMAN	USA	70	74	74	76	294	599
68	Kenneth TRIMBLE	Aus	71	71	83	75	300	596

COURSE: NATIONAL G.C. PARIS DATE: 25-28.6 YARDAGE: 6966 PAR: 71

WOOSNAM TAKES THE HAT-TRICK

Ian Woosnam beat the odds and recorded his third consecutive victory in Monte Carlo.

Certainly Ian Woosnam did not feel on top of the world when he arrived at Mont Agel for The European Monte Carlo Open. After a year without a victory on the Volvo Tour, his self-esteem was at a low scarcely paralleled since his days of baked beans and penury. A glance at his performance statistics for the season showed why. In the eight events he had played, he had finished worse than 33rd on five occasions, missed one cut and secured a top ten place only twice. A journeyman might have described that as an average start to the year; the 1991 US Masters champion called it a slump.

Woosnam has ever been a confidence player. If he believes he can win, he can; if he doesn't, he can't. Simple as that. Before he won the Monte Carlo Open in 1990, his caddie Phil Morbey can recall the Welshman looking doubtfully at short putts. 'He was over the ball thinking, I'm not going to get this in, I'm going to miss'.

But a sudden rush of confidence helped Woosnam to victory, and he defended his title successfully in 1991. Now Woosnam found himself at Mont Agel once again in that Catch-22 situation familiar to all professional golfers: unless he found self-assurance he wouldn't play well, and unless he played well he wouldn't find self-assurance. For the moment, at least, his dream of winning the same event three consecutive times, a feat unequalled since Peter Thomson won a trio of Open Championships in the mid-50s, seemed a distant goal.

The tournament began in typically inclement weather. Rain fell intermittently at first, but with increasing determination, and by mid-day was it bordering on the torrential. Seve Ballesteros, a resident of Monaco, teed off at the tenth and was making rapid strides when he reached the par five 17th. There he hit his four-iron approach shot into a tree, suspended four feet above the ground. Ballesteros took a penalty drop, shanked his recovery with a pitching wedge, and notched up an unattractive seven. He ended the day with a 70, six shots behind the leader, Costantino Rocca, who had gone out in 31 after making four birdies in a row from the 14th.

Woosnam's fine round owed much to the fact that he discovered that the reason he hadn't been able to hook the ball, though a draw is his natural shot, was because he had been setting up incorrectly. He had been so afraid of cutting the ball that he had been aiming straight at the pin. When he found the courage to hit it out to the right, he was rewarded with a score of 66. At the close of play he was level with Darren Clarke, Wraith Grant, Keith Waters and Manuel Pinero, a shot adrift of Paul McGinley and two behind Rocca. 'How much further does the ball fly at this altitude?' he was asked after his round. 'About ten per cent, usually,' he replied. 'And how much further do your putts travel?'

Essentially, the second round was dominated by Clarke, a resolute young Irishman whose previous best score in a professional event had been a 66 at Mont Agel in 1991, which included an outward 28. Clarke has the same powerful game and indomitable spirit as Woosnam, and both qualities worked to his advantage in the perfect scoring conditions. He swept all before him with two flawless halves of 30.

'I make this a 59,' said Ken Brown, his playing companion, when he came off the course. 'I wish it was,' Clarke told him, 'but it's not.' And signed for a 60 – two better than Ricardo Gonzalez – and a halfway total of 126, to lead McGinley and Woosnam by five shots.

Clarke now considered himself to be in

Darren Clarke toasts his record-equalling round of 60.

a no-lose situation. Nobody was expecting him to hold his position on the leaderboard, he reasoned, therefore there would be no pressure on him. He would be free to play his own game. But Clarke forgot that he might put pressure on himself. He slumped to a third day 73 and, at eight under par, was a shot adrift of Eduardo Romero and two behind Woosnam. Mark McNulty, the 1989 winner of the Monte Carlo Open, who has the extraordinary record of never finishing worse than third in any of the four tournaments he has played at Mont Agel, was on seven under par along with Eoghan O'Connell.

Woosnam's round of 66 was blighted by two lost balls. He couldn't remember when such a thing last happened to him. The bogey at the third hole he felt was justified – he had sliced his drive so far into the trees that he was not surprised to learn it was missing. But he was sore about the double-bogey five at the 14th. With 171 yards to the pin, he had taken a seven iron, and had last seen it clearing the green and vanishing into oblivion. Birdies at the 17th and 18th, where he holed putts of 20 and 14 feet, gave him the edge over his opponents. 'I've got to fancy my chances,' said Woosnam, 'but there are some good players out there. Anyone can shoot 60 and win.'

A pea-soup fog descended on the final round. It swirled white-fingered and clammy around the leading groups, causing a 40 minute postponement of play on the third hole and numerous other delays. The golf became an exercise in patience; whoever could concentrate the longest might win.

Johan Rystrom soon showed that he had more reserves of the former than most people. Unaffected by the mist and rain, he bounded ahead of the field, gathering birdies in astonishing profusion. After turning in 29, he picked up shots at the 12th, 14th, 15th and 16th, and was convinced he could become the first European player ever to score 59 in a professional event, when he stood on the 17th tee. Alas, it was not to be. He closed with two pars for a 60, to finish joint second with McNulty on 263.

But it was Woosnam who kept his

Ian Woosnam hits out at Mont Agel.

nerve to the last, Woosnam who compiled a round of 64, despite a bogey at 15th, and Woosnam who, six and a half hours after he teed off, became king of the mountains for the third successive time. 'I'm glad it's all over,' he said in relief when he came off the course. 'I really struggled over the last few holes, but I'm delighted to have come through it and won. Now I can go out there and believe in myself again.'

Crowds surround
the 13th green.

Johan Rystrom in agony as
putt for a 59 lips out.

COURSE: MONT AGEL GOLF CLUB, LA TURBE							
DATE:1-4.7		YARDAGE: 6198					PAR: 69
POS NAME	**CTY**	**1**	**2**	**3**	**4**	**TOTAL**	**PRIZE MONEY**
1 Ian WOOSNAM	Wal	66	65	66	64	261	£73474
2 Mark McNULTY	Zim	67	67	66	63	263	38281
Johan RYSTROM	Swe	70	64	69	60	263	38281
4 Darren CLARKE	N.Ire	66	60	73	65	264	22051
5 Eduardo ROMERO	Arg	67	66	65	68	266	18699
6 Anders FORSBRAND	Swe	73	67	65	64	269	13230
Paul McGINLEY	Ire	65	66	69	69	269	13230
Jonathan SEWELL	Eng	67	68	68	66	269	13230
9 Costantino ROCCA	It	64	71	67	68	270	9349
Stuart LITTLE	Eng	72	67	68	63	270	9349
11 Des SMYTH	Ire	72	67	64	68	271	7387
Jean VAN DE VELDE	Fr	71	67	65	68	271	7387
Eoghan O'CONNELL	Ire	70	66	64	71	271	7387
Miguel Angel JIMENEZ	Sp	67	68	67	69,	271	7387
15 Martin GATES	Eng	74	63	69	66	272	5752
Yasunobu KURAMOTO	Jap	68	71	70	63	272	5752
Per-Ulrik JOHANSSON	Swe	68	65	70	69	272	5752
Peter MITCHELL	Eng	68	65	70	69	272	5752
Richard BOXALL	Eng	74	62	69	67	272	5752
Philip WALTON	Ire	68	66	69	69	272	5752
Malcolm MACKENZIE	Eng	71	66	71	64	272	5752
22 Thomas LEVET	Fr	69	70	65	69	273	4763
Peter SENIOR	Aus	67	66	73	67	273	4763
Magnus SUNESSON	Swe	73	65	67	68	273	4763
Tony JOHNSTONE	Zim	71	66	67	69	273	4763
Steen TINNING	Den	74	64	66	69	273	4763
27 Ricardo GONZALEZ	Arg	71	62	71	70	274	4167
Lucien TINKLER	Aus	73	66	69	66	274	4167
Gery WATINE	Fr	70	69	69	66	274	4167
Seve BALLESTEROS	Sp	70	69	67	68	274	4167
31 Rodger DAVIS	Aus	68	66	68	73	275	3671
Dennis EDLUND	Swe	72	63	71	69	275	3671
Gordon J BRAND	Eng	67	71	68	69	275	3671
Jim RUTLEDGE	Can	73	67	71	64	275	3671
35 Miguel Angel MARTIN	Sp	71	69	70	66	276	3307
Hugh BAIOCCHI	SA	73	65	67	71	276	3307
Mike McLEAN	Eng	72	67	69	68	276	3307
Wraith GRANT	Eng	66	71	68	71	276	3307
39 Giuseppe CALI	It	67	71	68	71	277	2822
Wayne WESTNER	SA	74	66	69	68	277	2822
Jorge BERENDT	Arg	69	70	68	70	277	2822
Tim PLANCHIN	Fr	71	67	70	69	277	2822
Jose DAVILA	Sp	70	69	68	70	277	2822
Mike MILLER	Scot	70	67	73	67	277	2822
Danny MIJOVIC	Can	69	65	72	71	277	2822
46 David WILLIAMS	Eng	71	68	68	71	278	2249
Justin HOBDAY	SA	69	68	70	71	278	2249
Robert LEE	Eng	72	68	70	68	278	2249
Santiago LUNA	Sp	72	66	68	72	278	2249
Silvio GRAPPASONNI	It	68	72	68	70	278	2249
Mark MOULAND	Wal	69	69	70	70	278	2249
52 Jose COCERES	Arg	69	71	69	70	279	1852
Gavin LEVENSON	SA	69	68	71	71	279	1852
Bill MALLEY	USA	69	69	69	72	279	1852
55 Jose RIVERO	Sp	72	67	75	66	280	1508
Ross DRUMMOND	Scot	70	69	69	72	280	1508
Keith WATERS	Eng	66	70	67	77	280	1508
Mats HALLBERG	Swe	74	66	72	68	280	1508
Peter McWHINNEY	Aus	70	66	73	71	280	1508
60 Michael ALLEN	USA	70	70	69	72	281	1256
Ian PALMER	SA	73	67	70	71	281	1256
Manuel PINERO	Sp	66	73	73	69	281	1256
Jeff HAWKES	SA	72	68	69	72	281	1256
64 Stephen McALLISTER	Scot	70	70	71	71	282	970
Ronald STELTEN	USA	69	71	70	72	282	970
Robin MANN	Eng	71	69	73	69	282	970

O'MALLEY WINS IN SENSATIONAL STYLE

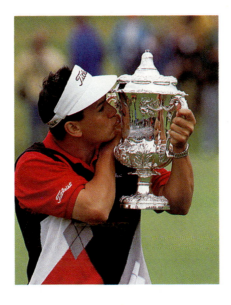

A seven-under-par burst over the final five holes enabled Australia's Peter O'Malley to capture the biggest title of his career.

It seemed like a dream come true. Finally, after five long years, a Scotsman was going to capture the prestigious Bell's Scottish Open at Gleneagles. It sounds like a bad joke, but an Englishman, an Irishman and a Welshman have all won the event. Even an American and Australian have won, but never a Scotsman. It was so close this year, but the Scotsman had the rug pulled from under him, actually from down under him, in the final round.

Dressed in a sweater bearing the St Andrews cross, Colin Montgomerie, who represents the Gleneagles Hotel, was striding towards victory over the King's course when 27-year old Australian Peter O'Malley produced what was arguably the best finish ever in tournament golf.

The Scottish crowds had turned out in their thousands to watch Montgomerie fulfil a promise he had made at the start of the week. The burly Scotsman had said it was time a Scotsman finally won the Scottish Open and he was that Scotsman.

Some 110,764 fans flocked to Gleneagles this year, with 28,546 turning up on the last day alone. Once again it set another attendance record, beating the 1991 mark by over 2,000. The large Bell's Scottish galleries weren't disappointed. For a start the field included 11 players from the 1991 Johnnie Walker Ryder Cup team, as well as Sandy Lyle, Ronan Rafferty, Mark McNulty and the defending champion Craig Parry. Thrown in were former Masters winners Larry Mize and Ben Crenshaw, and America's golden boy Phil Mickelson. The old guard

was represented by stylish swinger Tom Weiskopf and former Open and US Open Champion Tony Jacklin. This was a golf feast of gourmet proportions.

It was evident from the start that this would be another thrilling tournament when Bernhard Langer went round the King's Course in 62, establishing a two shot lead over Mats Lanner, and a three

shot lead over Montgomerie, O'Malley, Peter Baker, Jamie Spence, Derrick Cooper and American, Mark Brooks.

The high standards set in the first round continued on the second day when the halfway cut was set at two under par. Ian Woosnam went to eight under par, Nick Faldo was at nine under and Peter Senior and Montgomerie joined Langer at 11 under, one behind Mark Brooks and Paul Curry, who had the round of the day.

It's hard to imagine anyone shooting 62 on the King's Course. Three men have done so – Ian Woosnam, Jose Maria Olazabal previously and then Bernhard Langer in the first round. If 62 boggles the mind, then 60 was surely unattainable. Not for Paul Curry. He blitzed the King's Course with that figure on the second day. The quiet man from Essex had seven birdies, two eagles and one bogey in his round. The bogey came at the 15th. But for that he would have reached the magic figure of 59, a figure very few people have ever recorded. Not that Curry was unhappy – the new course record earned him £16,000 from the Johnnie Walker Tour Course Record Award.

Among the casualties to miss the final two days were Mark James, Scottish hopeful Sam Torrance, David Feherty and Steve Richardson. Tony Jacklin's return to the Tour wasn't a great success. He shot 76-72 to miss by ten shots. Phil Mickelson fared slightly better. He recorded rounds of 74-70 in his first European tournament as a professional, getting a painful insight into just how high the standards are on the Volvo Tour.

And so the tournament was Montgomerie's for the taking. All he had to do was play as he did in his first two rounds (65-64) and the tournament was his.

But the third day belonged to Bernhard Langer. The German shot a second successive 67 to take a three shot lead over Curry, Lanner and Montgomerie into the final round.

Montgomerie shot level par 70 in the third round and trailed Langer by three strokes. It seemed that he was to be denied. Langer's lead looked unassailable. One of the toughest competitors in the game, the German was unlikely to fold under pressure.

Langer never really folded. He just didn't get going on the last day. His final round of level par 70 would miss by four shots. Montgomerie, on the other hand, came out charging. By the sixth he had eradicated Langer's lead. The tournament was his, and the Scottish crowds were basking in his glory. Then came the O'Malley bombardment.

The Australian had gone quietly along shooting rounds of 65-70-65 to start the final round four shots behind Langer. It seemed that the young Aussie was going to accomplish two things at Gleneagles – make a good cheque and avoid the Open Qualifying by claiming one of the five exempt spots for Muirfield. He made sure of both when he went eagle, birdie, birdie, birdie, eagle over the last five holes. He covered the final five holes in seven under par.

Montgomerie did everything he could to win, shooting 65, but he still fell short by two strokes. He covered the final five holes in 19 strokes against O'Malley's 13. The former Australian Junior Champion and New Zealand Amateur Champion had finally lived up to expectations. He just saved his best until last.

Peter O'Malley en route to a birdie at the 71st hole.

Umbrellas frame Mark McNulty on the 12th hole.

A large Bell's for O'Malley.

Nick Faldo tuned up for Muirfield with a third place finish.

O'Malley phones home to Australia with the glad tidings.

Colin Montgomerie was in the driving seat prior to O'Malley's charge.

*O'Malley sinks eagle putt
to clinch the title.*

*Reflections on what might
have been from Montgomerie.*

*Bernhard Langer led
after 54 holes.*

COURSE: GLENEAGLES HOTEL, KING'S COURSE
DATE: 8-11.7   YARDAGE: 6739   PAR: 70

POS	NAME	CTY	1	2	3	4	TOTAL	PRIZE MONEY
1	Peter O'MALLEY	Aus	65	70	65	62	262	£100000
2	Colin MONTGOMERIE	Scot	65	64	70	65	264	66660
3	Nick FALDO	Eng	69	62	69	65	265	33780
	Mark McNULTY	Zim	68	68	66	63	265	33780
5	Bernhard LANGER	Ger	62	67	67	70	266	25400
6	Mats LANNER	Swe	64	69	66	68	267	21000
7	Craig PARRY	Aus	67	69	66	67	269	15480
	Costantino ROCCA	It	70	66	68	65	269	15480
	Ian WOOSNAM	Wal	66	66	70	67	269	15480
10	Rodger DAVIS	Aus	70	65	67	69	271	10740
	Philip WALTON	Ire	66	70	65	70	271	10740
	James SPENCE	Eng	65	67	69	70	271	10740
	Peter SENIOR	Aus	66	63	72	70	271	10740
14	Larry MIZE	USA	67	70	68	67	272	8820
	Carl MASON	Eng	69	67	68	68	272	8820
	David GILFORD	Eng	67	70	67	68	272	8820
17	Rocco MEDIATE	USA	69	67	68	69	273	7760
	Paul CURRY	Eng	68	60	71	74	273	7760
	Jose RIVERO	Sp	68	69	70	66	273	7760
20	Ben CRENSHAW	USA	71	64	68	71	274	6570
	Joakim HAEGGMAN	Swe	68	68	71	67	274	6570
	Howard CLARK	Eng	69	67	69	69	274	6570
	Miguel Angel MARTIN	Sp	66	67	72	69	274	6570
	Vijay SINGH	Fij	69	66	71	68	274	6570
	Duffy WALDORF	USA	66	67	69	72	274	6570
	Tom WEISKOPF	USA	69	65	71	69	274	6570
	Robert KARLSSON	Swe	70	65	68	71	274	6570
28	Anders SORENSEN	Den	68	70	66	71	275	5175
	Yasunobu KURAMOTO	Jap	69	67	70	69	275	5175
	Mark BROOKS	USA	65	63	73	74	275	5175
	Gavin LEVENSON	SA	68	68	71	68	275	5175
	Frank NOBILO	NZ	69	65	73	68	275	5175
	Craig MALTMAN	Scot	69	69	68	69	275	5175
	Sandy LYLE	Scot	66	65	72	72	275	5175
	Gary ORR	Scot	66	67	71	71	275	5175
36	Jose Maria CANIZARES	Sp	67	67	73	69	276	4260
	Lee JANZEN	USA	69	67	72	68	276	4260
	Manuel PINERO	Sp	68	67	71	70	276	4260
	Brian BARNES	Scot	70	66	72	68	276	4260
	Justin HOBDAY	SA	68	65	70	73	276	4260
	Paul BROADHURST	Eng	68	70	69	69	276	4260
42	Wayne WESTNER	SA	69	69	68	71	277	3660
	Hugh BAIOCCHI	SA	72	65	70	70	277	3660
	Vicente FERNANDEZ	Arg	69	65	75	68	277	3660
	Seve BALLESTEROS	Sp	70	68	69	70	277	3660
46	Peter BAKER	Eng	65	67	76	70	278	3060
	Juan QUIROS	Sp	69	66	71	72	278	3060
	Mike HARWOOD	Aus	69	69	72	68	278	3060
	Magnus SUNESSON	Swe	68	70	70	70	278	3060
	Andrew MURRAY	Eng	67	71	70	70	278	3060
	Mike McLEAN	Eng	67	67	72	72	278	3060
52	Barry LANE	Eng	72	66	74	67	279	2400
	Johan RYSTROM	Swe	69	69	70	71	279	2400
	Gary EVANS	Eng	67	71	67	74	279	2400
	Tony JOHNSTONE	Zim	73	65	67	74	279	2400
	Per-Ulrik JOHANSSON	Swe	73	65	70	71	279	2400
57	Isao AOKI	Jap	71	66	72	71	280	1872
	John McHENRY	Ire	68	70	69	73	280	1872
	Peter FOWLER	Aus	69	69	69	73	280	1872
	Robert LEE	Eng	70	68	73	69	280	1872
	Ronan RAFFERTY	N.Ire	68	67	72	73	280	1872
62	Gordon BRAND Jnr	Scot	69	67	73	72	281	1590
	Ross DRUMMOND	Scot	71	67	77	66	281	1590
	Peter SMITH	Scot	68	70	73	70	281	1590
	Stephen HAMILL	N.Ire	70	68	71	72	281	1590
66	Eamonn DARCY	Ire	67	68	74	73	282	900
67	Tony CHARNLEY	Eng	67	71	71	74	283	898
68	Mark ROE	Eng	69	68	73	74	284	896
69	Stephen FIELD	Eng	68	69	76	72	285	893
	Andrew OLDCORN	Eng	70	65	78	72	285	893

A TALE OF
TWO FIVE IRONS

In 1987 Nick Faldo struck a sumptuous five iron into the heart of Muirfield's 18th green to set up victory in the final round of the Open Championship. Five years later in the 121st Open Championship over the same course he struck another five-iron shot which, with hindsight, was the most telling of all the 272 strokes he hit *en route* to his third Open title.

During the period between those two shots Faldo established himself as the most formidable competitor in major championships since the hey day of Jack Nicklaus. He won the Open in 1990, the US Masters two years running (1989 and 1990), lost a play-off for the US Open in 1988, was one stroke out of the play-off for the 1990 US Open and finished outside the top 20 on only two occasions out of the 21 championships played in that spell.

In the light of this it was hardly surprising that Faldo was installed as favourite among the Honourable Company of International Golfers which gathered at the venerable links for an Open which marked the centenary of its first staging there.

The bookies know that Faldo has majors on his mind but despite their assessment there were a few niggling doubts concerning recent form. In the Carrolls Irish Open a month previously Faldo had squandered a four-stroke lead going into the final round and had only scraped to victory after a play-off. Then, in the Peugeot French Open at the end of June he had held a two-stroke lead with

In a thrilling finale Nick Faldo captured his third Open title

five holes to play but dropped five strokes in that stretch to lose. This was most un-Faldo like behaviour but the wounds were not mortal and his confidence was still high when the bell went for the start.

Scarcely a puff of wind greeted the players on the first morning and they were quick to cash in on the benign conditions. Leading the assault were Ray Floyd and Steve Pate, both coming in with seven-under-par 64s. Floyd, two months short of his 50th birthday, was enjoying an Indian Summer in his career and played impressively, picking up eight birdies, including one at the first which proved to be the

toughest hole all week, and dropping just one shot. 'The key is my suppleness and flexibility,' he said afterwards in answer to questions about the age factor. Pate confessed that he hadn't swung particularly well but seven single putts in his seven birdie effort made up for that.

One stroke behind them came Gordon Brand Junior with Ian Woosnam, standing on the 17th tee at seven under par, thinking in terms of a 63. A hooked drive and a long wait for the green to clear meant he had to settle for a par and a bunkered drive at the last turned it into a 65. Brand was steadiness personified and was rewarded with six birdies and no bogies.

Faldo made a most inauspicious start, turning away in disgust as he bunkered his opening drive. The resultant dropped shot was quickly forgotten when he chipped in for an eagle at the fifth followed by a hat-trick of birdies from the eighth and then another an the 13th. His 66 kept him well in touch with the lead and he was joined on that score by the Americans, John Cook and Lee Janzen and the young South African, Ernie Els.

The second day was perfect for golf, warm and sunny with a brisk enough wind to make a good score thoroughly earned. It was also the day when Nick Faldo delivered unto us 'the round'. He started quietly with four straight pars, birdied the fifth and sixth and then dropped a stroke at the seventh. A par-saving putt from 20 feet on the eighth gave him a boost but at this point he was three strokes behind Pate who had made

*Evening shade descends
on Muirfield.*

the running with an outward 32. On the ninth Faldo struck a three wood 241 yards into the wind – 'one of the best of my career' – to within four feet and down went the putt for an eagle. Now he was only one stroke behind Pate and the second nine became a glorious procession of scintillating iron play and magnificent putting. Faldo had been working with David Leadbetter on a new putting stroke for which Leadbetter had told him to 'watch it and brush it' and goodness, didn't it work. The ball dived into the hole for four birdies on the inward half so that by the time he completed the 16th with a par three he had played nine holes from the eighth in 29 strokes with six single putts. He let slip an opportunity at the

17th where, after a solid drive, he pulled his second wide of the green and had to settle for a five but a solid par up the last finished the job in 64.

Faldo's halfway total of 130 was a new Championship record, beating the one he shared with Greg Norman at St Andrews in 1990 and Henry Cotton had set at Royal St George's in 1934. It gave him a three-stroke lead over Cook and Brand whose rounds of 67 and 68 were highly respectable.

The cut fell at 143 and while Faldo was in his pomp, the man he replaced as the majors threat, Jack Nicklaus, was packing his bags after missing out for only the second time since he first appeared in 1962. Joining him were Tom Watson,

Colin Montgomerie, Fred Couples and saddest of all, Severiano Ballesteros who, as the evening shadows engulfed him, took six up the last.

What Faldo wanted in the third round was a consolidating performance that would give no quarter to his nearest rivals and that is what he achieved. In fact, his 69 enabled him to extend his lead to four strokes. It was not an easy day and when Faldo had reached the turn in a one under par 35 and then dropped a stroke

*Nick Faldo drives on the 18th in
the second round.*

Ernie Els experiences the severity of the Muirfield bunkers.

Gordon Brand Junior: Room for one angry man and his niblick.

Sweden's Robert Karlsson finished in fifth place.

at the tenth he found himself tied with Pate and only one ahead of Brand and two ahead of Cook.

Without leaning on his putting Faldo responded with the brand of relentless golf that has become watchword. While his challengers shed strokes on the difficult inward half, Faldo kept hitting fairways and greens, was rewarded with birdies at the 12th and 17th and was home in 34.

The positions after 54 holes were: Faldo – 199, Cook and Pate – 203, Brand, Els and Donnie Hammond – 205, Chip Beck and Jose Maria Olazabal – 206 and, as a matter of passing interest, John Daly – 223, a score which showed that it doesn't matter how far you hit it, at Muirfield there will always be a bunker lying in wait.

The agony continues for Severiano

Ballesteros.

What happened on the final day was the stuff of which legends are made, hearts are broken and Open Championships are lifted into the pantheon of the game. Muirfield became a battlefield, the whiff of cordite was in the air, the body-count was high and in the end, only one man was left staggering through the emotion of it all.

Faldo's mood for the day was set by his opening tee shot which found sand. From there on very little went right but he still reached the turn in a one-over-par 37. Ahead of him Cook had flared briefly with an eagle at the fifth but his impetus was halted when he drove out of bounds on the ninth to take seven. Pate turned in 36 to lie within three strokes of Faldo and the outcome still looked a foregone conclusion.

It's an old cliché that championships do not begin until the last nine holes of the final round but never did it carry more truth. Faldo suddenly went walkabout. He dumped a wedge into a bunker on

Late run from Jose Maria Olazabal gave

him third place.

the 11th to take five, he missed from three feet on the 13th to drop another shot and then bunkered his tee shot on the 14th to lose another stroke. Meanwhile, Cook had come alive again, birdieing the 12th, 15th and 16th to take a two stroke lead.

Faldo was far from finished and his torment was replaced by an almost fanatical conviction. 'I told myself I would have to play the best four holes of my life,' he said, as he stood on the 15th tee. And he did. And it started from the middle of the 15th fairway when with that faithful five iron he manoeuvred the ball through the cross-wind and fashioned it down to within five feet of the hole. It was a true champion's stroke and the birdie set him off and running again.

Cook, though, was still in control, that is to say that he had hit the 17th in two and had putted up to within three feet. Then the control was gone, the putt for a birdie slipped by and Cook was shattered. He drove well up the final fairway but hesitated between a two or three iron, decided on the former and secretly believing he had too much club, held back on the shot and sent the ball clattering into the crowd on the right. He received a free drop but could not get down in two more.

Faldo had made a great par-saving chip on the 16th and with a spring in his step had driven well down the 17th, following it with an imperious four iron to the green. As the crowd on the 18th informed him that something was amiss with Cook, he two-putted for a birdie and the retention of the lead.

A lovely drive up the final fairway and a thrilling three iron, banked into the wind, which covered the flag found him on the back of the green. The putt was fast and treacherous but he coaxed the ball down to within a foot and holed out before collapsing in a flood of emotion.

Between them, Cook and Faldo summed up the extraordinary sequence of events of the final round. Cook, who took defeat with grace and dignity, said: 'I was alive, dead, alive and then very much dead again. I've never gone through so many emotions during a round. That putt on the 17th, I expected it

Behind every great man

there's a woman.

to break a little but it didn't. I didn't hit the stroke well but at least it clipped the hole. The 17th was the key and I guess I gave away a major championship.'

Faldo too acknowledged the trauma he had been through. 'I could have just lost it all,' he recalled. 'Right there and that's a horrible feeling. I would have needed a big sticking plaster to heal the wound. At the end it just becomes a battle of the mind, a battle for control. You try so hard to do the right things, to relax, but pressure takes over. It wears you to a frazzle.'

Worn out or not, Faldo was champion for the third time and quite possibly the finest player ever to emerge from these shores. The Faldo era of major triumphs had been spanned by five years and two five iron shots but the tale certainly hasn't ended.

A pitch too far for Cook at the 72nd.

Faldo in trouble at the fifth in the final round.

Happiness is an Open
Championship victory.

The champion strikes
for home.

POS	NAME	CTY	1	2	3	4	TOTAL	PRIZE MONEY
	COURSE: MUIRFIELD	DATE:16-19.7		YARDAGE: 6970				PAR: 71
1	Nick FALDO	Eng	66	64	69	73	272	£95000
2	John COOK	Eng	66	67	70	70	273	75000
3	Jose Maria OLAZABAL	Sp	70	67	69	68	274	64000
4	Steve PATE	USA	64	70	69	73	276	53000
5	Donnie HAMMOND	USA	70	65	70	74	279	30071
	Andrew MAGEE	USA	67	72	70	70	279	30071
	Ernie ELS	SA	66	69	70	74	279	30071
	Ian WOOSNAM	Wal	65	73	70	71	279	30071
	Gordon BRAND Jnr	Scot	65	68	72	74	279	30071
	Malcolm MACKENZIE	Eng	71	67	70	71	279	30071
	Robert KARLSSON	Swe	70	68	70	71	279	30071
12	Mark O'MEARA	USA	71	68	72	69	280	17383
	Chip BECK	USA	71	68	67	74	280	17383
	Raymond FLOYD	USA	64	71	73	72	280	17383
	Sandy LYLE	Scot	68	70	70	72	280	17383
	James SPENCE	Eng	71	68	70	71	280	17383
	Larry RINKER	USA	69	68	70	73	280	17383
18	Greg NORMAN	Aus	71	72	70	68	281	13200
19	Hale IRWIN	USA	70	73	67	72	282	11066
	Ian BAKER-FINCH	Aus	71	71	72	68	282	11066
	Tom KITE	USA	70	69	71	72	282	11066
22	Peter MITCHELL	Eng	69	71	72	71	283	8950
	Paul LAWRIE	Scot	70	72	68	73	283	8950
	Tom PURTZER	USA	68	69	75	71	283	8950
25	Billy ANDRADE	USA	69	71	70	74	284	7700
	Duffy WALDORF	USA	69	70	73	72	284	7700
	Peter SENIOR	Aus	70	69	70	75	284	7700
28	Mark CALCAVECCHIA	USA	69	71	73	72	285	6658
	Mark McNULTY	Zim	71	70	70	74	285	6658
	Jodie MUDD	USA	71	69	74	71	285	6658
	Craig PARRY	Aus	67	71	76	71	285	6658
	Russ COCHRAN	USA	71	68	72	74	285	6658
	Mats LANNER	Swe	72	68	71	74	285	6658
34	Anders FORSBRAND	Swe	70	72	70	74	286	5760
	Corey PAVIN	USA	69	74	73	70	286	5760
	Payne STEWART	USA	70	73	71	72	286	5760
	Steve ELKINGTON	Aus	68	70	75	73	286	5760
	Tony JOHNSTONE	Zim	72	71	74	69	286	5760
39	De Wett BASSON	SA	71	71	71	74	287	5083
	Lee JANZEN	USA	66	73	73	75	287	5083
	Lee TREVINO	USA	69	71	73	74	287	5083
	Steven RICHARDSON	Eng	74	68	73	72	287	5083
	Wayne GRADY	Aus	73	69	71	74	287	5083
	Ronan RAFFERTY	N.Ire	69	71	75	72	287	5083
45	Lanny WADKINS	USA	69	69	75	75	288	4675
	Brian MARCHBANK	Scot	71	72	71	74	288	4675
	Craig MANN	Aus	74	69	72	73	288	4675
	Rocco MEDIATE	USA	67	75	73	73	288	4675
	Jose COCERES	Arg	74	69	73	72	288	4675
	Mike HARWOOD	Aus	72	68	76	72	288	4675
51	Roger MACKAY	Aus	73	70	73	73	289	4075
	Barry LANE	Eng	73	69	73	74	289	4075
	Vijay SINGH	Fij	69	72	76	72	289	4075
	Nick PRICE	Zim	69	73	73	74	289	4075
55	Costantino ROCCA	It	67	75	73	75	290	3875
	Orrin VINCENT III	USA	67	75	77	71	290	3875
	David FEHERTY	N.Ire	71	70	72	77	290	3875
	Mark BROOKS	USA	71	71	73	75	290	3875
59	Bernhard LANGER	Ger	70	72	76	73	291	3650
	Paul AZINGER	USA	70	69	75	77	291	3650
	Wayne RILEY	Aus	71	72	75	73	291	3650
	William GUY	Scot	72	71	70	78	291	3650
	Mike CLAYTON	Aus	72	70	75	74	291	3650
64	Hendrick BUHRMANN	SA	70	72	75	75	292	3425
	Craig STADLER	USA	72	70	75	75	292	3425
	Roger CHAPMAN	Eng	72	71	71	78	292	3425
	Danny MIJOVIC	Can	70	71	80	71	292	3425
68	Daren LEE (AM)	Eng	68	72	77	76	293	–
	Per-Ulrik JOHANSSON	Swe	67	74	77	75	293	3237
	Peter O'MALLEY	Aus	72	70	76	75	293	3237
	Andrew SHERBORNE	Eng	72	69	75	77	293	3237
	Jon ROBSON	Eng	70	71	78	74	293	3237

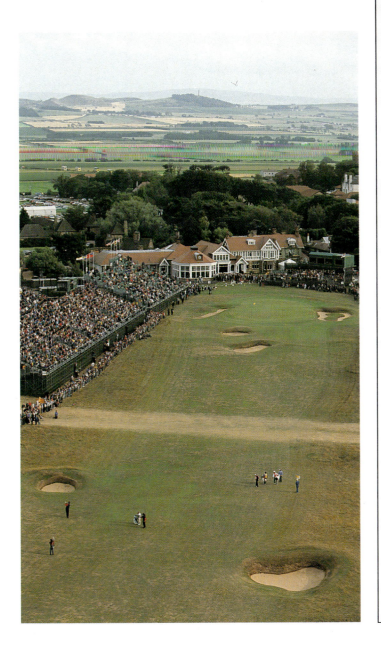

FOURIE'S A
JOLLY GOOD FELLOW

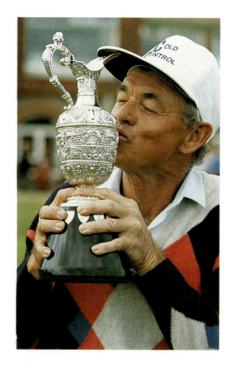

*John Fourie held off
some legendary figures
to become the fourth
South African Senior
British Open champion*

The Senior British Open Championship is an event of pure nostalgia, a gentler rhythm of golf, laced with vulnerability, humour and wry acceptance of passing years. At Royal Lytham and St Annes, a legend played alongside a local golfing dentist, Brian Waites was a walking wonder, and John Fourie turned back the clock with some *déjà vu* golf.

South African's Fourie emerged almost as astonishingly as he had 22 years previously when, as an amateur, he defeated the professionals to win the South African Dunlop Masters. Then, as now, the field included the presence of Gary Player. The pinnacle of Fourie's professional career in Europe was winning the 1977 Newcastle Open. Only two years later he returned home to slip into the life of a club professional.

The most famous club professional of them all, Brian Waites, had 11 months previously sustained such injury to limbs in a car crash, that he required 11 operations. Not once during three months in his hospital bed, did he contemplate being unable to play golf again. A slightly limping miracle – he was a competitor.

Those familiar names of Neil Coles, with a two-under-par 69, Arnold Palmer and Peter Butler on 70, and Bob Charles with a 71, came to the fore in the opening round.

Butler put his card on the Press conference table and remained standing. Were he to sit down, he explained, his increased long sight would prevent him from reading the numbers...simply a case of *tempus fugit*. These days he plays golf once a week with the Captain at his club.

No such problems for the optimistic 62-year old Arnold Palmer, who revels in playing the American Senior Tour, albeit in contact lenses. Palmer, whose hat to combat the wet and windy elements, was up at the back, down at the front in schoolgirl style, deemed his concentration

better, his mental errors fewer, in his opening 70. Everyone was pleased to see Palmer was there, and he in turn appreciated his playing companion of the first two days, 67-year old Christy O'Conner, still retaining that wonderful easy rhythmic swing, which took him to a share of joint 13th place.

The second day provided a headline-writer's dream as local dentist and three handicapper, Michael Noon, a Royal Lytham member, drilled his way to a 66 to lead the field by two shots from Neil Coles and Bob Charles.

'I've had a poor year, I'm astonished,' said the dazed dentist, who had to dash back to the surgery to fill a few more holes that evening. Known as the old Lytham nudger 'because I'm one of the faders of this world,' the modest winner of 39 medals was obviously tickled pink with his one eagle and four birdie round, saying, 'I never played that well at my best.'

The 59-year old Irish professional, Michael Murphy from Baltinglas, holed in one with a nine iron at the ninth, on a magical seven-under-par run in seven holes, which began at the sixth with an eagle, on the way to a 68. Exciting stuff for the man who has a club repair business and said: 'I had only seen seven under for seven holes on television.'

Day three and the big names were back in front: Charles and Coles at one under, Butler on level par, Palmer plus one, and the ever-competitive Player hauled himself upward with a 69 to finish four over. Noon's creditable 76

Trademark finish from Arnold

Palmer.

POS	NAME	CTY	1	2	3	4	TOTAL	PRIZE MONEY
1	John FOURIE	SA	75	67	71	69	282	£33330
2	Bob CHARLES	NZ	71	69	72	73	285	17360
	Neil COLES	Eng	69	71	72	73	285	17360
4	Peter BUTLER	Eng	70	71	72	73	286	10000
5	Tommy HORTON	Eng	74	70	69	75	288	7650
	Akio TOYODA	Jap	75	71	70	72	288	7650
7	Gary PLAYER	SA	73	76	69	71	289	5500
	Simon HOBDAY	SA	72	72	74	71	289	5500
9	Arthur PROCTOR	USA	72	74	70	74	290	4250
	Arnold PALMER	USA	70	72	72	76	290	4250
11	Dale DOUGLASS	USA	78	70	73	71	292	3390
	Jean GARAIALDE	Fr	75	74	68	75	292	3390
13	Jim FERREE	USA	76	75	73	70	293	3180
	Bob ZIMMERMAN	USA	73	73	75	72	293	3180
	Christy O'CONNOR	Ire	72	72	74	75	293	3180
	Joel S.HIRSCH (AM)	USA	71	72	70	80	293	-
16	Michel DAMIANO	Fr	75	75	70	74	294	2980
	Vincent TSHABALALA	SA	74	72	75	73	294	2980
18	Bobby VERWEY	SA	71	76	75	73	295	2860
19	Brian HUGGETT	Wal	75	74	70	77	296	2780
	Michael NOON (AM)	Eng	72	66	76	82	296	-
20	Dick SMITH	USA	77	71	74	75	297	2672
	Robert RAWLINS	USA	76	70	74	77	297	2672
22	Charles MEHOK	USA	76	71	75	76	298	2565
23	Jose Maria ROCA	Sp	78	67	77	77	299	2485
24	Bryan CARTER	Eng	76	72	74	78	300	2285
	Ralph TERRY	USA	75	71	75	79	300	2285
	Roger FIDLER	Eng	77	73	75	75	300	2285
	David JIMINEZ	USA	78	74	75	73	300	2285
	Brian WAITES	Eng	76	73	75	76	300	2285
	Roy SMETHURST (AM)	Eng	72	73	72	77	000	
	Gordon EDWARDS	Eng	73	76	73	78	300	-
29	James DOLAN II	USA	74	75	71	81	301	2075
	Rafe BOTTS	USA	77	71	81	72	301	2075
31	David BUTLER	Eng	74	73	76	79	302	1902
	Michael MURPHY	Ire	75	68	78	81	302	1902
	Ron NICHOL	USA	79	73	73	77	302	1902
	Hugh JACKSON	Ire	76	75	75	76	302	1902
	Daniel MORGAN	USA	79	70	77	76	302	1902
36	Ronald HASE	USA	73	73	82	75	303	1725

COURSE: ROYAL LYTHAM & ST ANNES

DATE:23-26.7   **YARDAGE: 6673**   **PAR: 72**

Th new champion drives from the

final tee.

gave him the thrill of playing with Palmer on the last day.

Fourie was lurking on level par, and as vulnerable nerves in some famous hands twitched a few shots, the South African broke clear of the legends with a great last round 69, strewn with birdies and the luxury of one or two wobbles, his action replay of so many years ago ended in triumph, on a two under par 282, three ahead of Charles and Coles.

Fourie was floating on air. On earth, Brian Waites finished tied 24th.

LANGER EXTENDS HIS RUN

Winning in Holland meant that Bernhard Langer extended his run of European victories to at least one every season for the past 14 years

The 1992 Heineken Dutch Open will probably always be remembered as the tournament Mike McLean lost, rather than the one Bernhard Langer won.

Even the German himself, although exhilarated at extending his sequence of European Tour victories to 14 years in succession by winning a dramatic play-off with Gordon Brand Junior, looked upon it as something of a hollow victory. 'It is the most unusual win of my life,' he said, after beating Brand at the second extra hole.

Only half-an-hour earlier, Langer had thought he had blown his chances, furiously smacking his head with his hand as McLean holed from 20 feet on the final green which he though had won him the £100,000 first prize at Noordwijkse.

McLean had sunk a huge putt off the green and twice chipped in on his way to a final round of 70, two under par, and when he rolled in that birdie putt on the last green, it should have taken him to 12-under-par 276 for the tournament. This was a stroke better than Langer, his playing companion closing with a 72, and than Brand, waiting in the clubhouse after surging through the field with a magnificent last-day 67.

But McLean, who had twice fallen flat on his back in delight as he chipped in, was to be floored by not knowing the Rules of Golf. On the 11th in the rough, he had unwittingly removed trailing strands of thorny bramble which had covered his ball – and that conflicts with the Rule which prevents a player improving his lie. Done in innocence, it was to cost the affable McLean the tournament, and

over £66,000. Hardly believing his final putt had gone in, for what he thought was his second victory on the Volvo Tour, McLean raised his arms in ecstasy and triumph on the last, but his ecstasy was almost immediately to turn to agony.

Warning him that to avoid possible disqualification he should not sign his card, Tournament Director Michael Tate informed him that a spectator had spotted

his indiscretion and reported it to a Dutch referee. He then showed the dismayed McLean the incident on a television recording. Realising his mistake, McLean saw his final round changed to a 72 by virtue of a two-stroke penalty for the breach of Rule, dropping him down to 10-under to tie third with Gary Evans.

The event was thus thrown into a play-off between Langer and Brand, and a bewildered Dutch crowd rushed to the short 17th to watch further drama. Both players made par-saving putts, Langer's from all of 15 feet, then a small misjudgment by Brand decided the destiny of the title at the 18th. His approach was just too strong and his ball rattled in and out of the grandstand. He received a free drop, but not from the dropping zone nearer the green, which would have given him a good chance to make par. Langer needed two putts to get down but, after pitching on, so did Brand. Langer's first win of the year was complete.

'It was very weird. All day I believed I'd win,' said Langer, who had snatched the tournament lead from Mark Mouland on the third day. 'Then when Mike's putt went in I thought I'd thrown it away. It was a very sad way to win.'

After recovering from missing out on his best chance to win in three years, Brand added: 'You feel so bad for Michael but you've got to play by the Rules.'

McLean took the blow on the chin. 'In the end it's just one of those things. I got it wrong. I moved this really long prickly creeper quite innocently, very carefully, and I was just happy I didn't accidently

move my ball while doing it. I obviously don't know my bushes, I'm not Percy Thrower, and didn't realise it was connected. As soon as I was told what I'd done I realised I'd broken the Rule and I couldn't question the decision.

'The worst of it was, though, I was about to play the shot with the creeper there, but Bernhard shouted over and asked if it was him to go first. I said it was, and while he was preparing to play thought, "Hang on, I might be able to move this and get a better look at the ball". It was not as if I even changed my club. I hit the seven iron I'd planned anyway. All I can say is I'd thought it was my lucky day when I chipped in twice, but perhaps I didn't deserve to win.'

As Langer collected the £100,000 first prize, Brand picked up £66,660, and McLean was left with the consolation of £33,780 for his third place with Evans.

Evans was sure he should have won, if McLean was not. The Worthing player, having a magnificent rookie season following his Walker Cup appearance at Portmarnock, three-putted the 15th green after mounting his challenge on the final afternoon, revelling in playing with Greg Norman rather than showing inhibition. Two more bogeys followed in quick succession, and his challenge was over. 'I had it in the palm of my hand,' said Evans. 'The tournament was mine, nobody else's. I just didn't finish it off.'

The other serious challenger was defending champion Payne Stewart, but a bogey on the 17th put him out of the race. He had borrowed a putter before the third round from Norman – who faded disappointingly on the final day to finish well down the field – and put it to good use, shooting a 63, just one off his course record, to haul himself back into contention.

The 1991 US Open champion lay one shot off the pace after a warm first round saw Mouland stamp his mark on the tournament, sharing the lead with Roger Winchester, Langer and Norman. Winchester put his 68 down to relaxing more on the course, not being so hard on himself. Norman, starting with a hat-trick of birdies, just felt he was playing too well not to have a chance of victory.

Langer was surprised the scoring was not better, even though the greens were much slower.

Mouland, who had won the Dutch Open in 1988, was relying on an old friend: the putter with which he had won his first tournament in 1986 and had last used when winning in Holland. Since then it had lain dormant in a bag of some 50 discarded putters. For round two, however, this putter came in for astonishingly little use. Mouland needed it only 19 times on the greens and once off it, establishing a new European record as he took a two-stroke lead, with a 66, over Langer and McLean.

McLean's 67 was a great feat of concentration. He had to return to the clubhouse with nine holes still to go when the late starters were held up for 75 minutes because of an electrical storm, accompanied by strong winds and heavy rain.

First round front-runner Winchester

ended up by bogeying the last two holes as the storm gathered in intensity. The cut came at 145 and that was goodbye to Sandy Lyle, Jose Maria Olazabal, also caught in the storm, Ian Baker-Finch and Ronan Rafferty, all of whom had been strong contenders for the title.

Mouland's putter got more use the next day as he slipped back into second place with McLean. Langer overcame a poor start, in which he drove into the tented village at the first and dropped two strokes in the opening four holes, to shoot a 69 for a one-stroke lead.

There were shades of 1991, too, as the course-record breakers from the year before, Stewart and Per-Ulrik Johansson,

Langer holes to stay alive in play-off
with Gordon Brand Junior.

Premature exultation
from McLean.

swapped birdie for birdie, the young Swede's 65 bringing him into the reckoning.

On a breezy last day scoring was tougher. The £600,000 event looked more and more likely to produce another six-way play-off before McLean conjured his way into the lead with an unnerving eye for the cup.

The final reckoning, though, came from fate, a bramble, and the rule book.

Prince Bernhard and

King Bernhard.

	COURSE: NOORDWIJKSE	DATE: 23-26.7			YARDAGE: 684		PAR: 72	
POS	**NAME**	**CTY**	**1**	**2**	**3**	**4**	**TOTAL**	**PRIZE MONEY**
1	Bernhard LANGER	Ger	68	68	69	72	277	£100000
2	Gordon BRAND Jnr	Scot	72	71	67	67	277	66660
3	Gary EVANS	Eng	70	67	71	70	278	33780
	Mike McLEAN	Eng	69	67	70	72	278	33780
5	Derrick COOPER	Eng	73	68	68	70	279	23200
	Payne STEWART	USA	69	75	63	72	279	23200
7	Per-Ulrik JOHANSSON	Swe	71	72	65	72	280	15480
	Wayne WESTNER	SA	71	71	68	70	280	15480
	Mark MOULAND	Wal	68	66	72	74	280	15480
10	Roger WINCHESTER	Eng	68	71	69	73	281	10428
	David FEHERTY	N.Ire	71	68	73	69	281	10428
	Glen DAY	USA	71	68	72	70	281	10428
	Greg J TURNER	NZ	71	69	69	72	281	10428
	Eamonn DARCY	Ire	71	66	73	71	281	10428
15	Vijay SINGH	Fij	71	70	70	71	282	8112
	Des SMYTH	Ire	71	70	71	70	282	8112
	Colin MONTGOMERIE	Scot	71	69	71	71	282	8112
	Greg NORMAN	Aus	68	69	71	74	282	8112
	Miguel Angel JIMENEZ	Sp	72	72	68	70	282	8112
20	Peter O'MALLEY	Aus	72	71	68	72	283	6840
	Jose RIVERO	Sp	71	68	71	73	283	6840
	De Wet BASSON	SA	72	70	70	71	283	6840
	Anders FORSBRAND	Swe	75	69	69	70	283	6840
	Howard CLARK	Eng	69	72	69	73	283	6840
25	Frank NOBILO	NZ	72	70	70	73	285	6210
	Jean VAN DE VELDE	Fr	71	71	69	74	285	6210
27	Jim PAYNE	Eng	73	71	69	73	286	5580
	Peter MITCHELL	Eng	71	71	72	72	286	5580
	David GILFORD	Eng	72	72	70	72	286	5580
	Barry LANE	Eng	71	70	72	73	286	5580
	Paul WAY	Eng	75	69	71	71	286	5580
32	Stephen FIELD	Eng	74	70	71	72	287	4560
	Danny MIJOVIC	Can	72	71	71	73	287	4560
	Robert KARLSSON	Swe	75	70	70	72	287	4560
	Tony JOHNSTONE	Zim	75	70	70	72	287	4560
	Rodger DAVIS	Aus	73	70	72	72	287	4560
	Mark ROE	Eng	72	69	72	74	287	4560
	Chris MOODY	Eng	73	68	74	72	287	4560
	Ernie ELS	SA	74	68	71	74	287	4560
	Russell CLAYDON	Eng	72	72	71	72	287	4560
41	Miguel Angel MARTIN	Sp	74	70	70	74	288	3720
	David R JONES	Eng	73	72	69	74	288	3720
	Glenn RALPH	Eng	73	70	74	71	288	3720
	Manuel PINERO	Sp	74	70	75	69	288	3720
	Fredrik LINDGREN	Swe	76	69	70	73	288	3720
46	Johan RYSTROM	Swe	72	70	73	74	289	3180
	Justin HOBDAY	SA	71	70	73	75	289	3180
	Anders SORENSEN	Den	73	69	74	73	289	3180
	Keith WATERS	Eng	71	69	72	77	289	3180
50	John WOOF	Eng	73	72	70	75	290	2520
	Peter BAKER	Eng	77	67	72	74	290	2520
	Robert LEE	Eng	70	72	74	74	290	2520
	Phillip PRICE	Wal	75	68	73	74	290	2520
	Rick HARTMANN	USA	71	73	71	75	290	2520
	Adam HUNTER	Scot	73	71	73	73	290	2520
	Andrew MURRAY	Eng	74	71	71	74	290	2520
57	Hugh BAIOCCHI	SA	71	71	74	75	291	1940
	Ross DRUMMOND	Scot	72	70	72	77	291	1940
	Stephen HAMILL	N.Ire	74	71	71	75	291	1940
60	Daniel SILVA	Port	71	72	71	78	292	1770
	Jonathan SEWELL	Eng	71	73	73	75	292	1770
62	David J RUSSELL	Eng	74	70	74	75	293	1359
	Juan QUIROS	Sp	73	71	73	76	293	1359
	Bernard GALLACHER	Scot	74	71	74	74	293	1359
	Vicente FERNANDEZ	Arg	70	74	71	78	293	1359
	Ross McFARLANE	Eng	73	71	74	75	293	1359
	Tony CHARNLEY	Eng	73	71	73	76	293	1359
68	Jesper PARNEVIK	Swe	75	70	73	76	294	896
69	Gary NICKLAUS	USA	72	73	75	75	295	891
	Ruud BOS	Hol	72	71	74	78	295	891
	Gavin LEVENSON	SA	73	72	70	80	295	891
	Richard BOXALL	Eng	71	71	75	78	295	891

FALDO
MASTERLY AGAIN

Fresh from his triumph in the Open Championship, Nick Faldo eased his way to victory in the Scandinavian Masters

In any tournament there are always deeper significances to be resolved beyond the obvious task of winning. Each player, it seems, has to answer some meaningful question about himself through the manner in which he plays.

That, at least, is how the media choose to perceive each given scenario on their week-to-week pilgrimage around the Volvo Tour in Europe. In fact, it is not just tabloid hype but does contain the substance of truth.

The Scandinavian Masters at Barsebacks near Malmo was a case in point. For the newly-crowned Open champion Nick Faldo it offered the opportunity to discover whether his game and resolve were still intact after the traumas of Muirfield; and equally to the point, if he was therefore in a fit state of readiness for the forthcoming American PGA Championship a week later – although he had no intention of treating this important Swedish event as a mere warm-up exercise.

Then, too, there was the perplexing case of Seve Ballesteros, a genius whose blinding displays were always built upon personal desire. Of late, that quality had somehow become mislaid. Here then, was yet another chance for him to rediscover those qualities that had once made him the greatest player in the world. And, of course, there were sub-plots to capture attention. Would Jose Maria Olazabal finally break free from his mystifying negative mood which constantly undermined his performances? Could Howard Clark come back to full competitive form after the injury to his left elbow? Could a

Swede really endorse the claims being made for the indigenous game by winning before a home crowd in this company? Was Sandy Lyle really ready for a comeback? Each character had his own separate narrative to follow.

But Faldo really was the main focus and he confessed to feeling 'physically and mentally knackered' after the Open exploits when he looked to have thrown

away the title then grabbed it back in remarkable style from American John Cook. It had become something of a disturbing Faldo trend of late that, when apparently in total control, he would falter without warning and indeed at least one title had slipped away from him in such a manner. Much later, when asked by a journalist about this pattern, he thrust both arms forward and said, 'Look, there's blood in there. I'm only human'.

There is about Faldo a compulsion to work that goes beyond the practical purposes of such effort and borders on spirituality as it did with Gary Player who drove himself because he considered it the only way to expect success. Consequently Faldo worked every day in the hotel gymnasium, building his strength. Even so, he had to concede first day prominence to his World Cup partner Steven Richardson, a performer who depends heavily on intuitive play and flair for his score and of late had been out of luck. In form, he is without question one of the most exciting players in European golf and confirmed that view with a sparkling opening display that included four successive birdies in a 66.

It was to be, however, a breathless pace he could not maintain and so throughout the week he slipped deeper down the list.

For Yorkshireman Clark, the first day was a rewarding experience. He had spent much of the season recovering from a serious case of tennis elbow in his right arm which had been caused, according to one specialist theory, by his attempts to

Nick Faldo takes a worm's

eye view.

impose a new golf swing on a 37-year old body whose muscles and bones were resisistant to change. His opening 67 at least gave him the evidence that he was still capable of good scoring and more importantly, that the old frame would withstand the rigours of tournament play, although he never quite reached similar sharpness throughout the week and finished in joint 18th place seven strokes behind the winning score.

Faldo had opened with a workmanlike 70 which left him comfortably placed and within reach of the leader but there was already concern for Seve Ballesteros whose opening 76 meant he needed an improved second round effort just to stay in the event. Ronan Rafferty who had struck such rich form at the beginning of the season faced a smiliar problem after

Alas! Per-Ulrik: Johansson

in despair.

his 75. So. too did former US Masters champion Craig Stadler following a 77.

By the end of the second day a new character had joined the drama as Jose Maria Olazabal produced a 67 which contained five birdies and was not bettered all day. It had been a difficult and windy day and the Spanish professional explained with simplistic frankness: 'The secret in scoring so well on a windy day is putting.' His halfway total of 139 left him three strokes clear of Faldo who had scored 72 and well placed for the crucial third day effort while a sad procession of players who failed to make the halfway cut packed up and headed for home. Seve was among them after a better, but not good enough, 72 and he confessed: 'I have no feeling for the game. No competitive desire. Mentally things are not right and my driving is bad. I don't want to play anywhere right now. I need a long rest.'

By custom, the third round sets the pattern for the final outcome. The contenders have safely beaten the halfway cut; they

have also judged the pace of scoring and it is now time to open up more aggressively. Accordingly, Faldo moved into top gear and dragged an exhilarating 66 from the 7,289 yard par 72 course. But the effort was not good enough to earn the Johnnie Walker bonus on offer for a new course record because PGA champion Tony Johnstone fashioned a remarkable display of putting for a 65 which earned him the additional £6,000. The Zimbabwean professional paid tribute to Scottish golf coach Bob Torrance and son Sam, who had helped him to make changes in his address position.

While each man's personal story of success and failure unfolded, the looming presence of Faldo simply would not go away. Danny Mijovic, New Zealander Frank Nobilo, Robert Allenby, a resurgent

Johansson gets the call.

Peter Baker as well as Peter O'Malley who won the Bell's Scottish Open in such spectacular style, had all closed in for an attempt at the title on the final day.

All of them were smart enough to keep an eye on the scoreboards to monitor news of Faldo's progress. They did not wait long. He eagled the long third and was looking for more chances. The pack could see the margin beginning to develop especially when Faldo scored three birdies in four holes from the 11th as he headed for home. He was clear of them all with a 69 for 277 total and even permitted himself the indulgence of three putts on the final green before picking up the £100,000 top prize which was £5,000 more than the Open winning cheque. He described that final round as a 'pleasant Sunday afternoon's work' but there was no suggestion that he intended to ease up on his phenomenal work-load

or the demands he placed upon himself.

Even as he was winning the title, he knew there was more work to be done to improve his technique and said; 'It's an old fault but at times my hips move too much. If I start the backswing with the hips instead of the arms and shoulders, I'm in trouble, I've got to quieten down my lower body and try to get my legs more solid.' No time, it seemed, for rest. Not with more titles to be won.

So the stars departed with some of their questions answered. Sandy Lyle would have to wait a little longer before the champion's touch returned although he had been encouraged by a last round 67. Olazabal may have been disgruntled with his share of second place but it was a status that delighted Peter Baker, the former Benson and Hedges International winner who went into mysterious decline but had suddenly regained the touch and

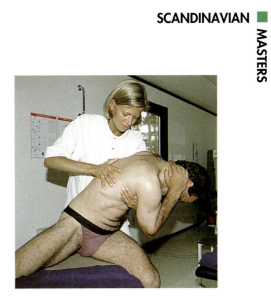

Danny Mijovic receives

physio attention.

Eighth green from

the tee.

View across the course

out to sea

Jose Maria Olazabal in

shadowy trouble.

The winner tests the comfort

of a Volvo.

Faldo parts the crowd.

POS	NAME	CTY	1	2	3	4	TOTAL	PRIZE MONEY
1	Nick FALDO	Eng	70	72	66	69	277	£100000
2	Danny MIJOVIC	Can	72	70	69	69	280	33103
	Frank NOBILO	NZ	72	70	68	70	280	33103
	Robert ALLENBY	Aus	71	71	70	68	280	33103
	Peter BAKER	Eng	72	69	70	69	280	33103
	Jose Maria OLAZABAL	Sp	72	67	72	69	280	33103
	Peter O'MALLEY	Aus	71	70	68	71	280	33103
8	Jamie SPENCE	Eng	70	72	68	71	281	13480
	Per-Ulrik JOHANSSON	Swe	70	70	73	68	281	13480
	Stephen FIELD	Eng	70	74	68	69	281	13480
11	Jim PAYNE	Eng	75	72	67	68	282	9792
	Wayne WESTNER	SA	69	74	70	69	282	9792
	Sandy LYLE	Scot	70	72	73	67	282	9792
	Carl MASON	Eng	72	71	72	67	282	9792
	Greg J TURNER	NZ	75	70	68	69	282	9792
16	Tony JOHNSTONE	Zim	72	73	65	73	283	8280
	Stephen McALLISTER	Scot	76	70	71	66	283	8280
18	Howard CLARK	Eng	67	73	72	72	284	7350
	Anders FORSBRAND	Swe	69	70	74	71	284	7350
	Santiago LUNA	Sp	71	74	69	70	284	7350
	Brett OGLE	Aus	72	71	69	72	284	7350
22	Jeremy ROBINSON	Eng	71	73	73	68	285	6570
	Anders GILLNER	Swe	74	72	72	67	285	6570
	Peter SENIOR	Aus	73	71	74	67	285	6570
	David FEHERTY	N.Ire	72	74	72	67	285	6570
26	Silvio GRAPPASONNI	It	72	74	67	73	286	5420
	Joakim HAEGGMAN	Swe	71	74	70	71	286	5420
	Chris MOODY	Eng	72	70	73	71	286	5420
	Steven RICHARDSON	Eng	66	75	73	72	286	5420
	Roger WINCHESTER	Eng	73	73	72	68	286	5420
	Philip WALTON	Ire	74	73	70	69	286	5420
	Vijay SINGH	Fij	68	74	72	72	286	5420
	Peter FOWLER	Aus	75	72	70	69	286	5420
	Andrew SHERBORNE	Eng	73	74	70	69	286	5420
35	Eamonn DARCY	Ire	70	76	71	70	287	4500
	Mark ROE	Eng	70	72	76	69	287	4500
	Vicente FERNANDEZ	Arg	71	73	75	68	287	4500
	Richard BOXALL	Eng	71	75	68	73	287	4500
	Nicklas FAST (AM)	Swe	72	73	70	72	287	—
39	Glen DAY	USA	70	74	74	70	288	3840
	Jean VAN DE VELDE	Fr	71	74	71	72	288	3840
	Rick HARTMANN	USA	72	72	74	70	288	3840
	Jay Don BLAKE	USA	69	73	71	75	288	3840
	Colin MONTGOMERIE	Scot	71	76	71	70	288	3840
	Jon ROBSON	Eng	72	75	73	68	288	3840
	Ross DRUMMOND	Scot	72	72	70	74	288	3840
	Mike HARWOOD	Aus	70	75	71	73	289	3240
	Bill MALLEY	USA	73	74	71	71	289	3240
	Gary NICKLAUS	USA	72	73	75	69	289	3240
49	Giuseppe CALI	It	74	71	74	71	290	2760
	Gavin LEVENSON	SA	71	74	72	73	290	2760
	Rodger DAVIS	Aus	72	73	74	71	290	2760
	Retief GOOSEN	SA	71	72	72	75	290	2760
	Adam HUNTER	Scot	70	75	75	70	290	2760
54	Anders SORENSEN	Den	74	73	75	69	291	2220
	Patrick HALL	Eng	71	75	74	71	291	2220
	Dennis EDLUND	Swe	69	76	75	71	291	2220
	Mark DAVIS	Eng	71	71	75	74	291	2220
58	Robert KARLSSON	Swe	70	69	77	76	292	1830
	Malcolm MACKENZIE	Eng	75	72	72	73	292	1830
	Hugh BAIOCCHI	SA	71	76	72	73	292	1830
	Jose Manuel CARRILES	Sp	70	76	73	73	292	1830
62	Steven BOWMAN	USA	77	70	75	71	293	1590
	Darren CLARKE	N.Ire	72	75	74	72	293	1590
	Peter SMITH	Scot	73	72	77	71	293	1590
	Jay TOWNSEND	USA	74	73	72	74	293	1590
66	Marc FARRY	Fr	71	75	76	72	294	893
	Eoghan O'CONNELL	Ire	72	74	79	69	294	893
	Fredrik LINDGREN	Swe	72	75	70	77	294	893
	Ian PALMER	SA	73	71	78	72	294	893
	Chris PLATTS	Eng	73	74	77	70	294	893
	Derrick COOPER	Eng	73	73	76	72	294	893
	Haydn SELBY-GREEN	Eng	75	72	76	71	294	893
	Peter LONARD	Aus	71	76	73	74	294	893

COURSE: BARSEBACK, SWEDEN DATE: 30.7-2.8 YARDAGE: 7290 PAR: 72

might well have finished in outright second place but for an error on the last hole which cost him a bogey.

There was to be no home Swedish triumph either, but for a time it was in prospect as Per-Ulrik Johansson made a determined charge that was sadly undermined by an untidy third round 73.

For those campaigners who departed Sweden still seeking the answers to their problems, the mood was hopeful. There is always next week. That after all, is the redemptive quality of professional sport. There is always another chance.

TOTAL PERFORMANCE.
IT RUNS IN THE FAMILY.

Whether it's carrying the fortunes of most of the world's Tour Pro's, or providing the margin of victory for most club champions, or simply carding better scores for serious golfers everywhere, there has never been the performance equal of the famous black script.

Today, that Titleist dedication to superior quality and consistency results in an extraordinary line-up for every golfer's performance needs.

THE TITLEIST TOUR.
No. 1 AT THE GAME'S HIGHEST LEVELS.

For more than a dozen years the wound balata covered Titleist has been the No. 1 ball on the Volvo Tour and on Tours throughout the world.

Its renowned spin, unique feel and unsurpassed control have made the Titleist Tour the most success-ful ball in the history of the game.

The Titleist Tour's performance among the game's most accomplished players and revered settings sets the standard for all Titleist golf balls.

THE TITLEIST PTS.
JUST LIKE THE PROS' ONLY TOUGHER.

The Titleist PTS's wound construction makes it as close as you can get to the pros' favourite ball and still play a cut-proof cover. Its Lithium-Surlyn cover makes the PTS the only ball with both that Titleist wound feel and a cut-proof guarantee.

The Titleist PTS delivers tremendous carry off the tee. But it's the PTS's consistent distance, accuracy and control that have made it the choice of serious golfers for over a decade.

THE TITLEIST HVC.
TWO-PIECE DISTANCE WITH TITLEIST ACCURACY.

Five years in the making, the Titleist HVC takes two-piece construction from simply a distance and durability idea to a truly total performance concept.

Hitting machine tests show the HVC is longer off the driver than other two-piece distance balls. But, more importantly, that distance is accurate distance.

A dramatic advance in total performance and better feel, the HVC is the first two-piece ball worthy of the Titleist stamp.

Titleist®
Nº1 ball in golf.

If you want more information on golf ball design and manufacture,
send self-addressed envelope to: Titleist, St. Ives, Cambs, PE17 4LS.

GOLF FOUNDATION

AZINGER COMES OUT OF THE CROWD

Paul Azinger was the survivor from a five-man play-off to capture his second BMW International title in three years

Paul Azinger had a distinct feeling of *déjà vu* standing on the 16th tee in a five-man play-off for the BMW International Open. Two years earlier at the Nord-Eichenried course he had birdied the 16th, the first play-off hole, from 18 feet to pip David Feherty for the title.

He was back at his happy hunting ground. Could history repeat itself? Azinger, who shot a closing 67, knew it would be tougher this time against the likes of local hero Bernhard Langer (66), fellow Ryder Cup man Mark James (64), Swede Anders Forsbrand (67) with two Volvo Tour wins already under his belt this year, and fellow American Glen Day (65) who had been knocking on the winner's door in recent weeks. All had finished on 22-under-par 266.

In fact, the play-off was something of an anti-climax. Azinger's birdie three from six feet at the 334-yard hole proved too much for his rivals. The US Ryder Cup man had completed his second play-off success in Europe, in contrast to two sudden-death defeats in his own backyard.

'The 16th has been kind to me,' he said with a large slice of understatement as he collected a cheque for £83,330. 'It's a long time since I had a putt to win a tournament and it's a nice feeling. I think I'll be back next year.'

Who could blame him? In three visits, Azinger had won twice and finished fourth to Sandy Lyle in 1991, his total take home pay in those years topping £165,000. Little wonder that he feels at home in Germany, while if he could dig up the 16th and transport it back home

to Florida, he would have no hesitation.

It was a week of sizzling scoring to match the blistering Munich weather. With the temperature up in the 90s, even touching 100° on the final day, little wind, a flat, uncomplicated course, and billiard table greens, a cut of five under par, a Tour record low was no surprise. What was surprising was that former US

Open champions Payne Stewart and Scott Simpson failed to beat it.

It was left to unsung heroes such as Darren Clarke and Denmark's Steen Tinning to show what could be done. Each equalled the course record of 62 in round two, Irishman Clarke, who shot 60 in The European Monte Carlo Open a few weeks earlier, grabbing ten birdies and coming close to a 61 when an eagle putt on his final hole finished inches away. Tinning's 62 was all the more remarkable because it contained a double-bogey six at the tenth when he hooked his drive into a ditch and took a drop. But that was offset by an eagle and ten birdies.

The great Dane, whose career was threatened when he shattered an arm in a car crash in Germany in early 1990, stayed on the title trail thanks to a hole-in-one in the final round. It came with a four iron at the 207-yard eighth. If it had been at the 12th, he would have won a BMW worth around £27,000.

At one stage on the final day Tinning was joint leader at 20 under par but was overtaken as the field came into the finishing straight. Any number of players could have made the play-off and Colin Montgomerie and Sandy Lyle probably felt they should have made it.

Montgomerie, so close to victory with two seconds and two thirds already in the bag, finished with a 64 for 268, two strokes too many. Coming in the wake of his 65 in the final round of the Bell's Scottish Open at Gleneagles and being devastated by Peter O'Malley's 62,

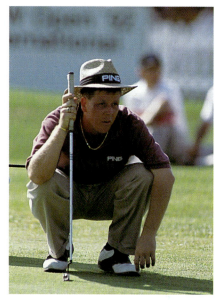
Bernhard Langer was play-off victim.

Heat protection for defending champion Sandy Lyle.

Colin Montgomerie came close again.

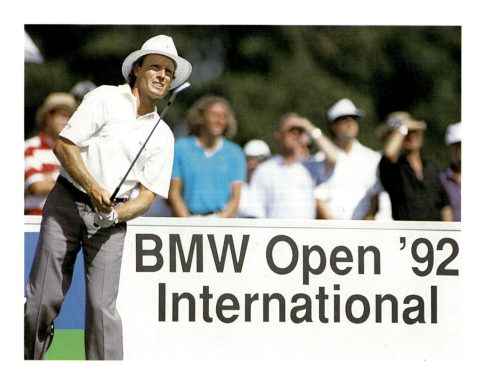

Monty must have wondered what he'd done to deserve such treatment. But he wasn't a bit dispirited. 'Counting my 64 in the pro-am, I'm 28 under par for five rounds,' he remarked. 'I missed five or six putts so on a good putting day it could easily have been a 58.'

Lyle, who ended his three-year slump by winning the 1991 BMW, made a brave defence of the title with a closing 67 for 269, one more than his winning tally. He was also in the frame to the bitter end but needed a last hole eagle to get into the play-off. Unfortunately, he drove left into the lake and finished with a bogey.

'I played well but you expect to make a few birdies on the finishing holes,' he said. 'I played them in one over but I had to go for the eagle. It was a gamble that didn't come off. I'm afraid it's the same old pattern, I get into a winning position and finish poorly.'

You had to sympathise with the big Scot but one man who didn't finish poorly was Azinger. He had the bit between his teeth all week, especially on his sweet 16th.

| | COURSE: GOLFPLATZ MUNCHEN NORD-EICHENRIED MUNICH | | | | | | | |
| | DATE: 6-9.8 YARDAGE: 6910 PAR: 72 | | | | | | | |

POS	NAME	CTY	1	2	3	4	TOTAL	PRIZE MONEY
1	Paul AZINGER	USA	66	67	66	67	266	£83330
2	Glen DAY	USA	66	70	65	65	266	33262
	Bernhard LANGER	Ger	66	69	65	66	266	33262
	Anders FORSBRAND	Swe	68	65	66	67	266	33262
	Mark JAMES	Eng	69	66	67	64	266	33262
6	Colin MONTGOMERIE	Scot	65	67	72	64	268	16250
	Steen TINNING	Den	70	62	70	66	268	16250
8	Sandy LYLE	Scot	70	67	65	67	269	12500
9	Costantino ROCCA	It	65	69	66	70	270	9394
	Frank NOBILO	NZ	68	68	71	63	270	9394
	Ross McFARLANE	Eng	67	68	67	68	270	9394
	Stephen McALLISTER	Scot	70	66	67	67	270	9394
	Darren CLARKE	N.Ire	68	62	71	69	270	9394
14	David GILFORD	Eng	67	68	68	68	271	7500
	Jamie SPENCE	Eng	68	68	65	70	271	7500
16	Peter FOWLER	Aus	67	67	70	68	272	6612
	Corey PAVIN	USA	71	64	66	71	272	6612
	David FEHERTY	N.Ire	66	67	69	70	272	6612
	Miguel Angel JIMENEZ	Sp	69	67	67	69	272	6612
20	Danny MIJOVIC	Can	67	70	68	68	273	5925
	Malcolm MACKENZIE	Eng	66	71	69	67	273	5925
22	Adam MEDNICK	Swe	66	70	68	70	274	5625
	Gordon J BRAND	Eng	69	68	66	71	274	5625
24	Alexander CEJKA	Ger	69	68	69	69	275	5250
	Silvio GRAPPASONNI	It	67	71	69	68	275	5250
	David J RUSSELL	Eng	69	69	67	70	275	5250
27	Anders SORENSEN	Den	68	69	70	69	276	4443
	Roger CHAPMAN	Eng	68	65	77	66	276	4443
	Russell CLAYDON	Eng	67	70	68	71	276	4443
	Peter TERAVAINEN	USA	68	69	69	70	276	4443
	Philip WALTON	Ire	66	68	73	69	276	4443
	Andrew SHERBORNE	Eng	69	70	72	65	276	4443
	Hugh BAIOCCHI	SA	70	68	66	72	276	4443
	Miguel Angel MARTIN	Sp	66	71	68	71	276	4443
35	Brett OGLE	Aus	67	69	71	70	277	3650
	Gordon BRAND Jnr	Scot	69	69	70	69	277	3650
	Rodger DAVIS	Aus	70	67	68	72	277	3650
	Davis LOVE III	USA	71	68	69	69	277	3650
	Ian SPENCER	Eng	67	72	71	67	277	3650
	Mike CLAYTON	Aus	68	71	68	70	277	3650
41	Kenneth TRIMBLE	Aus	69	70	71	68	278	3200
	David CURRY	Eng	69	70	71	68	278	3200
	Manuel MORENO	Sp	70	67	72	69	278	3200
44	Jim CARTER	USA	69	70	69	71	279	2750
	Wayne RILEY	Aus	67	70	75	67	279	2750
	Heinz P THUEL	Ger	69	69	72	69	279	2750
	Gavin LEVENSON	SA	70	69	72	68	279	2750
	Santiago LUNA	Sp	70	67	73	69	279	2750
	Derrick COOPER	Eng	68	71	69	71	279	2750
50	Thomas LEVET	Fr	65	72	71	72	280	2200
	Steven RICHARDSON	Eng	67	71	71	71	280	2200
	Robert LEE	Eng	66	72	69	73	280	2200
	Ralf BERHORST	Ger	68	71	71	70	280	2200
	Jose Manuel CARRILES	Sp	68	68	72	72	280	2200
55	Orrin VINCENT III	USA	71	68	72	70	281	1583
	Andrew HARE	Eng	69	68	72	72	281	1583
	Mike MILLER	Scot	70	68	69	74	281	1583
	Olle NORDBERG	Swe	66	73	71	71	281	1583
	Daniel SILVA	Port	68	70	71	72	281	1583
	Ove SELLBERG	Swe	65	72	71	73	281	1583
	Glenn RALPH	Eng	66	72	69	74	281	1583
	Juan QUIROS	Sp	65	73	72	71	281	1583
	Jim PAYNE	Eng	69	68	73	71	281	1583
64	Peter SENIOR	Aus	68	68	74	72	282	1275
	Bill MALLEY	USA	69	70	72	71	282	1275
66	Torsten GIEDEON	Ger	69	69	72	73	283	750
67	Jay TOWNSEND	USA	64	74	74	73	285	747
	David WILLIAMS	Eng	69	70	68	78	285	747

SINGH IS SIMPLY BRILLIANT

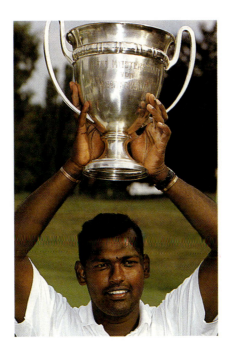

Records tumbled in Dusseldorf as Vijay Singh destroyed the field with an 11-stroke victory margin, highlighted by two course record equalling rounds

After the five-man play-off in Munich two weeks before, things were somewhat different in the Volvo German Open. Vijay Singh saw to that.

In an imperious display the tall Fijian left the best of the rest trailing 11 shots behind. Everybody knew he was good, but this was better than good. It was simply brilliant. Statistically, it was a performance bettered only once in European Tour history. Canadian Jerry Anderson was 27-under par in winning the European Masters-Swiss Open in 1984. Singh finished 26 under.

Bear in mind, too, that the rolling tree-lined Hubbelrath course, unlike the 6,000 feet high Crans-sur-Sierre, offers no thin air assistance. The ball travels normal distances and every birdie has to be worked for. Singh had 25 of them and two eagles. Only one bogey and one double bogey – they both came at the start of the second round – disfigured four cards that the 29-year-old will always treasure.

A week earlier Singh had played his first major championship in America, the invitation a reward for the strides forward he had made in Europe since coming second at the 1988 PGA European Tour Qualifying School and since twice topping the Safari circuit money list.

A 48th place finish in the US PGA might not appear the basis for such a *tour de force* on his return, but Singh felt his play at Bellerive was not accurately reflected in his score. Hence his confidence on arrival in Dusseldorf. As everyone was to discover shortly, it was not misplaced.

Ian Woosnam's form in St Louis was accurately reflected. He shot 73-80 to miss the cut by three shots and headed for Germany swathed in doom and gloom. It was as if his three previous European finishes of first in Monte Carlo, seventh at Gleneagles and fifth at Muirfield had never happened. A holiday in Barbados might have helped his tan but it did nothing for this game.

So on the eve of the £525,000 tournament – in odd-numbered years the last qualifying event for the Ryder Cup – Woosnam said; 'If the match was next month I wouldn't want to play. I'm waiting to play well, but it may be next year before I do.' Two days later this man of moods led the field by two. An opening 67 which left him three behind Barry Lane was followed by a 65.

Wales's former world number one was still not fully trusting of his driver and used it on only three holes, but he was prospering from the discovery on the practice range that he was standing too far from the ball at address. By shuffling forward and swinging with a towel tucked under his arms he had started to cure a damaging push-slice. If only it were as easy as that for mere mortals.

A pretty hot pace had been set then by halfway. Lane's 64 equalled the course record and Woosnam's 132 total for 36 holes left the remainder of the field stretched out behind him. The cut came on one under par, four too few to give rookie Gary Evans an Alfred Dunhill Cup debut. Jamie Spence joined Steven Richardson and David Gilford instead.

Singh stayed in touch with 66-68, then went into overdrive. After birdies on the third, fifth and sixth came a chip-in two at the 209-yard seventh and on the 492-yard eighth all he required was a three-

Bonanza for runner-up
Jose Manuel Carriles.

Germany's
Sven Struer.

wood and seven-iron to set up an eagle from 18 feet.

It added up to an outward 30 and, with Woosnam taking 36, he was four clear. By the end of the round it was seven, a birdie on the last giving him a 64 to set alongside those of Lane in round one and Wayne Grady earlier the same day.

Singh had not forgotten that in the 1989 Ivory Coast Open he had led by six with 18 holes to play and had scraped home by a single stroke. But he did not expect the same to happen and any hopes his closest challengers – Woosnam had been joined by Grady, Bell's Scottish Open champion Peter O'Malley, South African Gavin Levenson and Spain's Jose Manuel Carriles – had

of him relaxing enough to open the door were quickly snuffed out.

Singh went to the turn in 32 and, courtesy of another birdie on the last, came home in 32. It was another course record-equalling effort, it was the best score of the day by three, it was the biggest one-man show since Colin Montgomerie won by the same 11-stroke margin in Portugal in 1989, it was the lowest total ever recorded in the German Open.

In the distant battle for second place

HOLE	1	2	3	4	5	6	7	8	9	10	11	12	13	14	15	16	17	18		TOTAL
PAR	4	4	4	3	4	5	3	5	4	4	4	3	5	4	3	4	5	4		288
18 SINGH	18	18	19	19	20	21	21	22	22	22	22	22	23	23	24	24	25	26	★	262
11 GRADY	11	11	11	11	12	12	12	13	13	13	13	14	14	14	14	14	13	14		274
HAWKSWORTH	10	10	10	10	10	10	10	11	11	11	10	11	10	10	10	11	11	10		278
9 NOBILO	9	9	10	9	10	10	11	11	10	11	11	12	12	12	12	12	12	12		276
11 WOOSNAM	12	12	12	12	13	14	14	14	14	14	14	13	14	14	14	14		13		275
11 CARRILES	11	10	10	11	11	11	10	11	12	12	13	14	14	14	14	15	15			273
7 FARRY	7	8	9	9	9	10	11	10	10	10	10	10	10	10	10	10				278
10 MACKENZIE	10	10	10	10	11	11	11	12	12	12	13	12	12	13	12	12	12	12		276
8 SHERBORNE	8	8	9	9	10	9	10	9	10	10	11	11	12	11	10	11	11			277
11 LEVENSON	11	11	11	11	11	10	10	11	10	10		11	12	12	11	11	11	9		279

Scoreboard reveals
Vijay Singh's domination.

The course was wide open
for Singh.

Ian Woosnam had to take
a back seat.

there was a surprise outcome. Grady, the 1990 US PGA champion, playing in the event for the first time since he won it in 1984, finished on 14 under and 1991 Masters champion Woosnam on 13 under, but on 15 under after a birdie on the final green was Carriles, for whom the £58,275 cheque represented more than twice what he had earned all season. 'The greatest day of my golfing life,' said the 29-year-old Tour School qualifier. 'My life will change because now I've kept my card for next year.'

Singh's reaction was calmer, but he took immense pride in his fourth Volvo Tour victory. It stood out above the others not only because of how well he won it, but also because of whom he had beaten. They were just about visible in his rear-view mirror.

The 18th at Hubbelrath.

Home hero Bernhard Langer.

		COURSE: HUBBELRATH DUSSELDORF						
		DATE: 20-23.8		YARDAGE: 6777				PAR: 72

POS	NAME	CTY	1	2	3	4	TOTAL	PRIZE MONEY
1	Vijay SINGH	Fij	66	68	64	64	262	£87500
2	Jose Manuel CARRILES	Sp	69	69	67	68	273	58275
3	Wayne GRADY	Aus	70	71	64	69	274	32850
4	Ian WOOSNAM	Wal	67	65	73	70	275	26250
5	Malcolm MACKENZIE	Eng	68	69	69	70	276	20317
	Frank NOBILO	NZ	65	71	71	69	276	20317
7	Andrew SHERBORNE	Eng	71	68	69	69	277	15750
8	Peter O'MALLEY	Aus	68	68	69	73	278	11265
	Eduardo ROMERO	Arg	69	66	71	72	278	11265
	John HAWKSWORTH	Eng	66	69	71	72	278	11265
	Marc FARRY	Fr	69	69	71	69	278	11265
12	Barry LANE	Eng	64	70	74	71	279	7958
	Jamie SPENCE	Eng	69	70	69	71	279	7958
	Ross McFARLANE	Eng	72	66	72	69	279	7958
	Carl MASON	Eng	72	66	69	72	279	7958
	David GILFORD	Eng	71	68	69	71	279	7958
	Gavin LEVENSON	SA	68	66	71	74	279	7958
18	Greg J TURNER	NZ	70	66	74	70	280	6526
	Miguel Angel JIMENEZ	Sp	71	72	65	72	280	6526
	Jose RIVERO	Sp	74	68	68	70	280	6526
21	Rodger DAVIS	Aus	69	66	75	71	281	5605
	Jonathan SEWELL	Eng	69	70	75	67	281	5605
	Peter BAKER	Eng	71	70	69	71	281	5605
	Fredrik LINDGREN	Swe	70	68	69	74	281	5605
	Paul WAY	Eng	68	69	70	74	281	5605
	Silvio GRAPPASONNI	It	70	69	69	73	281	5605
	Stephen McALLISTER	Scot	68	70	70	73	281	5605
28	Mike McLEAN	Eng	72	68	74	68	282	4740
	Don POOLEY	USA	69	71	72	70	282	4740
	Robert LEE	Eng	70	71	70	71	282	4740
	Mark ROE	Eng	70	72	69	71	282	4740
	Jose Maria CANIZARES	Sp	69	70	71	72	282	4740
	Sven STRUVER	Ger	70	69	71	72	282	4740
34	Mark DAVIS	Eng	72	68	70	73	283	3900
	Glen DAY	USA	68	68	72	75	283	3900
	Costantino ROCCA	It	67	69	71	76	283	3900
	Brett OGLE	Aus	71	71	72	69	283	3900
	Martin GATES	Eng	72	69	67	75	283	3900
	Joakim HAEGGMAN	Swe	70	71	69	73	283	3900
	Bernhard LANGER	Ger	72	71	72	68	283	3900
	Alexander CEJKA	Ger	69	73	67	74	283	3900
42	Heinz P THUEL	Ger	71	69	72	72	284	3120
	Mark BROOKS	USA	69	72	72	71	284	3120
	Eric GIRAUD	Fr	67	69	71	77	284	3120
	Sam TORRANCE	Scot	74	69	70	71	284	3120
	Michael ALLEN	USA	74	69	71	70	284	3120
47	Jorge BERENDT	Arg	71	71	70	73	285	2540
	Peter MITCHELL	Eng	73	69	68	75	285	2540
	Hugh BAIOCCHI	SA	70	72	71	72	285	2540
	Brian MARCHBANK	Scot	73	70	72	70	285	2540
	Wayne WESTNER	SA	72	69	73	71	285	2540
52	Stephen FIELD	Eng	73	69	68	76	286	2067
	Steen TINNING	Den	74	69	72	71	286	2067
	Jose COCERES	Arg	69	69	71	77	286	2067
	Antonio POSTIGLIONE	Ger	69	74	69	74	286	2067
56	Martin POXON	Eng	70	72	73	72	287	1680
	Paul McGINLEY	Ire	73	69	76	69	287	1680
	Paul CURRY	Eng	70	70	72	75	287	1680
	Anders SORENSEN	Den	72	69	73	73	287	1680
	Torsten GIEDEON	Ger	72	70	75	70	287	1680
	Giuseppe CALI	It	71	71	71	74	287	1680
	Gordon J BRAND	Eng	72	70	76	69	287	1680
63	Mike CLAYTON	Aus	73	70	71	74	288	1410
	Ross DRUMMOND	Scot	74	69	70	75	288	1410
65	Andrew MURRAY	Eng	72	71	72	74	289	872
	Jose DAVILA	Sp	73	70	73	73	289	872
	Manuel MORENO	Sp	70	73	70	76	289	872
	Peter FOWLER	Aus	75	68	75	71	289	872
	Adam HUNTER	Scot	73	70	74	72	289	872
	Jesper PARNEVIK	Swe	70	73	70	76	289	872
71	Philip WALTON	Ire	70	73	75	73	291	777

Tour Proven TP
Most Preferred
FORGED MILD STEEL BLADES

TP18: Innovation-grind hosel enables clearer view of club face for extra confidence.

TP19: The blade developed with Nick Faldo's know-how. Ideal model for competitive, serious golfers who want a professional tour winner.

PGA European Tour Quality: Awarded to Mizuno as the first clubmaker to achieve excellence in producing the fine tournament blades used on the PGA European Tour.

TP18 · TP19

FERNANDEZ STEALS IT WITH 'THE PUTT'

Vicente Fernandez snatched the Murphy's English Open Title with a sensational putt on the final green

The age of 46 is when a professional golfer is prone to moments of self-doubt. The physical erosion of former powers is self-evident and unstoppable but it is the mental turmoil that the ticking away of the years produces that really accelerates the decline.

At the start of the 1992 Volvo Tour, 46-year old Vicente Fernandez took a cold, hard look at himself. In the previous six years, he had won just one tournament. His putting stroke had lost its silken touch, but equally, here was a career that was a testament to indomitable will. Born with a paralysed lower right leg, Fernandez's football ambitions never reached the first corner post yet, once introduced to golf, he strove to put in what nature had omitted. And in doing so he compiled a distinguished portfolio with many victories in his native South America and also in Europe too, where perhaps the most notable was winning the 1979 PGA Championship.

Now, 13 years on, did he still have it within him to win? Could he overcome the twin peaks imposed not only by maintaining his own standard but, if anything, improving on it to compete on a Tour where the competition only gets stiffer all the time?

Inside, Fernandez felt strong. He had retained his inner faith. But still, he needed an outside voice to tell him he wasn't embroiled in an inglorious exercise in self-delusion. He turned to his old friend, Severiano Ballesteros. He knew this was a voice he could trust. Ballesteros had no doubts: 'You still have the spirit,' he said.

Nothing on his season's *c.v.* suggested that Fernandez could win the Murphy's English Open, yet how a player feels is more important than what is written on paper. Fernandez had started to hit his driver accurately, and just as importantly, felt comfortable from the off on The Belfry greens.

He opened with a 69 to be just two shots behind the first round leader, Rodger Davis, and following rounds of 72 and 73 tucked him in behind Fredrik Lindgren and Per-Ulrik Johansson. Then, 18 holes later, Fernandez gathered the title from out of the mouths of the two young Swedes.

In American sports they're fond of putting the definite article in front of memorable happenings and in similar vein, Fernandez may be said to have won with 'The Putt'.

The 18th hole on the Brabazon Course has become a home for drama since it was first opened 16 years ago, and Fernandez scripted a tale as thrillingly unlikely as any that has previously been witnessed. His second shot on the final day had finished on the bottom tier of a three-tier green and the flag was way back on the top. How far back? Fernandez thought 75 feet, yet it was measured the next day and it came out at 87 feet. It was so far back, Fernandez needed the pin attended, and when his caddie took the flag out he hadn't a clue where the hole was. By this time the ball had progressed three-quarters of its journey.

In the packed stands, the crowd egged it on. They knew it was good. On and on the ball came. Then, with five feet of its travels to complete, the ball turned ever so slightly to the left, just as Fernandez could only have dreamed.

The little man may not have seen the hole, but he knew what to do when the ball disappeared. He threw his arms outwards and whirled like a dervish, then did a somersault, touched his toes, and waved joyfully to the gods. You could say he was touch pleased.

And how good it was to see a player revel so much in the possibility of victory, to indulge in a spontaneous, unexpected, and exuberant ode to joy, and when he got his breath back, Fernandez muttered the same word, over and over again. 'Unbelievable,' he said.

Back on the 18th tee, the cheers echoed and when they reached the ears of Johansson and Lindgren it must have chilled their hearts. Particularly Johansson's.

He had just missed from four feet at the 17th to register a bogey six on a hole where he had gone for the green in two. Golf is a game played at a leisurely pace but fortunes can change in the blink of an eye. Standing on the 17th tee, Johansson had been two shots ahead of Fernandez. Now he needed a birdie on possibly the British game's toughest finishing hole to register a tie.

So too did Lindgren, but here ambition did not weigh quite so great. He was having the week of his life, and enjoying

a moment where, whatever happened, he had taken his career to a new peak. Johansson, on the other hand, felt the burden of expectation. He was a young man who had impressed everyone with his form in the 18 months since he turned professional.

He had been in position to win. On the 18th, a fine drive was matched by an approach of equal virtue and he was left with a birdie putt of about 20 feet. Lindgren was 25 feet away.

To a small press gathering, Fernandez was sharing some thoughts, and one stuck in the mind as the Swedes prepared to putt. 'When something has to be yours, it will be,' he said, and fate had certainly

The winner receives the trophy from Miles Templeman of Murphy's.

Fredrik Lindgren reached new heights.

Mark Roe made a good run for the title.

The start of something big, above, as Vicente Fernandez goes into victory roll, right.

Brett Ogle birdies the 15th in the final round.

___

___

Joint second place for Per-Ulrik Johansson.

wrapped a kindly arm around his shoulder and in doing so had put an obstacle in the way of Scandinavian hopes that proved to be insurmountable.

Johansson's putt slipped by. Lindgren's came up short. When something has to be yours it will be.

POS	NAME	CTY	1	2	3	4	TOTAL	PRIZE MONEY
1	Vicente FERNANDEZ	Arg	69	72	73	69	283	£91660
2	Fredrik LINDGREN	Swe	69	68	74	73	284	47765
	Per-Ulrik JOHANSSON	Swe	71	68	72	73	284	47765
4	Barry LANE	Eng	70	69	78	68	285	27500
5	Mark ROE	Eng	69	69	75	73	286	21275
	Brett OGLE	Aus	72	67	75	72	286	21275
7	Silvio GRAPPASONNI	It	70	69	74	74	287	15125
	Keith WATERS	Eng	71	69	76	71	287	15125
9	Santiago LUNA	Sp	73	71	74	70	288	12280
10	Rodger DAVIS	Aus	67	72	78	72	289	10555
	Gordon J BRAND	Eng	75	71	74	69	289	10555
12	Chris WILLIAMS	Eng	72	71	80	67	290	8906
	Paul WAY	Eng	74	71	74	71	290	8906
	Peter MITCHELL	Eng	75	71	73	71	290	8906
15	Stephen FIELD	Eng	75	72	74	70	291	7590
	Mats HALLBERG	Swe	72	72	77	70	291	7590
	Jay TOWNSEND	USA	72	75	72	72	291	7590
	Colin MONTGOMERIE	Scot	71	71	79	70	291	7590
19	Phillip PRICE	Wal	72	69	77	74	292	6446
	Steen TINNING	Den	76	71	73	72	292	6446
	Mark DAVIS	Eng	72	75	74	71	292	6446
	Peter O'MALLEY	Aus	75	72	71	74	292	6446
	Robert LEE	Eng	75	72	72	73	292	6446
24	Jim RUTLEDGE	Can	74	70	77	72	293	5527
	Jon ROBSON	Eng	75	72	73	73	293	5527
	Alberto BINAGHI	It	73	73	71	76	293	5527
	Vijay SINGH	Fij	73	71	75	74	293	5527
	Costantino ROCCA	It	72	70	77	74	293	5527
	Joakim HAEGGMAN	Swe	70	76	75	72	293	5527
30	Adam HUNTER	Scot	73	72	76	73	294	4716
	Mats LANNER	Swe	75	71	75	73	294	4716
	Mike McLEAN	Eng	71	73	79	71	294	4716
	Roger CHAPMAN	Eng	72	69	76	77	294	4716
34	Howard CLARK	Eng	73	71	76	75	295	3960
	Stuart LITTLE	Eng	76	70	74	75	295	3960
	Jorge BERENDT	Arg	75	71	81	68	295	3960
	Carl MASON	Eng	75	68	78	74	295	3960
	Anders SORENSEN	Den	74	72	79	70	295	3960
	Peter LONARD	Aus	72	74	73	76	295	3960
	Bernard GALLACHER	Scot	74	71	77	73	295	3960
	Jean VAN DE VELDE	Fr	71	76	77	71	295	3960
	Stephen McALLISTER	Scot	70	71	78	76	295	3960
43	David R JONES	Eng	72	74	76	74	296	3135
	Thomas LEVET	Fr	74	71	79	72	296	3135
	John BLAND	SA	72	75	75	74	296	3135
	Giuseppe CALI	It	71	72	76	77	296	3135
	Robert ALLENBY	Aus	75	70	75	76	296	3135
	Andrew MURRAY	Eng	70	70	80	76	296	3135
49	Paul BROADHURST	Eng	69	71	80	77	297	2420
	Jose COCERES	Arg	72	74	74	77	297	2420
	Roger WINCHESTER	Eng	75	66	79	77	297	2420
	Jesper PARNEVIK	Swe	73	71	77	76	297	2420
	Stephen BENNETT	Eng	71	70	82	74	297	2420
	Kevin DICKENS	Eng	72	73	81	71	297	2420
	Sam TORRANCE	Scot	75	72	77	73	297	2420
56	David CURRY	Eng	74	73	74	77	298	1760
	Jeremy ROBINSON	Eng	74	72	76	76	298	1760
	Wayne WESTNER	SA	74	73	73	78	298	1760
	Chris MOODY	Eng	72	69	85	72	298	1760
	Kenneth TRIMBLE	Aus	74	71	76	77	298	1760
	Russell CLAYDON	Eng	73	73	74	78	298	1760
62	Stephen HAMILL	N.Ire	73	73	78	75	299	1485
	Johan RYSTROM	Swe	69	78	75	77	299	1485
	Lucien TINKLER	Aus	70	72	74	83	299	1485
65	Ian PALMER	SA	76	71	76	77	300	1100
	Wraith GRANT	Eng	75	72	82	71	300	1100
67	John McHENRY	Ire	72	75	80	74	301	822
	Gavin LEVENSON	SA	75	71	79	76	301	822
69	Ricky WILLISON	Eng	75	72	78	77	302	816
	David GILFORD	Eng	72	71	83	76	302	816

COURSE: THE BELFRY (BRABAZON COURSE)
DATE: 28-31.8   YARDAGE: 7276   PAR: 72

Knowing your greens.

MURPHY'S. A LORE UNTO ITSELF.

 OFFICIAL SPONSORS OF THE
ENGLISH OPEN.

SPENCE SCALES THE PEAK

Like a hero from a Hans Christian Anderson story, the tall young man picked his way carefully through the snow, his followers crunching behind him. Above them the white peaks towered; on either side of them the ground fell away sharply, revealing a breathtaking panorama of forests and glens. At last the leader paused, and his assistant motioned for silence. He narrowed his eyes and focused on some distant point in the gloom. 'How far is it to the green?' he asked.

Snow, sleet and blizzards are uncommon foe for most professional golfers, Jamie Spence too, but these were what he faced during the Canon European Masters at beautiful Crans-sur-Sierre in the Swiss Alps and he treated those imposters just the same.

When the sun finally came out, it was Spence that it shone on: his final round 60, twelve under par, equalled Baldovino Dassu's 21-year old record (except that then the par of the course had been 71), was the joint lowest of any player ever in Europe, and gave him the courage to overcome Anders Forsbrand with a putt of 20 feet at the second extra hole for his first Volvo Tour win.

Altogether, the Canon European Masters was the tournament that had everything, including: birth – Seve Ballestero's wife Carmen had her second baby at 8.15 on Thursday night; gunfighting – Ballesteros defeated Bernhard Langer to win the Canon Shoot-Out final; tragedy – Paul Way fell from the door frame he was swinging on and had to

A final round of 60 enabled Jamie Spence to capture his first Volvo Tour title in the exhilerating atmosphere of the Swiss Alps

withdraw after having two stiches in his nose; hole-in-one – Manuel Pinero aced the 208 yard 11th with a five-iron.

The weather, of course, was the dominant topic of conversation. All four seasons passed through Crans Montana during the course of the tournament, often in the same hour. In the first round it was

spring in the morning and summer in the afternoon, and the hills were alive with the cheers of Colin Montgomerie's gallery. He bounded up slope and down dale, as if to the manner born, recording a nine-under-par 63 and narrowly missing out on a 62. Close on his heels was Jose Rivero with a 64, followed by the 1988 champion Chris Moody, Peter Fowler, Chris Van der Velde, Jonathan Sewell and Mark James – who had been lured to Switzerland by the promise of Ryder Cup points, all with 66's.

On the second day, play was alternately halted by rain, mist and sleet, and delays stretched to three hours. Only Montgomerie had the patience to weather them. He secured five birdies in his last five holes in the worst of the conditions to finish three strokes clear of Mats Lanner, his nearest rival, at 6.30pm. His tee-off time had been 9.15am. At that point, night descended and play was stopped for the day – meaning that another two and a half hours were lost. Ballesteros had not even laced up his golf shoes.

The second round was completed the following morning with little ado, barring a brief suspension at the start while snow was cleared from the greens. The main subject of interest was Italian Giuseppe Cali, who had once worked as a chef in Turin. Having started his round at 3.50 the previous day, when he made only one birdie in five holes, he resumed on the sixth and in no time at all had made up two strokes to turn in 33, three under par. More strokes were snatched back from par at the 13th, 15th and 18th, his only misadventure occurring at the par five 14th, where a hooked second shot came to a halt precisely one inch from out of bounds. As luck would have it, his ball was deemed to be in ground under repair, and he escaped with a free drop and a par for an eventual 67.

When the leaders teed off in the third round, the scoreboard looked something like this: Montgomerie, 133 (11 under par); Cali, 134; Jose Maria Canizares, Lanner and Per-Ulrik Johansson, 136. The Scotsman could not suppress a feeling of trepidation: 'I haven't won for over a year,' he had said after the first round, 'and I feel I should have done. I get myself into position and then throw it away in the third round. It's a challenge for me now and I enjoy challenges.'

The spectre of the penultimate round, which had loomed so large over Montgomerie's season, was laid to rest on the back nine. After going out in 35, one under par, he made four birdies in six holes before darkness drew the curtain on play. By that time he was leading Cali, Lanner, Forsbrand, Fowler and Canizares by a comfortable five strokes and left the course full of hope for the morrow. Spence, who had been a contender after two rounds, slept less well. A three-putt at the 18th in fading light cost him a double-bogey and a 73.

On the final day the sky cleared, and though the air was bitter conditions were perfect for golf. Spence, a racehorse owner, would not have even considered himself a rank outsider for the title. Neither would anyone else. At the start of the round he was ten strokes behind Montgomerie, whom not many people could give a head start. But then not many people could make five birdies and an eagle in the last six holes of a tournament. While Montgomerie could only muster a one-under-par 71, Spence played the inward half in an incredible 29 strokes to finish with a 17-under-par total. The threat came eventually from Forsbrand.

He birdied the last five holes to tie Spence and force a play-off, and it was only with the greatest skill and daring that the young Englishman won his prize. It was a fairy-tale ending, for the victory also gave Spence an immediate lead in the points table for a place in the Johnnie Walker European Ryder Cup team.

Jamie Spence drives on the final hole.

Above left, chocolate box scenery at Crans.

Severiano Ballesteros on snow-laden fairway.

Trouble for Colin Montgomerie in the final round.

The top three take the rostrum.

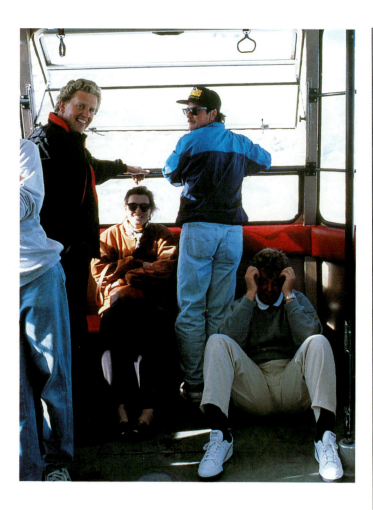

Montgomerie
gets a lift.

─────────

─────────

Runner-up Anders Forsbrand
approaches the last green.

								PRIZE
POS	**NAME**	**CTY**	**1**	**2**	**3**	**4**	**TOTAL**	**MONEY**
1	Jamie SPENCE	Eng	67	71	73	60	271	£93859
2	Anders FORSBRAND	Swe	68	70	68	65	271	62535
3	Colin MONTGOMERIE	Scot	63	70	68	71	272	35267
4	Sandy LYLE	Scot	71	70	66	67	274	28169
5	Sven STRUVER	Ger	68	72	67	68	275	20169
	Jose RIVERO	Sp	64	73	69	69	275	20169
	Per-Ulrik JOHANSSON	Swe	68	68	74	65	275	20169
8	Jim PAYNE	Eng	69	72	72	63	276	14084
9	Mats LANNER	Swe	68	68	70	71	277	11943
	Robert LEE	Eng	69	71	70	67	277	11943
11	Phillip PRICE	Wal	67	75	69	67	278	9708
	Silvio GRAPPASONNI	It	69	70	69	70	278	9708
	Jose Maria CANIZARES	Sp	67	69	71	71	278	9708
14	Mark JAMES	Eng	66	75	70	68	279	7943
	Bill LONGMUIR	Scot	71	70	70	68	279	7943
	Russell CLAYDON	Eng	69	71	68	71	279	7943
	Peter FOWLER	Aus	66	72	68	73	279	7943
	Giuseppe CALI	It	67	67	72	73	279	7943
19	Bernhard LANGER	Ger	72	68	72	68	280	6779
	Sam TORRANCE	Scot	70	72	68	70	280	6779
	Mike MILLER	Scot	69	69	73	69	280	6779
22	Jeremy ROBINSON	Eng	70	72	70	69	281	6000
	Gavin LEVENSON	SA	70	71	72	68	281	6000
	Santiago LUNA	Sp	69	71	69	72	281	6000
	Mats HALLBERG	Swe	68	71	71	71	281	6000
	Marc FARRY	Fr	70	72	73	66	281	6000
	Stephen BENNETT	Eng	69	71	73	68	281	6000
28	Eduardo ROMERO	Arg	69	70	75	68	282	5323
	Barry LANE	Eng	69	71	73	69	282	5323
30	Seve BALLESTEROS	Sp	72	69	71	71	283	4704
	Gordon BRAND Jnr	Scot	72	70	70	71	283	4704
	Ian PALMER	SA	72	68	74	69	283	4704
	Manuel PINERO	Sp	73	69	70	71	283	4704
	Patrick HALL	Eng	67	72	71	73	283	4704
	Daniel SILVA	Port	69	71	74	69	283	4704
36	Chris MOODY	Eng	66	74	73	71	284	3943
	Jose Manuel CARRILES	Sp	69	72	71	72	284	3943
	Roger WINCHESTER	Eng	71	71	70	72	284	3943
	David J RUSSELL	Eng	70	71	73	70	284	3943
	Stephen HAMILL	N.Ire	70	72	71	71	284	3943
	Mark MOULAND	Wal	69	73	66	76	284	3943
	Roger CHAPMAN	Eng	69	72	74	69	284	3943
43	Ole ESKILDSEN	Den	70	71	72	72	285	3211
	Fredrik LINDGREN	Swe	71	71	75	68	285	3211
	Costantino ROCCA	It	70	72	73	70	285	3211
	Jonathan SEWELL	Eng	66	75	72	72	285	3211
	Mark ROE	Eng	70	70	69	76	285	3211
	Peter MITCHELL	Eng	67	72	75	71	285	3211
49	Ian WOOSNAM	Wal	67	74	76	69	286	2535
	Yasunobu KURAMOTO	Jap	68	73	73	72	286	2535
	Anders SORENSEN	Den	73	68	73	72	286	2535
	Gabriel HJERSTEDT	Swe	71	71	69	75	286	2535
	Chris VAN DER VELDE	Hol	66	73	74	73	286	2535
	Thomas LEVET	Fr	69	68	75	74	286	2535
55	Peter SMITH	Scot	67	70	74	77	288	2084
	Haydn SELBY-GREEN	Eng	68	71	74	75	288	2084
57	Danny MIJOVIC	Can	72	70	72	75	289	1821
	Richard BOXALL	Eng	68	74	77	70	289	1821
	Chris WILLIAMS	Eng	70	71	74	74	289	1821
60	Jeff HALL	Eng	69	73	73	75	290	1690
61	Andrew HARE	Eng	68	74	77	72	291	1633
62	Malcolm MACKENZIE	Eng	69	73	76	74	292	1577
	Dimitri BIERRI (AM)	Swi	72	70	74	78	294	–
63	Eamonn DARCY	Ire	69	73	77	83	302	1521
64	Glenn RALPH	Eng	75	68			143	920
	Justin HOBDAY	SA	70	73			143	920
	Paul McGINLEY	Ire	71	72			143	920
	Jim RUTLEDGE	Can	70	73			143	920
	Paul CURRY	Eng	69	74			143	920

COURSE: CRANS SUR-SIERRE, SWITZERLAND
DATE: 3-6.9 **YARDAGE: 6745** **PAR: 72**

Canon's expertise helps transform professional tournaments into a relaxing game of golf

Professional golfers know that performing well under pressure is the secret of success. Canon has exactly the same attitude. Behind the scenes at many major golf tournaments, Canon is making sure that everything runs smoothly.
As official copier and facsimile, Canon supports a number of events sanctioned by the PGA European Tour. Canon, therefore, plays an important role in ensuring problem-free communication, so everyone can relax....and enjoy a good game of golf.

PGA EUROPEAN TOUR

OFFICIAL COPIER AND FACSIMILE OF THE PGA EUROPEAN TOUR

Canon

SUPPORTING THE WORLD OF SPORTS

Canon
SHOOT-OUT SERIES

ON A DIFFERENT PLANE

With a compelling performance Nick Faldo recorded his third successive triumph amid the splendours of Sunningdale

Nick Faldo produced an almost flawless performance to win the GA European Open at Sunningdale and then warned his contemporaries that he believed his best was still to come.

Faldo went over par just twice in 72 holes while recording rounds of 67, 66, 64 and 65 on a venerable Old Course which was in magnificent condition for its farewell to big-time Tour golf. His 18-under-par aggregate of 262 saw him finish three shots ahead of the young Swede, Robert Karlsson, and four in front of Mark James. Barry Lane and Jose Maria Olazabal tied for fourth place at distant nine shots behind.

'Not bad,' was the expression Faldo used to describe a remorseless performance which consolidated his position at the top of the Volvo Tour Order of Merit and gave him an ideal start in the biennial battle to secure one of the automatic places in the Johnnie Walker European Ryder Cup team. The captain, Bernard Gallacher, put it rather differently. 'Faldo is on a different plane to the rest of us right now,' said the combative Scot who at Sunningdale was heading for his best finish of the season before a final round of 76 saw him drop into a tie for 49th place. 'There is no doubt that he is number one in the world at the moment and that he will hold that place for some time to come.'

Gallacher's sentiments were clearly borne out by a glance at the statistics. Faldo's win in the GA European Open was his fourth in six starts on the Volvo Tour and his third in a row. At that stage he hadn't finished outside the top eight in any of his previous 12 outings and that included a tie for fourth in the US Open and a tie for second in the USPGA.

'Faldo is the greatest player in the world,' said Karlsson, who had made a name for himself while finishing tied for fifth behind Faldo at the Open at Muirfield and whose performance at Sunningdale confirmed that he has a bright future ahead of him.

'In different circumstances I might have been disappointed about finishing second here,' the genial young Swede added. 'But it's no disgrace to lose out to someone who has been in the sort of form that Nick has been all season.'

Karlsson had started his quest for his first Volvo Tour title with a six under par 64. That was three shots better than Faldo could manage but still wasn't enough to set the pace.

South Africa's Ian Palmer who started the season with a win in the Johnnie Walker Asian Classic in Thailand came to Sunningdale desperate to end a run which had seen him miss 11 cuts in his previous 17 starts. Out at the head of the field on a sun-drenched and still autumnal morning, Palmer birdied the first three holes and raced to the turn in 31. He then glided home in 32 to lead a strong international field which included three members of Europe's big five and no less than 18 out of the top 20 on the Volvo Tour Order of Merit.

Given such a cast list it came as no surprise that at the end of the second round the big names had started to emerge. Karlsson was out in front after adding a three under par 67 to his opening 64 but he was only one shot ahead of Mark James and just two in front of Faldo and Mats Lanner. Also in close attendance was Jamie Spence, who the week before had won his first Volvo Tour title at the Canon European Masters, and who was among those on 136. One behind was a group which included Ryder Cup men Jose Maria Olazabal and Paul Broadhurst on 137 and David Gilford on 138.

Nick Faldo on the ninth green.

When the cut fell, just about the only major casualties were Anders Forsbrand and Seve Ballesteros who both finished on 143, one shot outside the mark. Forsbrand had come to Sunningdale hoping to close the gap on Faldo at the top of the Volvo Order of Merit. Ballesteros was much less optimistic. He arrived at one of his favourite venues having missed two cuts in his previous three starts and struggling to overcome a niggling back injury which had been troubling him for most of the season. He departed with a resigned smile on his face. 'I did my best,' he said after rounds of 70 and 73. 'I couldn't have done any better.'

Meanwhile, Faldo was experiencing no such difficulties. During the opening two rounds he had dropped shots at both the seventh and the 35th but there were to be no similar lapses from thereon. The Open champion was in remorseless form as he shrugged off his nearest challengers. He produced 11 birdies and 25 pars in his last 36 holes and never had as much as a five on his card. His six-under-par 64 in the third round transformed a two shot deficit into a one shot lead and his final round of 65 increased his lead to three

Robert Karlsson receives hole-in-one award from Denys Pasche of Ebel.

Karlsson was

impressive.

The amphitheatre of

the 18th

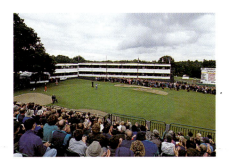

Third successive trophy for

Nick Faldo.

Jose Maria Olazabal receives

treatment in the Tour Physio Unit.

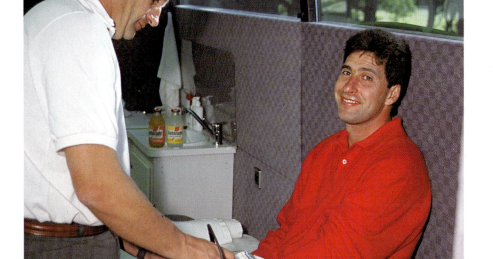

Players at charity fashion show

during the tournament.

— 179 —

and might have done more had it not been for the impressive manner that Karlsson stuck to his task, including a hole-in-one at the 13th during the third round, to win an Ebel '1911' gold watch.

After he had collected his fourth Volvo Tour title of the season Faldo took time to praise the Swede before switching his attention to his own game. 'I was very impressed,' he said. 'He's a fine player.'

'I'm delighted with the way things are going right now. This is probably as well as I've ever played. The half shots that I have now have really helped me but there's still a long way to go.'

'I honestly believe I can still improve,' he added with a smile.

It was a thought which must have alarmed other Volvo Tour regulars who all season long have struggled to keep pace with a man already out on his own.

Faldo didn't have it all

his own way.

POS	NAME	CTY	1	2	3	4	TOTAL	PRIZE MONEY
COURSE: SUNNINGDALE OLD COURSE								
DATE: 10-13.9			**YARDAGE: 6607**					**PAR: 70**
1	Nick FALDO	Eng	67	66	64	65	262	£100000
2	Robert KARLSSON	Swe	64	67	67	67	265	66660
3	Mark JAMES	Eng	64	68	69	65	266	37560
4	Jose Maria OLAZABAL	Sp	70	67	69	65	271	27700
	Barry LANE	Eng	66	68	69	68	271	27700
6	Steven RICHARDSON	Eng	68	71	66	67	272	21000
7	Mats LANNER	Swe	65	68	71	69	273	16500
	Jose RIVERO	Sp	68	69	69	67	273	16500
9	Philip WALTON	Ire	66	71	69	68	274	11280
	Frank NOBILO	NZ	64	72	70	68	274	11280
	Ian PALMER	SA	63	74	69	68	274	11280
	Jamie SPENCE	Eng	69	67	67	71	274	11280
	Rodger DAVIS	Aus	70	69	68	67	274	11280
14	Paul BROADHURST	Eng	71	66	69	69	275	8640
	Glen DAY	USA	71	69	66	69	275	8640
	Russell CLAYDON	Eng	67	71	71	66	275	8640
	Santiago LUNA	Sp	67	69	71	68	275	8640
18	David GILFORD	Eng	68	70	69	69	276	7150
	Malcolm MACKENZIE	Eng	70	70	70	66	276	7150
	Kenneth TRIMBLE	Aus	72	70	65	69	276	7150
	Marc FARRY	Fr	71	65	69	71	276	7150
	Sandy LYLE	Scot	71	70	68	67	276	7150
	Magnus SUNESSON	Swe	70	72	67	67	276	7150
24	Jim PAYNE	Eng	68	73	66	70	277	6300
	Juan QUIROS	Sp	70	70	68	69	277	6300
	David J RUSSELL	Eng	73	68	69	67	277	6300
27	Peter FOWLER	Aus	71	69	68	70	278	5490
	Paul WAY	Eng	66	72	70	70	278	5490
	Colin MONTGOMERIE	Scot	71	68	69	70	278	5490
	Des SMYTH	Ire	72	69	70	67	278	5490
	Paul CURRY	Eng	69	70	68	71	278	5490
33	Roger WINCHESTER	Eng	67	72	73	67	279	4560
	Jean VAN DE VELDE	Fr	70	69	72	68	279	4560
	Mark MOULAND	Wal	72	68	71	68	279	4560
	Stephen McALLISTER	Scot	71	69	68	71	279	4560
	Jay TOWNSEND	USA	71	68	69	71	279	4560
	Joakim HAEGGMAN	Swe	74	68	68	69	279	4560
	Jeff HAWKES	SA	66	68	75	70	279	4560
40	Christy O'CONNOR Jnr	Ire	74	67	70	69	280	3600
	Carl MASON	Eng	68	74	69	69	280	3600
	Jonathan SEWELL	Eng	70	71	71	68	280	3600
	Ronan RAFFERTY	N.Ire	71	69	69	71	280	3600
	Mike HARWOOD	Aus	71	69	70	70	280	3600
	Chris MOODY	Eng	69	72	70	69	280	3600
	Ricky WILLISON	Eng	70	70	69	71	280	3600
	Mark ROE	Eng	70	71	71	68	280	3600
	Vicente FERNANDEZ	Arg	72	69	69	70	280	3600
49	Peter BAKER	Eng	70	70	69	72	281	2640
	Mike McLEAN	Eng	73	69	65	74	281	2640
	Tony JOHNSTONE	Zim	69	69	69	74	281	2640
	Manuel MORENO	Sp	68	69	74	70	281	2640
	Alberto BINAGHI	It	69	69	70	73	281	2640
	Rick HARTMANN	USA	70	72	68	71	281	2640
	Bernard GALLACHER	Scot	70	66	69	76	281	2640
56	Bill LONGMUIR	Scot	75	67	73	67	282	2100
	Stephen FIELD	Eng	70	70	72	70	282	2100
58	John BLAND	SA	69	70	72	72	283	1740
	Ernie ELS	SA	71	69	68	75	283	1740
	Peter SENIOR	Aus	69	72	71	71	283	1740
	Eamonn DARCY	Ire	72	70	70	71	283	1740
	Miguel Angel MARTIN	Sp	71	71	71	70	283	1740
	Derrick COOPER	Eng	70	72	70	71	283	1740
	Bill MALLEY	USA	67	73	74	69	283	1740
65	Roger CHAPMAN	Eng	70	70	70	74	284	1200
	Gordon BRAND Jnr	Scot	71	71	69	73	284	1200
67	David R JONES	Eng	69	71	72	73	285	896
	Martin GATES	Eng	72	70	71	72	285	896
	Wayne RILEY	Aus	69	72	71	73	285	896
70	Peter O'MALLEY	Aus	66	73	70	77	286	891
	Heinz P THUEL	Ger	68	73	69	76	286	891
72	Anders SORENSEN	Den	71	70	68	79	288	887

OUR VIEW OF THE TOUR

British Airways is the official airline to the
PGA European Tour.

BRITISH AIRWAYS

FORSBRAND LANDS UNIQUE DOUBLE

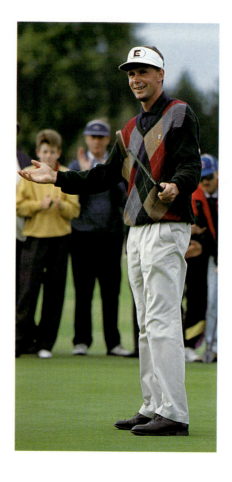

Anders Forsbrand topped the Equity & Law table throughout the season and then romped to victory in the final at Royal Mid-Surrey

Having garnered enough birdies and eagles throughout the season to start a fair-sized aviary, Anders Forsbrand arrived at Royal Mid-Surrey as the clear favourite for the final of the Equity & Law Challenge.

In 84 rounds on the Volvo Tour, Forsbrand had collected 316 birdies and 11 eagles to leave him well ahead of his nearest challengers, Barry Lane, Malcolm Mackenzie and David Gilford. All of them however, qualified for the bonus pool of £25,000, £13,000, £9,000 and £6,000 respectively by competing in the final.

With a points format of one for a birdie, two for an eagle and three for an albatross in operation, the message was attack. In the first round, Australia's Robert Allenby did just that, picking up nine points over the 5,968 yard composite course to lead by one point from Grant Turner with Russell Claydon, Roger Chapman and Mackenzie a further point behind. Forsbrand lay four points adrift of the lead.

In the morning round of the final day, Forsbrand began to show the form that had already landed him two Volvo Tour titles in the year. Five birdies between the seventh and 14th followed by a holed sand wedge for an eagle two at the 16th

gave him seven points. Allenby had only collected one point in his morning round and it was Mackenzie, with five points, who joined the Swede at the top of the leader board with 12 points apiece.

As the wind freshened in the afternoon, Forsbrand was out on his own. Driving the ball a massive distance, he reeled off a succession of birdies and, when he holed a putt of 15 feet on the 13th for an eagle two, he was six points clear. Mackenzie could only gather three points in his round and so the battle for second place came down to Claydon and Allenby.

In the end it was the 15-stone Claydon who prevailed over the slim Australian with a seven-point round against six points from his rival. Claydon won £13,000 while Allenby pocketed £9,000 in his last event before flying home south for the winter.

Forsbrand thus became the first man to win the season-long table and the final, a unique double which earned him a total of £50,000.

The defending champion, Brian Marchbank, who was going for a hat-trick of Equity & Law titles finished in sixth place but he, like everyone else, was well beaten on points by the outstanding Anders Forsbrand.

POS	NAME	CTY	R1	R2	R3	AGG	PARS	PRIZE MONEY
	COURSE: ROYAL MID SURREY DATE: 14-15.9 YARDAGE: 5968 PAR: 68							
1	Anders FORSBRAND	Swe	5	7	8	20	(29)	£25000
2	Russell CLAYDON	Eng	7	3	7	17	(32)	13000
3	Robert ALLENBY	Aus	9	1	6	16	(27)	9000
4	Mark MOULAND	Wal	5	6	4	15	(35)	6000
5	Malcolm MACKENZIE	Eng	7	5	3	15	(31)	4250
6	Brian MARCHBANK	Scot	5	6	3	14	(31)	3500
7	David GILFORD	Eng	6	2	5	13	(35)	2750
	Paul LAWRIE	Scot	4	3	6	13	(35)	2750
9	Patrick HALL	Eng	2	6	5	13	(30)	2000
10	Paul BROADHURST	Eng	3	5	4	12	(34)	1450
	Martin GATES	Eng	5	2	5	12	(34)	1450
12	Darren CLARKE	N.Ire	3	4	5	12	(33)	1100
13	Jay TOWNSEND	USA	3	6	2	11	(36)	950
14	Stephen FIELD	Eng	3	3	5	11	(35)	900
15	Grant TURNER	Eng	8	1	2	11	(32)	820
16	Roger CHAPMAN	Eng	7	3	1	11	(27)	780
17	Carl MASON	Eng	3	1	6	10	(33)	740
18	Vijay SINGH	Fij	4	2	4	10	(32)	700
19	Philip WALTON	Ire	4	2	3	9	(39)	680
20	Robert LEE	Eng	3	3	3	9	(38)	650
	Roger WINCHESTER	Eng	4	3	2	9	(38)	650
22	David R JONES	Eng	3	4	2	9	(37)	640
23	Jon ROBSON	Eng	4	3	2	9	(33)	630
	Jonathan SEWELL	Eng	4	1	4	9	(33)	630
25	Glenn RALPH	Eng	2	2	5	9	(32)	620
26	Peter BAKER	Eng	3	0	4	7	(34)	620
	Gordon J BRAND	Eng	3	3	1	7	(34)	620
28	Richard BOXALL	Eng	5	0	1	6	(36)	620
29	Barry LANE	Eng	2	1	2	5	(39)	600
	Derrick COOPER	Eng	1	Disq				600
	Peter SENIOR	Aus	2	Disq				600

Anders Forsbrand was the birdie machine.

First round leader Robert Allenby.

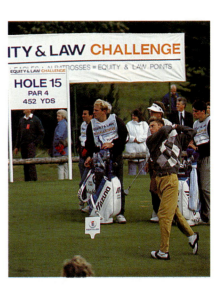

Richard Boxall, Roger Winchester and Forsbrand on the 14th green.

ROE BOUNCES TO SUCCESS

Trampoline enthusiast Mark Roe hit new heights in Paris to secure the second Volvo Tour title of his career

All roads in France on the third Sunday of September led to the polling booth as the nation went to vote on the burning issue of Maastricht and an even more united Europe. To the foreign visitor it was a bit like gate-crashing a party as the French played at politics.

Meanwhile, down the road from the wondrous palace of Versailles, where 200-odd years before Louis Quatorze had himself played a mean hand in the affairs of state, there was another distraction to appeal to the sports-loving citizens of Paris and its suburbs. It was Trophée Lancôme time, and for a while the beautiful people could forget about the ballot box and indulge themselves in a game of another sort.

No matter how many or how few turn up at St-Nom-la-Breteche, there is always a special atmosphere for this most up-market of tournaments. With its elite field and no halfway cut, it is a unique event which has seen the great European names of the modern era – Langer, Ballesteros, Olazabal – holding aloft the most unusual trophy on the Volvo Tour.

Well, this year it was not to be one of the legends of the game who stepped up coyly to receive a kiss from Isabella Rosselini, the face of Lancôme, but rather, in these times of sporting stereotypes, a character, a one-off, a bit of a lad. To whit, one Mark Adrian Roe, who won the peck on the cheek from Ms Rosselini and a cheque for £79,000 with a total of 267, 13 under par.

Roe, a hyper-active Jiminy Cricket of a man who once hit exploding golf balls on the practice ground at the Open championship while wearing a paper bag over his head, the former schoolboy diving champion who loves nothing more to this day than bouncing around on a trampoline, whose one-time party trick was once to stroll around the room on his hands, had for years been a chronic under-achiever. It seemed at least possible that at the age of 29 his golfing ability, while undoubted and undenied by even his sternest critic, wouyld never be matched by his talent for eccentric behaviour.

But there was always another side to Roe, and one that he never quite succeeded in hiding behind the clown's mask. He was, and is, a born competitor; catch him anywhere between the first tee and the 18th green and you're watching a man who is seriously devoted to his job. None the less, it had been three years since he had had his only other Volvo Tour success – at the Catalan Open in 1989 – and even he, confident fellow that he is, must have been wondering where the next victory was coming from.

If, before the tournament started, you had been given 20 chances of picking a winner other than Nick Faldo, the runaway leader of the Volvo Order of Merit, or Ian Woosnam, or even Jose Maria Olazabal, a former winner of the event, only by closing your eyes and using a pin might you have come up with the name of Roe. Oh, he was handily enough placed in the money list after a couple of narrow failures earlier in the season in the Jersey European Airways Open and the Murphy's English Open, but a winner in the face of all this high-octane opposition? Hardly.

Roe did not make his first genuinely threatening appearance on the leader-board until the third day when with Eduardo Romero, Jim Payne, and most dangerous of all, Jose Maria Olazabal, he was a stroke behind the leader, Peter Senior. Few may have suspected it then, but he was timing his burst for the tape to perfection.

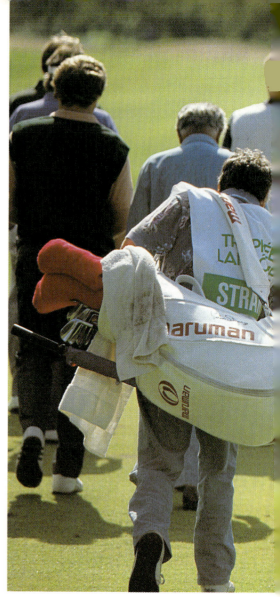

*Splash of sand from
Jose Maria Olazabal.*

*Tree trouble for
Barry Lane.*

*Phalanx of caddies
follow their masters.*

Olazabal, for instance, led after the first day, then said he couldn't understand how he'd done it: 'I'm only playing about 50 per cent as well as I can. I'm not going for the flag like I used to. My confidence is just not there. I don't feel anything when I stand over the ball.' Does that sound like a man who had just had his third competitive round of 65 on the trot?

The litany of complaints did not end there: 'I missed a lot of shots left and right. Here you need to be on the fairway to have any control, and I'm not sure I can do it this week. I don't think I can keep up this scoring.' Oh, the misery of it.

A little while later Faldo, who had had a level-par 70, was told of his Johnnie Walker Ryder Cup colleague's doleful utterances. Faldo smiled indulgently, like you might when told of the words of a young and slightly dotty nephew. 'He's young and fussy,' he said. 'When he's ten years older he'll take it and run.'

Olazabal, in spite of his protestations to the contrary was still there or thereabouts at the conclusion of the second

Nick Faldo checks the

exchange rates.

round, when he shot a 69 to stand alongside Tony Johnstone and Woosnam to be a shot behind Romero, himself a former winner at St Nom. And Roe? He had a 69 to add to a first-round 67 to be a couple of shots further back.

Sunny dawned Saturday, and with it came a new leader as the determined figure of Senior thrust his way into the limelight with a near-flawless 66, including four birdies and not a sniff of a dropped shot.

Even now Roe would not have been the punter's choice, but he soon changed that on the final day. He read a huge right-to-left break to the millimetre to birdie the first from 20 feet, made life easy for himself at the second by hitting a pitching wedge to five feet, and put the finishing touch to a perfect start by sinking a putt of 25 feet for his third birdie in succession on the next.

He reached the turn in 32 and saw Olazabal challenge briefly on the back nine only to bogey two of the last four holes, while Payne and Romero huffed and puffed but made no real headway. In the end it was left to Vicente Fernandez, the veteran winner of the Murphy's English Open the previous month, to keep Roe's mind on the job. Roe, however, would not be denied. He birdied the tenth from eight feet, and narrowly missed with an eagle putt on the 16th. He could have bogeyed the last and still won. In the event, a par three was never in doubt.

Before long he was sitting down and reflecting on his success. 'Mark, is this the biggest win of your life?' somebody asked. Roe thought about it for a bit, then answered, po-faced. 'Well, I did win a couple of Sheffield and District Alliances last winter'. Told you he was a character.

Severiano Ballesteros, Lane and Olazabal in first tee discussion.

Mark Roe had the last word.

POS	NAME	CTY	1	2	3	4	TOTAL	PRIZE MONEY
1	Mark ROE	Eng	67	69	66	65	267	£79000
2	Vicente FERNANDEZ	Arg	66	70	69	64	269	52700
3	Eduardo ROMERO	Arg	66	67	69	68	270	24700
	Jim PAYNE	Eng	69	68	65	68	270	24700
	Steven RICHARDSON	Eng	68	68	71	63	270	24700
6	Jose Maria OLAZABAL	Sp	65	69	68	69	271	16800
7	Peter SENIOR	Aus	69	66	66	71	272	14300
8	Barry LANE	Eng	66	69	68	70	273	11250
	Tony JOHNSTONE	Zim	67	67	69	70	273	11250
10	Jamie SPENCE	Eng	72	67	68	67	274	8455
	Ian WOOSNAM	Wal	66	68	76	64	274	8455
	Christy O'CONNOR Jnr	Ire	70	67	68	69	274	8455
	Peter MITCHELL	Eng	71	65	68	70	274	8455
14	Howard CLARK	Eng	67	69	70	69	275	6843
	Frank NOBILO	NZ	69	70	67	69	275	6843
	Bob MAY	USA	68	70	70	67	275	6843
17	Wayne RILEY	Aus	68	71	67	70	276	5925
	Gordon BRAND Jnr.	Scot	69	66	72	69	276	5925
	Jose Manuel CARRILES	Sp	66	71	67	72	276	5925
	Nick FALDO	Eng	70	74	65	67	276	5925
21	Mark JAMES	Eng	69	70	68	70	277	5350
	Bernhard LANGER	Ger	70	68	72	67	277	5350
	Colin MONTGOMERIE	Scot	73	69	69	66	277	5350
24	Robert KARLSSON	Swe	71	69	66	72	278	4900
	Costantino ROCCA	It	68	75	69	66	278	4900
	David GILFORD	Eng	72	70	68	68	278	4900
27	Ian BAKER-FINCH	Aus	71	67	73	68	279	4266
	Curtis STRANGE	USA	72	67	69	71	279	4266
	Marc FARRY	Fr	67	71	71	70	279	4266
	Sam TORRANCE	Scot	69	69	72	69	279	4266
	Jose RIVERO	Sp	70	73	71	65	279	4266
	Ronan RAFFERTY	N.Ire	72	69	70	68	279	4266
33	Ian PALMER	SA	71	67	72	70	280	3900
34	Paul BROADHURST	Eng	71	72	67	71	281	3750
	Malcolm MACKENZIE	Eng	72	68	72	69	281	3750
36	Brett OGLE	Aus	71	71	68	72	282	3350
	Glen DAY	USA	68	71	70	73	282	3350
	Rodger DAVIS	Aus	70	73	72	67	282	3350
	Ove SELLBERG	Swe	67	73	71	71	282	3350
	Joakim HAEGGMAN	Swe	76	70	68	68	282	3350
	Johan RYSTROM	Swe	69	67	74	72	282	3350
42	Miguel Angel JIMENEZ	Sp	70	72	72	69	283	2950
	Grant WAITE	NZ	71	69	74	69	283	2950
44	Mike MCLEAN	Eng	73	70	70	71	284	2700
	Fredrik LINDGREN	Swe	71	74	68	71	284	2700
	David FEHERTY	N.Ire	71	73	73	67	284	2700
47	Anders FORSBRAND	Swe	75	74	69	67	285	2400
	Mats LANNER	Swe	74	69	72	70	285	2400
	Thomas LEVET	Fr	71	68	72	74	285	2400
50	Carl MASON	Eng	68	73	76	69	286	2120
	Philip WALTON	Ire	69	72	72	73	286	2120
	Santiago LUNA	Sp	68	73	75	70	286	2120
53	Jean VAN DE VELDE	Fr	70	70	74	73	287	1880
	Daniel SILVA	Port	72	73	70	72	287	1880
	Mark DAVIS	Eng	75	68	74	70	287	1880
56	Michel BESANCENEY	Fr	73	72	72	71	288	1750
57	Jose Maria CANIZARES	Sp	72	69	74	74	289	1625
	David J RUSSELL	Eng	75	72	66	76	289	1625
	Vijay SINGH	Fij	73	71	73	72	289	1625
	Andrew SHERBORNE	Eng	73	70	71	75	289	1625
61	Per-Ulrik JOHANSSON	Swe	75	72	72	71	290	1500
62	Miguel Angel MARTIN	Sp	71	73	74	73	291	1425
	Peter BAKER	Eng	74	74	71	72	291	1425
64	Bernard GALLACHER	Scot	72	74	72	75	293	1325
	Wayne WESTNER	SA	74	70	75	74	293	1325
66	Mike HARWOOD	Aus	70	72	75	DISQ	217	1250

COURSE: ST-NOM-LA-BRETECHE DATE:17-20.9 YARDAGE: 6756 PAR: 70

SURPRISINGLY, THIS IS NO LONGER THE BEST WAY TO VIEW THE BRITISH OPEN.

Recently, a piece of equipment more at home in the Atlantic surfaced on the golf course.

We have to admit that the idea is nothing short of brilliant.

Sadly, though, the view is not.

Spotting frigates is one thing. Trying to keep your eye on a golf ball on a twenty-foot putt is another.

With a Sony Video Walkman, you'd have a perfect view and the best television com-mentary, whatever the obstruction.

You wouldn't miss any of the action, or action replays, on its three-inch colour LCD screen. And if, perish the thought, a downpour should stop play, you could see what's on the other channel or catch up on that programme you've recorded but haven't had the chance to see. You could even watch a pre-recorded film on Video 8.

The Video Walkman is only slightly larger than a filofax and weighs little more than a portable phone.

Wherever you're standing, it'll give a view head and shoulders above the competition.

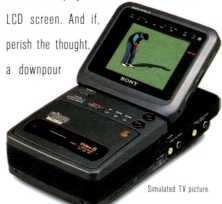

Simulated TV picture.

Sony is the sponsor of the World Golf Ranking.

SONY.

WHY COMPROMISE?

JIMENEZ FULFILS A DREAM

Miguel Angel Jimenez seized his opportunity in Belgium to become the seventh first time winner of the Volvo Tour this season

The first Piaget Open will be remembered for a host of things. A testing and beautiful golf course, huge crowds, sunshine and a first time winner – all will stick in the memory of those who were lucky enough to be in the smart resort of Knokke-Heist for this new event incorporating the Belgian Open. But most of all, perhaps, it will be recalled for one stunning revelation. Nick Faldo is human, after all.

Faldo went into the tournament on the wonderful links at Royal Zoute as a red-hot favourite. Nothing new in that, you might say, in this, his *annus mirabilis*, and you would be right. He was a mere couple of shots off the pace after the first round, and shared the lead after the second and third.

The winner's booty had his name written all over it, and another £100,000 in his hopeful march towards becoming the first man to win £1 million in a European season was as good in the Faldo piggy bank. After eight holes of the last round he led the field by three strokes, and there were no prizes for guessing where the smart money was going.

This was, after all, the season in which he had proved beyond all question that he was the best. He was thousands of feet further up the mountain than his rivals, that much nearer to the summit than the rest. Well, if he was up there on that warm Sunday afternoon in Belgium, he was suffering from altitude sickness. Because suddenly, shockingly, and totally without warning, it all went wrong.

He dropped six strokes in the last ten holes, eventually signed for a closing 74, and finished with a share of fifth place with Sandy Lyle, Per-Ulrik Johansson and Ian Woosnam. It was awful to watch a man for whom perfection is the norm suffering from the helpless sensation of a game under seige. Suddenly, the sepulchral all-black in which he was clad seemed grotesquely appropriate.

And what was happening while Faldo was hurtling out of the frame? One Miguel Angel Jimenez was revealing to all who had written him off at the start of the final day that they were making a serious error of judgment.

They didn't know their man – but then, not many did, to be honest. However, when Jimenez, former caddie, former teaching professional, four times a visitor to the PGA European Tour Qualifying School, got his chance, he took it. Boy, how he took it.

The record books will show that Jimenez, playing alongside Faldo on the last day (after a third day 64 had won him a £14,000 Johnnie Walker Course Record Award and put him into a share of the lead with the great man), won with a final 69 for a total of 274, ten under par. What they will not reveal is how, as a frail and flustered Faldo was gripped by that dreadful bout of self-destruction, eventually to finish five strokes behind, Jiminez maintained his form and determination to complete the greatest day of his sporting life.

He went into the tournament in 52nd place in the Volvo Order of Merit money list, using a set of clubs that he was still bedding in after three months' use and a putter that was so new it almost still had the price tag on it. He had been suffering on the greens, and the previous week his old putter had had, he said in charmingly fractured English 'an accident.'

It was never made entirely clear what the accident was, but the suggestion was that the shaft was not necessarily joined to

*Nick Faldo was ambushed
in the final round.*

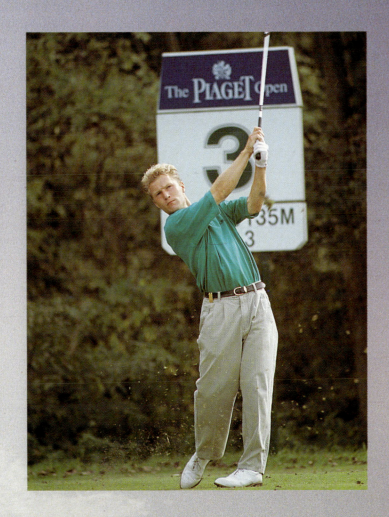

Another top ten finish for
Per-Ulrik Johansson.

the head after one particularly frustrating miss on the practice green. So along came the new weapon and, 21 birdies later, came also the winner's laurels. It was whatever the Spanish is for *Boys' Own Paper* stuff.

But let us put some flesh on the grisly bones of Faldo's demise. After birdieing the first two holes, he led by three strokes and all seemed well. It started to go wrong on the eighth, where he dropped a shot after missing the green. A leaked second shot from the rough on the 12th brought him a bogey six. He missed the green by no more than eight yards on the next, but had a grotesquely hanging lie in thick rough. Result: another bogey.

While all this increasingly desperate hacking was going on, Jimenez birdied the ninth, then took the lead for the first time with a putt from 12 feet on the 12th. From that moment on, with the 28-year-old Spaniard's game holding together supremely well with par golf to the end and Faldo's disintegrating, there was going to be only one winner.

Faldo marked another bogey on his card after being forced to take a penalty

Barry Lane's good form
continued.

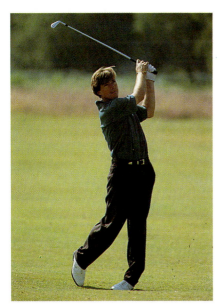

Twilight setting as Miguel Angel
Jiminez pitches, left.

drop on the 15th after hitting his ball deep into bushes and declaring it unplayable. His chance of victory had by now long disappeared, and further dropped shots on the 16th and 18th, both of which he three-putted, were in the end mere irrelevancies. He still won £19,850, enough to take him past Woosnam's previous money record – it was, to a man whose second name might be Flawless, a small consolation indeed.

While all this was going on Barry Lane, one of the Volvo Tour's nice guys, was producing his 12th top ten finish of an impressive season to finish second, three shots behind the winner; while Severiano Ballesteros played his best golf for months to finish third alongside Torsten Giedeon, who had a final 65 to clinch his Tour card for 1993.

Miguel Angel Jimenez can remember with crystal clarity when he hit his first golf shot. It was in September, 1979, and he was fooling around with his fellow caddies at Torrequebrada, the club to which he is still attached, near his home in Malaga.

He was 15 ½ years of age, and he knew from that moment that he wanted to be a professional golfer. The road was not always smooth for him after that, but 13 years later, almost to the day, he finally arrived. And to think it all started with a hopeful swing with a rusty old mid-iron behind the caddie shack where once he seemed destined to spend most of his life. Who says there's no romance left in sport?

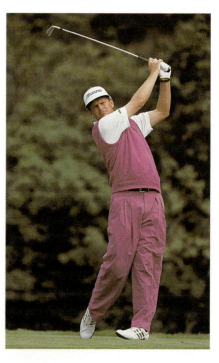

Sandy Lyle was in

the pink.

Steven Richardson blasts

from sand.

Severiano Ballesteros

showed some old form

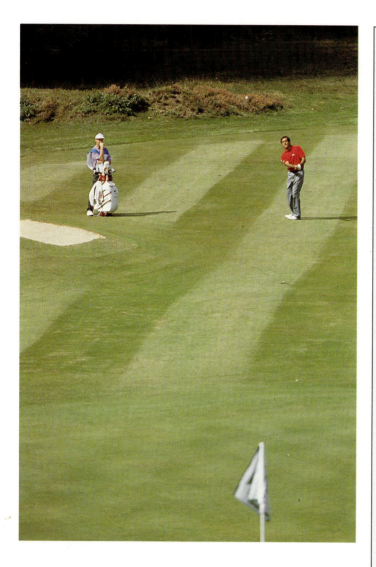

Ballesteros kept it on line.

*Jimenez claims his first
Volvo Tour trophy.*

COURSE: ROYAL ZOUTE G. C.   DATE: 24-27.9   YARDAGE: 6882   PAR: 71

POS	NAME	CTY	1	2	3	4	TOTAL	PRIZE MONEY
1	Miguel Angel JIMENEZ	Sp	71	70	64	69	274	£100000
2	Barry LANE	Eng	68	68	71	70	277	66660
3	Seve BALLESTEROS	Sp	70	71	70	67	278	33780
	Torsten GIEDEON	Ger	72	70	71	65	278	33780
5	Per-Ulrik JOHANSSON	Swe	72	69	69	69	279	19850
	Ian WOOSNAM	Wal	67	70	71	71	279	19850
	Nick FALDO	Eng	69	67	69	74	279	19850
	Sandy LYLE	Scot	69	70	72	68	279	19850
9	Philip WALTON	Ire	70	73	71	66	280	12720
	Darren CLARKE	N.Ire	69	72	68	71	280	12720
11	Ronan RAFFERTY	N.Ire	71	70	71	69	281	10320
	Vijay SINGH	Fij	75	70	66	70	281	10320
	Jim PAYNE	Eng	68	72	71	70	281	10320
14	Russell CLAYDON	Eng	73	73	67	69	282	9000
	Frank NOBILO	NZ	74	71	69	68	282	9000
16	Peter SENIOR	Aus	72	67	73	71	283	8100
	Danny MIJOVIC	Can	71	69	74	69	283	8100
	Tony CHARNLEY	Eng	69	70	75	69	283	8100
19	Rick HARTMANN	USA	73	74	69	68	284	6940
	John BLAND	SA	70	71	73	70	284	6940
	Bernhard LANGER	Ger	75	70	71	68	284	6940
	Richard BOXALL	Eng	75	69	68	72	284	6940
	Steven RICHARDSON	Eng	71	70	71	72	284	6940
	Peter MITCHELL	Eng	75	70	72	67	284	6940
25	Jesper PARNEVIK	Swe	71	76	71	67	285	5940
	Peter BAKER	Eng	71	69	75	70	285	5940
	Fredrik LINDGREN	Swe	73	74	70	68	285	5940
	Peter FOWLER	Aus	71	72	72	70	285	5940
	Patrick HALL	Eng	69	74	72	70	285	5940
30	Wayne RILEY	Aus	73	71	70	72	286	4945
	Jose RIVERO	Sp	74	73	71	68	286	4945
	Manuel PINERO	Sp	76	71	71	68	286	4945
	Paul WAY	Eng	72	70	70	74	286	4945
	Brett OGLE	Aus	71	73	72	70	286	4945
	Adam HUNTER	Scot	71	74	71	70	286	4945
	Roger CHAPMAN	Eng	76	71	70	69	286	4945
37	Mark JAMES	Eng	70	74	74	69	287	4200
	Colin MONTGOMERIE	Scot	73	69	72	73	287	4200
	Michael ALLEN	USA	79	68	69	71	287	4200
	Gordon BRAND Jnr.	Scot	72	74	70	71	287	4200
	Ernie ELS	SA	73	71	69	74	287	4200
42	Jay TOWNSEND	USA	73	69	75	71	288	3660
	Jean VAN DE VELDE	Fr	75	70	73	70	288	3660
	Jonathan SEWELL	Eng	73	72	71	72	288	3660
	Stephen FIELD	Eng	74	69	75	70	288	3660
46	Paul CURRY	Eng	72	70	73	74	289	3120
	Kenneth TRIMBLE	Aus	74	69	71	75	289	3120
	Costantino ROCCA	It	74	73	70	72	289	3120
	Grant TURNER	Eng	72	74	72	71	289	3120
	Bill MALLEY	USA	74	73	71	71	289	3120
51	Eduardo ROMERO	Arg	70	73	76	71	290	2460
	Sam TORRANCE	Scot	71	76	73	70	290	2460
	Keith WATERS	Eng	74	69	73	74	290	2460
	Ross DRUMMOND	Scot	72	71	72	75	290	2460
	David WILLIAMS	Eng	74	71	72	73	290	2460
	Chris MORTON	Eng	71	72	72	75	290	2460
57	Wayne WESTNER	SA	72	72	75	72	291	1905
	Robert KARLSSON	Swe	71	73	75	72	291	1905
	Mark DAVIS	Eng	72	71	75	73	291	1905
	Chris MOODY	Eng	76	70	75	70	291	1905
61	Stephen BENNETT	Eng	71	75	75	71	292	1500
	Glen DAY	USA	72	75	72	73	292	1500
	Stephen McALLISTER	Scot	72	74	74	72	292	1500
	Martin POXON	Eng	71	74	73	74	292	1500
	John HAWKSWORTH	Eng	75	71	75	71	292	1500
	Derrick COOPER	Eng	74	71	74	73	292	1500
67	Manuel MORENO	Sp	73	72	75	73	293	896
	Eamonn DARCY	Ire	76	70	75	72	293	896
	Andrew SHERBORNE	Eng	72	73	70	78	293	896
70	Hugh BAIOCCHI	SA	73	72	74	75	294	892
71	David J RUSSELL	Eng	73	71	74	77	295	890

Gouverneur
Own a Piaget
and wear
a work of art.

PIAGET

LANE FINDS WINNING PATH IN GERMANY

Although he was beginning to feel the effects of a six-week run on the Volvo Tour there was never any doubt really that Barry Lane would enter the Mercedes German Masters. It was not just because the tournament, run by Bernhard Langer and his brother, Erwin, has become one of the Volvo Tour's most successful, but rather that Lane enjoys playing golf in Germany. Just why he does not know but it was appropriate that in Stuttgart he should finally add to his lone Volvo Tour success scored four years earlier at Gleneagles in the Bell's Scottish Open.

The surprise was that he had not won more often in between. In Scotland he had won from a field that included a number of top American challengers. In Stuttgart, Lane, who had had 12 top ten finishes during the season, five in his last six starts, again triumphed over a field of class performers.

Indeed Erwin Langer's proud boast in pre-tournament publicity was that the top five in the Sony World rankings would be battling for the first prize of £100,000, Brother Bernhard would be defending the title he won in a play-off against Rodger Davis the year before, just seven days after his dramatic Ryder Cup experience at Kiawah Island. Ian Woosnam was in the field, as was Seve Ballesteros, Jose Maria Olazabal, a former winner of the title and Fred Couples starting a three-week swing through Europe where he admits he enjoys playing. The big bonus

Consistently high finishes over a six-week spell finally bore fruit for Barry Lane when he captured the second Volvo Tour title of his career

was that Nick Faldo, the runaway number one in the rankings, had included the event on his carefully worked out schedule. Sadly Faldo would fail to make it. He was a late withdrawal, mentally and physically tired from having been in contention so many times.

Such has been the growth of golf in Germany that the Volvo Tour now touches

down four times in that country. Vijay Singh had won the Volvo German Open where Langer, a winner on Tour each year for the past 14, had had an indifferent week. In Munich, at the BMW International Open, he had lost to Paul Azinger after a five-way play-off but he was hopeful that he might again pick up a first prize cheque at Stuttgart where he won the German Open in 1981 and where he had won twice and come second once in the Masters.

It was a course he did well on, a course he had helped improve. Langer is building his own new course not far away and had been telling the international press corps of the extensive lengths to which he had had to go to meet new environmental regulations. The environmentalists had indirectly caused a problem at the Solitude Club where green staff had been unable to use sprays to cope with the problem of worms burrowing up through the compacted ground for air. Not every fairway was affected but on some there were little worm casts which meant mud and earth clung to balls, prompting Ian Woosnam to make the point that this prevented him producing the precision golf he wanted to play. Tournament Director Andy McFee did not allow players to prefer their lies on the fairways until the weekend but the problem did not prevent the talented young Swede Robert Karlsson, who had been second to David Gilford in Morocco and to Nick Faldo at Sunningdale in the GA European Open, from shooting a 64 to lead on the first day or Christy O'Connor Junior, the 44-year-old Dunhill Masters champion, from easing his way into a one-shot lead from the ever-consistent Costantino Rocca on 11-under-par 133 at halfway. The Irishman's secret weapon had been his five-wood. While Woosnam and company were having to cope with mud on the ball and the inevitable misdirected iron shot, Christy, with all the skill and timing of his famous uncle, hit his five-wood like a dream.

Of the Sony Ranking top five Olazabal missed the cut, but after three rounds Woosnam and Rocca were ahead on 14-under-par 202, first round leader Karlsson was just a shot behind with Langer and Lane on 12-under and O'Connor, Rodger Davis, Ballesteros and Sam Torrance on 11-under. Torrance might have been even better but for a temporary switch back to a more tradition-al putter from the broomstick one he uses so well. Torrance explained he had had to find out whether a return to normality was a possibility. It was not. 'I ended up thinking only about putting even on the tee and before hitting my second shots,' he said. 'I'll stick with the broomstick.'

Severiano Ballesteros and Bernhard Langer in green discussion.

Frustration for Langer, left, and birthday celebration for Fred Couples, below.

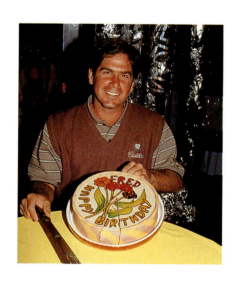

Eamonn Darcy steers in

a pitch.

For Torrance, another former Stuttgart winner whose season had been indifferent for several reasons – injury, the disruption of a move from Scotland to Wentworth, and the welcome arrival of a new baby daughter Phoebe – victory was important to get him to the end-of-season Volvo Masters. He had a chance but, going into the final day, the favourite was Woosnam, despite his problems with the worms. Early on the final day the Welshman had moved into the lead but he could not sustain his challenge. Rocca slipped back with a closing 73, Karlsson felt the pressure and tumbled down and off the leader board with a 77, Seve eagled the seventh gloriously to be two shots back then curiously found birdies tough to get, and Langer, Davis and O'Connor, too, could not cope with the winning last round 68 returned by Lane.

He had been given just the boost he needed for his last round charge to victory when shooting 66 on the third day in the company of Ballesteros. He had enjoyed the experience of playing with the maestro, not maybe at his best, but still trying and simply refusing to give up. That got Lane in the right mood for a last day charge. Three birdie putts and an eagle from 20 feet at the downwind seventh

Fore right from

Costantino Rocca.

Victory at last for

Barry Lane.

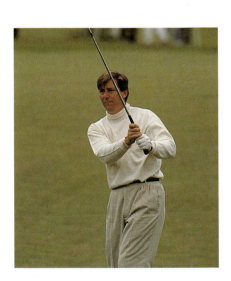

where he hit a drive over 330 yards, set him up for the victory he had known for two months was not far away.

He embarrassingly took two in a bunker at the last when, for the first time that day, he momentarily lost concentration, but in the end he had a two-shot winning margin over Langer, Woosnam and Davis with a 16-under-par total of 272 that brought with it the special bonus of a place in the Johnnie Walker World Championship at Tryall in Jamaica.

Lane, second in the Piaget Open a week earlier, had had to wait for his end of season win but he could not deny he was delighted at achieving it on a very important week.

For the seven events leading up to and including the Mercedes German Masters Lane was 57 under par and had won £246,000 in prize money. His popular win moved him into third spot behind Faldo in the Volvo Order of Merit with £357,000 and swept him to the top of the Johnnie Walker Ryder Cup table with 210,000 points, more than half of what he knows he will need to achieve his goal of an automatic place in the team next year.

──────────

Pro-am dinner high jinks for Ian Woosnam and team member.

POS	NAME	CTY	1	2	3	4	TOTAL	PRIZE MONEY
	COURSE: STUTTGARTER		DATE: 1-4.10		YARDAGE: 6839			PAR: 72
1	Barry LANE	Eng	71	67	66	68	272	£100000
2	Rodger DAVIS	Aus	67	69	69	69	274	44740
	Bernhard LANGER	Ger	65	71	68	70	274	44740
	Ian WOOSNAM	Wal	68	68	66	72	274	44740
5	Costantino ROCCA	It	65	69	68	73	275	23200
	Steven RICHARDSON	Eng	70	71	68	66	275	23200
7	Paul BROADHURST	Eng	67	68	73	68	276	16500
	Christy O'CONNOR Jnr	Ire	67	66	72	71	276	16500
9	Chris MOODY	Eng	69	70	70	68	277	12720
	Miguel Angel JIMENEZ	Sp	67	71	69	70	277	12720
11	Ronan RAFFERTY	N.Ire	68	69	72	69	278	11020
12	Martin POXON	Eng	73	69	71	66	279	9280
	Stephen McALLISTER	Scot	69	73	69	68	279	9280
	Jose RIVERO	Sp	71	69	68	71	279	9280
	Sam TORRANCE	Scot	65	70	70	74	279	9280
	Seve BALLESTEROS	Sp	68	70	67	74	279	9280
17	Chris WILLIAMS	Eng	68	72	67	73	280	7620
	Peter SENIOR	Aus	72	73	66	69	280	7620
	Robert KARLSSON	Swe	63	72	68	77	280	7620
	Colin MONTGOMERIE	Scot	74	69	70	67	280	7620
21	Jean VAN DE VELDE	Fr	72	71	71	68	282	6570
	Mark ROE	Eng	70	75	67	70	282	6570
	Michael ALLEN	USA	66	69	73	74	282	6570
	Santiago LUNA	Sp	72	71	65	74	282	6570
	Jamie SPENCE	Eng	71	68	69	74	282	6570
	Eamonn DARCY	Ire	70	71	71	70	282	6570
27	Danny MIJOVIC	Can	72	70	67	74	283	5580
	Ian PALMER	SA	67	68	72	76	283	5580
	Fred COUPLES	USA	70	71	73	69	283	5580
	Sandy LYLE	Scot	67	74	70	72	283	5580
	Anders SORENSEN	Den	68	71	73	71	283	5580
32	Howard CLARK	Eng	69	73	73	69	284	4740
	Peter FOWLER	Aus	72	72	71	69	284	4740
	Malcolm MACKENZIE	Eng	67	75	73	69	284	4740
	David GILFORD	Eng	71	72	70	71	284	4740
	Peter MITCHELL	Eng	71	68	74	71	284	4740
	Torsten GIEDEON	Ger	73	69	70	72	284	4740
38	Paul CURRY	Eng	73	70	71	71	285	4080
	Keith WATERS	Eng	73	71	68	73	285	4080
	Andrew SHERBORNE	Eng	70	72	69	74	285	4080
	Chris VAN DER VELDE	Hol	72	72	72	69	285	4080
	Andrew MURRAY	Eng	69	72	72	72	285	4080
43	Heinz P THUEL	Ger	72	71	72	71	286	3420
	Joakim HAEGGMAN	Swe	73	70	70	73	286	3420
	Peter TERAVAINEN	USA	75	70	71	70	286	3420
	Frank NOBILO	NZ	69	71	74	72	286	3420
	Philip WALTON	Ire	70	70	76	70	286	3420
	Peter O'MALLEY	Aus	72	73	70	71	286	3420
49	Sven STRUVER	Ger	72	72	74	69	287	2880
	Vijay SINGH	Fij	71	70	74	72	287	2880
	Hugh BAIOCCHI	SA	71	73	72	71	287	2880
52	Alberto BINAGHI	It	75	70	72	71	288	2400
	Wayne WESTNER	SA	74	71	69	74	288	2400
	Alexander CEJKA	Ger	67	78	72	71	288	2400
	Mark DAVIS	Eng	72	70	70	76	288	2400
	Jesper PARNEVIK	Swe	74	70	71	73	288	2400
57	Grant TURNER	Eng	74	71	71	73	289	1872
	Jeff HAWKES	SA	71	73	72	73	289	1872
	Jim PAYNE	Eng	69	74	72	74	289	1872
	Mark McNULTY	Zim	74	71	72	72	289	1872
	Ross DRUMMOND	Scot	72	73	72	72	289	1872
62	Eric GIRAUD	Fr	72	70	69	79	290	1680
63	Martin GATES	Eng	68	76	75	74	293	1560
	Derrick COOPER	Eng	69	76	73	75	293	1560
	Per-Ulrik JOHANSSON	Swe	71	73	72	77	293	1560
66	Phillip PRICE	Wal	71	74	73	76	294	899
	Patrick HALL	Eng	73	72	73	76	294	899
68	Peter BAKER	Eng	75	70	74	78	297	895
	Daniel SILVA	Port	70	69	77	81	297	895
70	Mark MOULAND	Wal	72	72	79	W/D	223	892

KING LANGER
THE SEVENTH

Bernhard Langer made it seven titles on his home soil when he captured the inaugural Honda Open

Whoever wrote the script for this blockbuster deserved an Oscar. For a new tournament with a new sponsor looking to establish itself on the Volvo Tour, the organisers of the Honda Open were naturally praying for a combination of memorable golf and a popular winner. By the end of the week they had both.

Played near Hamburg, over the tree-lined Gut Kaden course, little was predictable before the first blow was struck, except that the crowds would be huge. When Bernhard Langer plays in Germany the crowds are always huge. The man only needs to tee up there to take on the air of the Pied Piper. And, after his second place finish in the Mercedes German Masters the previous weekend, the whole country was willing the 35-year old folk hero to go one better. They were not to be disappointed.

'Perfect,' whispered tournament promoter, Harald Hartmann, as Langer's languid seven-iron approach to the 72nd green finished five feet from the flag. It set up a showpiece birdie for the German, giving him victory by three shots from the rapidly-improving Irishman, Darren Clarke, and by five from England's Roger Chapman.

It was Langer's seventh win on German soil in his 14-year career (which includes four German Open and two German Masters titles) and his second win of the season, following his earlier success in the Heineken Dutch Open. His 15-under-par victory, with rounds of 69, 65, 70 and 69, underlined his status as number three in the Sony Ranking, while the £75,000 first prize pushed him to second

place in both the Volvo Order of Merit and the Johnnie Walker European Ryder Cup points list. It was also Langer's 27th win of his European Tour career.

This time the statistics told the true story: Bernhard Langer was officially the second best golfer in Europe. Or rather, put another way, the first best golfer in Europe – bar Nick Faldo.

It was a stylish victory in Hamburg by Langer, with the highlight being his

second round 65, when he tore apart Gut Kaden with eight birdies, equalling the course record which Roger Chapman had set a few hours earlier. Having stormed to the top of the leaderboard at the halfway mark, Langer maintained his three-shot lead after three rounds, and again after four.

While the German never looked like faltering, Darren Clarke clearly had the bit between his teeth after a number of near misses, and threatened for a time to come up on the blind side. His runner-up spot represented his sixth top-ten finish of the season. In the third round, the 24-year-old from Ulster got the better of playing companion and current US Masters champion, Fred Couples, (who eventually finished joint fifth) when he shot 67 to the American's 70, and set up a final day showdown with Langer.

A former Irish amateur champion, and the only player from that country to have ever held the elusive plus-four handicap, Clarke always looked well-equipped to mount a challenge. He had shot a round of 60 earlier in the season, when finishing fourth in Monte Carlo, and a 62 when temporarily taking the lead at the BMW International Open, in Munich.

Unintimidated by the German crowds who had turned up to see their hero, Clarke's short game, in particular, was formidable. A putt from 30 feet on the 11th on the final afternoon took him to within a shot of the leader.

An upset looked possible, until a stroke of German brilliance turned the tables. Having hit a poor one-iron short of the

Lowering skies over Gut Kaden course.

Inset, Sven Struver exults after course record.

Fred Couples unleashes a drive.

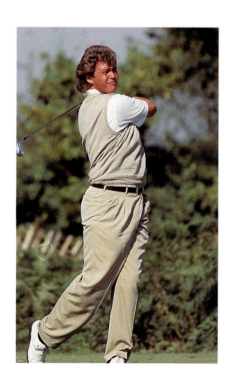

Runner-up Darren Clarke.

green at the demanding 235-yard, par-three 14th, Langer holed his pitch from the semi-rough, 60 feet away, for an unlikely birdie. With some daylight now restored, the German relaxed into an easier gear and added two closing birdies to cross the 't's and dot the 'i's.

Clarke's runner-up cheque for £50,000 moved him up 17 places to 42nd in the Volvo Order of Merit in his second season on Tour and brought him into the reckoning as a serious contender for the Johnnie Walker European Ryder Cup team at The Belfry.

The new Honda Open champion was the first to acknowledge Clarke's potential: 'He's a wonderful player. I'm sure we're going to hear a lot more about him,' said Langer. 'I won't be surprised if he wins a tournament soon.'

But it was a good day for Irish golf elsewhere, and Clarke was particularly pleased for his friend and travelling companion, Eoghan O'Connell, who emerged triumphantly in the battle for exemption which intensified in Hamburg.

The former Walker Cup player started

the week in 126th place in the Volvo Order of Merit and in severe danger of losing his card – with only the Iberia Madrid Open to go for those seeking the sanctuary of the top 124. However, with a final round 67, which contained a hole-in-one at the 16th, O'Connell picked up the £3,375 needed to raise him to 119th in the table and grasp virtual safety. A £20,000 Honda Accord car in recognition of an inch-perfect seven iron, was a pleasant bonus for the Irishman.

Epitomising the plight of the players scrambling for a lifeline was Bill Malley, who finished tied for tenth with two other players after a fine tournament in which he made much of the early running. But the American, who has played in Europe since 1985, agonisingly three-putted the final green when tenth place outright would have seen him, too, home and dry for next season.

As if the crowd might not go home happy enough, the best round of the week was a stunning closing 64 by another German player, this time local Hamburg man, Sven Struver. It brought

him £4,000 for the Johnnie Walker Tour Course Record Award, but his seventh place finish came too late to earn him a spot in the German Alfred Dunhill Cup side at St Andrews the following week.

It was not a happy return to Germany for Sandy Lyle – exactly one year to the week since his famous 'comeback' victory at the BMW International Open in Munich. The Scot departed after rounds of 78 and 73 which left him four shots adrift of the halfway cut. 'I haven't a clue what's wrong,' said a dejected Lyle as he trudged off the course. 'Just a bad attitude,' he suggested.

US Ryder Cup star, Payne Stewart, was another big-name casualty. Despite posting the best professional score in the pro-am tournament – a 66 on Wednesday – the American, cutting a dash in his Union Jack outfit, slumped to a 36-hole total of 150 – three shots too many.

In the end, Bernhard Langer was quite happy to host his own 'At Home' party. For him, at least, golf in Hamburg was the only game in town.

HONDA OPEN

COURSE: GUT KADEN, HAMBURG DATE: 8-11.10 YARDAGE: 6810 PAR: 72

POS	NAME	CTY	1	2	3	4	TOTAL	PRIZE MONEY
1	Bernhard LANGER	Ger	69	65	70	69	273	£75000
2	Darren CLARKE	N.Ire	71	69	67	69	276	50000
3	Roger CHAPMAN	Eng	72	65	72	69	278	28170
4	Russell CLAYDON	Eng	68	77	68	66	279	22500
5	Mark ROE	Eng	70	71	70	69	280	17405
	Fred COUPLES	USA	69	70	70	71	280	17405
7	Wayne WESTNER	SA	72	70	66	73	281	11600
	Ernie ELS	SA	71	70	71	69	281	11600
	Sven STRUVER	Ger	74	72	71	64	281	11600
10	Gordon J BRAND	Eng	70	69	74	69	282	8340
	Bill MALLEY	USA	68	70	72	72	282	8340
	Jesper PARNEVIK	Swe	71	71	69	71	282	8340
13	Danny MIJOVIC	Can	72	72	71	68	283	6906
	Peter MITCHELL	Eng	70	70	73	70	283	6906
	Paul BROADHURST	Eng	73	69	70	71	283	6906
16	Gordon BRAND Jnr	Scot	72	71	68	73	284	5656
	John McHENRY	Ire	73	71	72	68	284	5656
	Martin POXON	Eng	71	74	71	68	284	5656
	Mats LANNER	Swe	74	70	71	69	284	5656
	David GILFORD	Eng	74	70	69	71	284	5656
	Keith WATERS	Eng	75	71	68	70	284	5656
	Yasunobu KURAMOTO	Jap	70	73	67	74	284	5656
23	Glenn RALPH	Eng	71	72	69	73	285	4590
	Paul CURRY	Eng	70	74	68	73	285	4590
	Heinz P THUEL	Ger	72	72	73	68	285	4590
	Ian PALMER	SA	72	69	70	74	285	4590
	Tony CHARNLEY	Eng	72	73	71	69	285	4590
	Chris WILLIAMS	Eng	75	70	68	72	285	4590
	Johan RYSTROM	Swe	71	71	74	69	285	4590
30	Steen TINNING	Den	76	70	71	69	286	3858
	Stephen McALLISTER	Scot	73	70	70	73	286	3858
	Mats HALLBERG	Swe	71	72	72	71	286	3858
	Mark JAMES	Eng	75	70	74	67	286	3858
34	Jim PAYNE	Eng	74	72	71	70	287	3375
	Peter FOWLER	Aus	69	72	74	72	287	3375
	Andrew MURRAY	Eng	73	71	71	72	287	3375
	Eoghan O'CONNELL	Ire	72	74	74	67	287	3375
	Juan QUIROS	Sp	71	72	73	71	287	3375
	Alberto BINAGHI	It	71	76	70	70	287	3375
40	Neal BRIGGS	Eng	74	73	70	71	288	2655
	Richard BOXALL	Eng	72	72	73	71	288	2655
	Eamonn DARCY	Ire	73	73	74	68	288	2655
	Sam TORRANCE	Scot	71	75	69	73	288	2655
	Mike McLEAN	Eng	77	67	73	71	288	2655
	Paul WAY	Eng	72	73	73	70	288	2655
	Peter LONARD	Aus	73	71	76	68	288	2655
	Thomas GOEGELE	Ger	74	72	73	69	288	2655
	Joakim HAEGGMAN	Swe	75	71	70	72	288	2655
	Peter SMITH	Scot	72	71	70	75	288	2655
50	Rick HARTMANN	USA	71	72	74	72	289	2025
	Jeremy ROBINSON	Eng	70	74	73	72	289	2025
	Peter O'MALLEY	Aus	79	66	74	70	289	2025
	Gary EVANS	Eng	72	73	71	73	289	2025
54	Adam MEDNICK	Swe	74	73	73	70	290	1665
	Andrew SHERBORNE	Eng	74	73	71	72	290	1665
	Daniel SILVA	Port	78	69	75	68	290	1665
	Ricardo GONZALEZ	Arg	71	74	70	75	290	1665
58	Jim RUTLEDGE	Can	74	73	73	71	291	1417
	John METCALFE	Eng	73	70	74	74	291	1417
60	Michael ALLEN	USA	73	74	74	71	292	1305
	Mark MCNULTY	Zim	72	75	74	71	292	1305
	Andrew HARE	Eng	74	71	73	74	292	1305
63	Paul McGINLEY	Ire	75	72	70	76	293	1170
	Grant TURNER	Eng	74	70	72	77	293	1170
	Lucien TINKLER	Aus	71	74	77	71	293	1170
66	Jean VAN DE VELDE	Fr	74	73	75	72	294	674
	Manuel PINERO	Sp	73	70	74	77	294	674
68	Carl MASON	Eng	72	73	75	75	295	671
69	Stuart LITTLE	Eng	76	71	71	78	296	668
	Thomas LEVET	Fr	70	76	74	76	296	668
71	Brian MARCHBANK	Scot	77	70	77	73	297	664

FALDO'S
DEMOLITION JOB

Nick Faldo was relentless as he strode to his second World Match-Play Championship title

When Nick Faldo examined his swing on video the day before the Toyota World Match-Play Championship, he was not best pleased with what he saw. 'It was pretty awful,' he pronounced. Yet 72 hours later he had added another monumental record to a houseful of gold discs by beating America's Jeff Sluman by 8 & 7, the biggest final margin in the 29-year history of this illustrious tournament.

The uninitiated will never know what that kink was in Faldo's swing but in his remorseless pursuit of perfection he had his game in sufficiently good order to dismiss the challenges of Mark O'Meara by 5 & 3 and the reigning US PGA champion Nick Price by 2 & 1 (having been behind in both matches) before demolishing the aspirations of Sluman, the 1988 US PGA champion, in a match that was virtually over before it began and certainly long before most spectators had arrived.

After three holes, Faldo found himself three up, thanks to a birdie of his own at the second and Sluman missing each of the first three greens, underclubbing, over-clubbing and underclubbing in turn. 'My local knowledge helped. It was so cold that the ball wasn't going so far. He made some misjudgments and I got away from him,' explained the winner later.

Poor Sluman, having then failed to cash in on half an hour of Faldo hiccups when the great man leaked four shots in three holes from the 13th, found himself six adrift at half-time. The 5ft 7in New Yorker, who was conceding Faldo almost

seven inches in height and 26 rungs on the Sony Ranking, found out that when you shoot 75 against the world's number one you're as dead as a dodo.

At one stage, as the match moved inexorably towards its only possible conclusion, Sluman turned to a policeman patrolling the vast crowds and said wearily: 'You know, my mother always told me I'd have days like this.' Not that he had anything to be ashamed of after claiming the formidable scalps of Vijay Singh, defending champion Seve

Ballesteros and dual winner Woosnam on the way to a six-figure payday.

In order to pick up a record first prize of £160,000, Faldo played 97 holes in approximately 17 under par (official figures made it more because of one or two generous 'concessions'). Price, ground down after leading by two at lunch, called Faldo's afternoon display 'flawless'. Sluman simply called him 'the best — no-one in America seriously disputes that'. When Faldo had won his first Match-Play title in 1989 he had been 38 under par for 105 holes, but this was a far tougher Burma Road. Faldo called it 'the longest I have ever seen Wentworth play' after requiring a two iron for his second shots at 13 and 15, both par fours, against O'Meara.

Length has never been one of Ian Woosnam's problems and the Welshman injected much of the sparkle into the Championship with his record-breaking contribution, seven consecutive birdies which turned the week's potentially most intriguing showdown, against Jose Maria Olazabal, into 8 & 7 drubbing.

After routing the outgunned Japanese veteran Norio Suzuki by 8 & 6 on day one and then Olazabal by an almost identical margin, Woosnam quite astonishingly had recorded an eagle and 23 birdies in the space of 59 holes. Breathtaking stuff, and all apparently due to a left hand adjustment of his putting grip. From the fifth hole to the 11th of his afternoon round against the Spaniard, Woosnam pieced together a 2-3-3-3-3-2-3 burst the like of which the noble

Burma Road can never before have experienced.

Only the final birdie, from a yard, was not holed out but by then the enchanting but disenchanted Olazabal decided he had had enough. Falling to his knees in mock surrender beside the 11th green and cupping his hands together in a plea for mercy, he may have lost a battle but he must have won new admirers the world over for his mastery of the art of losing graciously.

Woosnam's words as he celebrated his second runaway win came back to haunt him: 'It could all go wrong tomorrow,' he said, 'but at the moment I feel I can beat anybody in the world.'

It did all go wrong, horribly wrong, against Sluman. He lost a three-up lead and then a golf ball as he surrendered meekly by 3 & 2 to the American, who could hardly believe his luck. 'That's my golf these days,' explained the loser. 'No consistency.'

It wasn't a good week for those with a grandstand view of the 18th hole. Only three matches reached the 36th green – and one didn't even make the 18th. Greg Norman created his own record-book niche by becoming the first player ever to withdraw in mid-match. The Australian drew stumps after 'bunting the ball less than 200 yards down the sixth' against Price, by which time the neck injury he had mentioned the previous day had become too painful for him to carry on. Norman blamed his demise on sleeping in a strange position on his first night in Britain. Three down and unable to make a proper turn, Norman called it quits, leaving Price the first semi-finalist ever to have reached that stage after only five holes of golf.

Greg had not looked his usual happy self in his first match, a last-hole victory over young American Brad Faxon. He frittered away a three up lead with a series of sliced drives and it took a shot of pure genius, a long 48-yard bunker explosion that pulled up four feet short of the 36th flag to bale him out of an ever-worsening situation.

Joining Faxon and Suzuki as first-day casualties were the European Tour pair Anders Forsbrand and Vijay Singh. The

Severiano Ballesteros

let it go again.

*Birdie for Nick Price
at the second.*

*Greg Norman signs off in his match
against Price.*

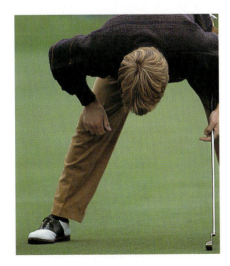

Brad Faxon in hole search.

Swede was the loser of the only match to go into extra holes, against O'Meara, and Singh was punished 4 & 3 by Sluman for a six-bogey display.

Day two saw the entrance and exit of five-times champion Severiano Ballesteros. A shadow of his old self in going down on the home green to an equally uninspired Sluman, who was only seven under par for the 132 holes he played during the week. Seve could have got himself out of jail with an eagle at the last and the magician of past years might well have conjured one up. But the 1992 vintage took four shots to reach the green and an absorbing, if sub-standard contest, subsided into anti-climax. 'I play bad, he play bad, that's why it was such a close game,' explained a philosophical ex-champion. He will be back.

So too will Faldo, who to celebrate the 30th staging of the tournament next year would like to see the inaugural winner Arnold Palmer and the other 13 past heroes involved as well. Not that too many would have a chance against the man who dwarfed his 1992 rivals in more ways than one. Faldo's fifth win of the year showed him to be on a different planet, though being the perfectionist he is, Faldo would be reluctant to agree. 'I still have faults and want to get on and correct them,' he said, explaining his insatiable need to achieve even more.

If there were faults, Jeff Sluman didn't spot too many of them: 'I only hope that if I make the Ryder Cup team for The Belfry, I'll draw someone else in the singles,' he said feelingly.

Next time they may have to give Faldo's opponents a start if they want to make a fair fight of it.

Rare moment of trouble for Nick Faldo.

COURSE: WENTWORTH CLUB (WEST COURSE)					
DATE: 8-11.10		YARDAGE: 6945			PAR: 72

NAME	CTY	NAME	CTY	TOTAL	PRIZE MONEY
FIRST ROUND					
Jeff SLUMAN	USA beat	Vijay SINGH	Fij	4&3	£22500
Ian WOOSNAM	Wal beat	Norio SUZUKI	Jap	8&6	22500
Greg NORMAN	Aus beat	Brad FAXON	USA	1hole	22500
Mark O'MEARA	USA beat	Anders FORSBRAND	Swe	at 37th	22500
SECOND ROUND					
Jeff SLUMAN	USA beat	Seve BALLESTEROS	Sp	2holes	27500
Ian WOOSNAM	Wal beat	JoseMaria OLAZABAL	Sp	8&7	27500
Nick PRICE	Zim beat	Greg NORMAN	Aus	retd	27500
Nick FALDO	Eng beat	Mark O'MEARA	USA	5&3	27500
SEMI-FINALS					
Jeff SLUMAN	USA beat	Ian WOOSNAM	Wal	3&2	
Nick FALDO	Eng beat	Nick PRICE	Zim	2&1	
PLAY-OFF FOR THIRD AND FOURTH PLACES					
Nick PRICE	Zim beat	Ian WOOSNAM	Wal	4&3	40000 (4th)
					50000 (3rd)
FINAL					
Nick FALDO	Eng beat	Jeff SLUMAN	USA	8&7	100000 (2nd)
					160000 (1st)

Perfect patterns on the fourth fairway at Wentworth.

THE SHOT OF A LIFETIME

lifetime™ line
0800 21 4000

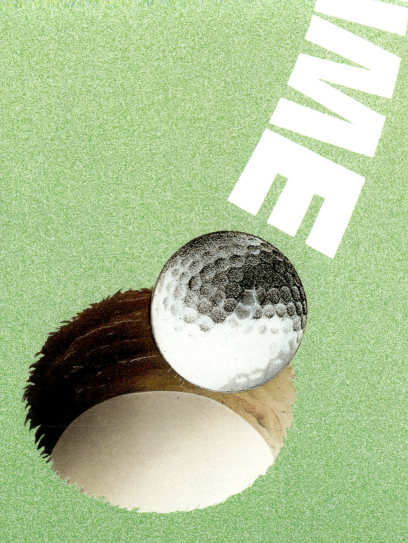

cellnet
The nearest phone.

Lifetime™ is a special service
from Cellnet (the world's largest
network operator), which can
significantly reduce the cost of
using a mobile phone.
For more information phone the
Lifetime line above.

Telecom Securicor Cellular Radio Limited.

ENGLAND ARE THE DREAM TEAM

England indicated that there is a life without Nick Faldo when, rather against the odds David Gilford, Steven Richardson and Jamie Spence won the newly-named Alfred Dunhill Cup over the Old course at St. Andrews, beating Scotland in the final.

It was a victory against the odds because England began as the fifth seeds and then triumphed in style without firing on all three cylinders. Gilford, rising from the ashes of his disappointment in the 1991 Johnnie Walker Ryder Cup when he was left out of the singles because of an injury to Steve Pate, was unbeaten in his five singles, Richardson won four of his five, while Spence, whom the other two had elected captain, did not win any in a competition that, until the semi-finals, was for the first time decided by round robin.

Hitherto in what had previously been called the Dunhill Cup, it had been by straight knock-out all the way through, the change being made to give the lesser teams who, like Korea and Thailand, otherwise would have travelled halfway round the world with the expectation of just one game. Now they were guaranteed three even if, as was predictable, they lost them all.

It did however lead to some confusion, particularly on the last day of the round robin when there were so many possible permutations that either a head for figures or the use of a calculator was necessary

England defied the odds to triumph at St Andrews

to decide the outcome. England, for instance, made the semi-final stage not so much by their own hand as by the hand of Silvio Grappasonni, an Italian, when playing against a Japanese, Nobumitsu Yuhara.

The putt Grappasonni holed for a birdie three at the 19th meant that Italy had beaten Japan 2-1 just as England were about to go down by the same margin to Spain. Had Japan beaten Italy, it was they who would have gone through with a superior stroke difference for the three games. This method of deciding ties was at the root of the confusion because it could and did change, hole by hole,

but it also added to the excitement. It might have been clearer if a point had been awarded for each winning game rather than just a single point for a whole match won. The only trouble with that is that a team which won all its three matches by 2-1 for six points would have come second to another which won two by 3-0 but lost the other 1-2, thereby collecting seven points overall.

As it was, three of the four groups were decided on strokes, the United States by a substantial margin from Ireland and New Zealand who both also won twice; Scotland from Canada and Sweden, all with two victories out of three; and England from Spain, both also with two out of three. Only group four was clear cut, Australia winning all their three round robin games.

For the first time in the eight years of the competition, there was more than a hint of winter in the air. Snow lay on the distant Grampians and the players were wrapped, certainly on the first day when there were also icy squalls of rain, in every piece of protective clothing they could find.

Most went according to plan, though Ireland had a close call against Korea, winning only 2-1 and then on the disqualification of Park Nam Sin in a match with Christy O'Connor Junior. O'Connor led by a stroke as they came to the 17th hole and when Park carved his drive apparently way out of bounds in the direction the Old Course hotel, he immediately produced another ball, first showing it to the Irishman, before driving again.

Unexpectedly however, the first ball was found on the fairway and Park played it to the green, despite protests from O'Connor that he could not because he had failed to declare his second ball a 'provisional'. Technically therefore the second ball had become the ball in play and on reference to the referee, David Garland, the Korean was disqualified for playing a wrong ball under Rule 15-3. The fact that Park did not speak English did not help a delicate situation though the Rules are, of course universal and have to be observed. Park agreed that he had not declared his second ball a provisional and O'Connor knew that he

---

David Gilford was England's anchor man.

Ice-cream was cold comfort for Fred Couples.

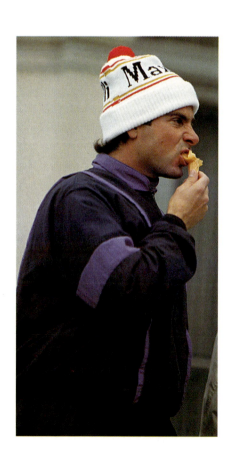

Davis Love III drives on the 18th.

could not be party to any rule violation.

Subsequently the Americans rather unwisely threw some petrol on the embers, expressing the opinion that O'Connor had acted within the letter rather than the spirit of the rule and his clash with Fred Couples in the semi-finals was regarded in some quarters as a 'grudge match', not least also because it was a repeat of their Ryder Cup single in 1989. O'Connor won it again, peacefully, 69-73, but a 2-1 defeat did not stop the Americans from taking their appointed semi-final place against England, with Scotland playing Australia.

If the likelihood was a final between America and Australia, for whom Greg Norman was in a rich vein of form,

expectation was very wide of the mark. Scotland, with Colin Montgomerie round in 68 and Sandy Lyle in 69, had strokes to spare over Ian Baker-Finch and Rodger Davis and Gordon Brand Junior's defeat at the hands of Norman (68) was therefore immaterial.

England's defeat of America was closer. Richardson recovered the form he had lost for his only defeat the previous day and a 68 was too good for Davis Love III. However Spence was always trailing the dependable Tom Kite and all rested on Gilford against Couples, the US Masters champion.

Rising to the occasion magnificently, particularly over the closing holes, Gilford gained a most notable scalp with a 69 to

a 70 and in the final did so again, breaking a long deadlock with Lyle with birdies at the 14th and 16th.

As Richardson had already accounted for Brand with some ease, Spence's stern tussle with Montgomerie, both of whom went round in 69 and were still tied after the first extra hole, was declared a draw. It was consolation for Spence but not for Scotland, who have twice now lost to England in the final and five times altogether.

Steven Richardson and Gordon Brand Junior set off in the final.

A hard round ahead for Gilford.

Colin Montgomerie couldn't alter the final score.

Jamie Spence on birdie march.

DAY1

GROUP 1

USA beat New Zealand 3-0

Fred COUPLES	70	beat	Frank NOBILO	75
Davis LOVE III	70	beat	Grant WAITE	76
Tom KITE	71	beat	Greg TURNER	73

Ireland beat Korea 2-1

Philip WALTON	77	beat	Cho CHUI-SANG	80
Christy O'CONNOR Jnr	77	beat	Park NAM-SIN	Disq
Ronan RAFFERTY	74	lost to	Choi SANG-HO	72

GROUP 2

Spain beat Italy 2-1

Miguel Angel JIMENEZ	69	beat	Giuseppe CALI	77
Jose RIVERO	77	lost to	Costantino ROCCA	74
Jose Maria OLAZABAL	76	beat	Silvio GRAPPASONNI	76

(on 1st play-off hole)

England beat Japan 2-1

Steven RICHARDSON	70	beat	Masahiro KURAMOTO	72
David GILFORD	76	beat	Nobumitsu YUHARA	76

(on 1st play-off hole)

Jamie SPENCE	77	lost to	Hiroshi MAKINO	70

GROUP 3

Scotland beat Canada 3-0

Gordon BRAND Jnr	75	beat	Danny MIJOVIC	81
Colin MONTGOMERIE	71	beat	Brent FRANKLIN	72
Sandy LYLE	71	beat	Richard ZOKOL	74

Sweden beat France 2-1

Robert KARLSSON	77	lost to	Jean VAN DE VELDE	73
Per-Ulrlk JOHANSSON	75	beat	Thomas LEVET	77
Anders FORSBRAND	74	beat	Marc FARRY	75

GROUP 4

Australia beat Germany 2-0

Greg NORMAN	72	tied with	Bernhard LANGER	72
Rodger DAVIS	78	beat	Heinz-Peter THUL	81
Ian BAKER-FINCH	75	beat	Torsten GIEDEON	81

South Africa beat Thailand 3-0

John BLAND	78	beat	Santi SOPHON	80
Ernie ELS	77	beat	Boonchu RUANGKIT	82
David FROST	78	beat	Thaworn WIRATCHANT	85

DAY 2

GROUP 4

Australia beat Thailand 3-0

Greg NORMAN	69	beat	Boonchu RUANGKIT	76
Ian BAKER-FINCH	74	beat	Santi SOPHON	78
Rodger DAVIS	73	beat	Thaworn WIRATCHANT	78

Germany beat South Africa 2-1

Bernhard Langer	72	beat	John BLAND	77
Torsten GIEDEON	72	lost to	David FROST	69
Heinz-Peter THUL	75	beat	Ernie ELS	75

(on 1st play-off hole)

GROUP 3

Scotland beat France 3-0

Gordon BRAND Jnr	75	beat	Marc FARRY	78
Colin MONTGOMERIE	71	beat	Thomas LEVET	78
Sandy LYLE	70	beat	Jean VAN DE VELDE	71

Canada beat Sweden 3-0

Brent FRANKLIN	71	beat	Robert KARLSSON	75
Richard ZOKOL	72	beat	Anders FORSBRAND	74
Danny MIJOVIC	74	beat	Per-Ulrik JOHANSSON	75

GROUP 2

Japan beat Spain 3-0

Nobumitsu YUHARA	72	beat	Miguel Angel JIMENEZ	77
Hiroshi MAKINO	71	beat	Jose RIVERO	76
Masahiro KUROMOTO	71	beat	Jose Maria OLAZABAL	72

England beat Italy 2-1

Jamie SPENCE	71	lost to	Costantino ROCCA	70
David GILFORD	71	beat	Giuseppe CALI	74
Steven RICHARDSON	70	beat	Silvio GRAPPASONNI	78

GROUP 1

USA beat Korea 3-0

Fred COUPLES	70	beat	Park NAM-SIN	78
Tom KITE	70	beat	Choi SANG-HO	74
Davis LOVE III	72	beat	Cho CHUI-SANG	79

New Zealand beat Ireland 2-1

Frank NOBILO	67	beat	Ronan RAFFERTY	68
Grant WAITE	70	beat	Philip WALTON	72
Greg TURNER	74	lost to	Christy O'CONNOR Jnr	68

DAY3

GROUP 4

Germany beat Thailand 2-1 — Germany win £45,000 — Thailand win £22,500

Torsten GIDEON	79	lost to	Thaworn WIRATCHANT	77
Bernhard LANGER	72	beat	Boonchu RUANGKIT	77
Heinz-Peter THUL	76	beat	Santi SOPHON	76

(on 1st play-off hole)

Australia beat South Africa 2-0 — South Africa win £22,500

Ian BAKER-FINCH	74	beat	David FROST	75
Rodger DAVIS	75	tied with	John BLAND	75
Greg Norman	67	beat	Ernie ELS	70

GROUP 2

Italy beat Japan 2-0 — Italy win £22,500 — Japan win £22,500

Costantino ROCCA	70	beat	Hiroshi MAKINO	74
Giuseppe CALI	71	tied with	Masahiro KURAMOTO	71
Silvio GRAPPASONNI	75	beat	Nobumitsu YUHARA	75

(on 1st play-off hole)

Spain beat England 2-1 — Spain win £45,000

Jose Maria OLAZABAL	70	beat	Jamie SPENCE	72
Miguel Angel JIMENEZ	73	beat	Steven RICHARDSON	77
Jose Rivero	73	lost to	David GILFORD	69

GROUP 1

New Zealand beat Korea 2-1 — New Zealand win £33,750 — Korea win £22,500

Frank NOBILO	75	lost to	Choi SANG-HO	73
Greg TURNER	70	beat	Park NAM-SIN	76
Grant WAITE	72	beat	Cho CHUL-SANG	72

(on 2nd play-off hole)

Ireland beat USA 2-1 — Ireland win £33,750

Christy O'CONNOR Jnr	69	beat	Fred COUPLES	73
Philip WALTON	72	beat	Davis LOVE III	74
Ronan RAFFERTY	71	lost to	Tom KITE	70

GROUP 3

Sweden beat Scotland 2-1 — Sweden win £33,750

Robert KARLSSON	71	beat	Gordon BRAND Jnr	75
Per-Ulrik JOHANSSON	74	lost to	Colin MONTGOMERIE	70
Anders FORSBRAND	70	beat	Sandy LYLE	74

Canada beat France 2-1 — Canada win £33,750 — France win £22,500

Danny MIJOVIC	73	beat	Jean VAN DE VELDE	75
Brent FRANKLIN	73	beat	Marc FARRY	76
Richard ZOKOL	75	lost to	Thomas LEVET	73

SEMI-FINALS

England beat USA 2-1 — USA win £95,000

David GILFORD	69	beat	Fred COUPLES	70
Steven RICHARDSON	68	beat	Davis LOVE III	71
Jamie Spence	72	lost to	Tom KITE	71

Scotland beat Australia 2-1 — Australia win £95,000

Colin MONTGOMERIE	68	beat	Ian BAKER-FINCH	72
Sandy LYLE	69	beat	Rodger DAVIS	73
Gordon BRAND Jnr	73	lost to	Greg NORMAN	68

FINAL

England beat Scotland 2-0 — England win £300,000 — Scotland win £150,000

Steven RICHARDSON	71	beat	Gordon BRAND Jnr	73
Jamie SPENCE	69	tied with	Colin MONTGOMERIE	69
David GILFORD	71	beat	Sandy LYLE	74

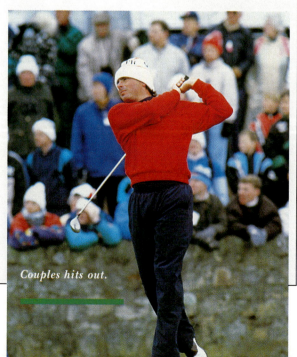

Couples hits out.

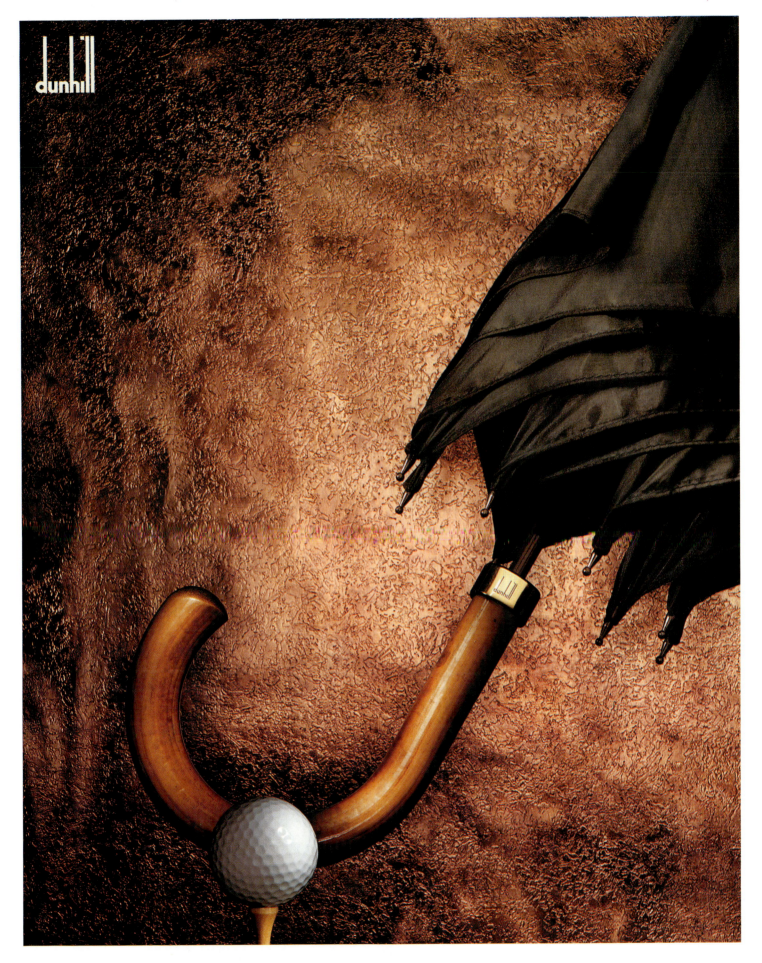

ALFRED DUNHILL

THE ALFRED DUNHILL CUP

Old Course, St Andrews 14-17 October 1993.

— Sought after since 1893. —

FEHERTY SAVES HIS SEASON

Remember David Feherty? He of the ready wit. He of the snake bite in practice for the Volvo PGA championship at Wentworth in May. The 34-year old Ryder Cup player had, on his own admission, hardly looked like a Ryder Cup player of late. He had slipped into what he called 'comfortable mediocrity'.

The year had started well enough with victory in the Bell's Cup in South Africa, a tie for third in the Dubai Desert Classic in Dubai and joint fourth in the Australian Masters, but therein lay the problems over the coming months.

Feherty continued to globe-trot. His wife was in South Africa expecting their second child and the Ulsterman divided his time not just between there and Europe but also America, as well having qualified for the three majors there by finishing seventh in the 1991 US PGA championship. 'I lost my confidence early on, didn't play enough to get it back – then played too much,' said Feherty.

So it was that his position in the Volvo Order of Merit was a sorry 83rd as he clocked in at the Iberia Madrid Open at Puerta de Hierro against a field that included John Daly, the 1991 US PGA champion. Daly was not to come to the fore, but Feherty was.

The opening day had a distinctly Scottish flavour to it, however. Not just in the weather – those who had survived wintry St Andrews were not expecting the Spanish capital to be almost as cold – but also on the leaderboard. Ross Drummond and Sam Torrance both shot 67s and Colin Montgomerie went one better to set

Injury and loss of form were forgotten as David Feherty came back to win at Puerta de Hierro

a pace that only Zimbabwean Mark McNulty, late in the day, could match.

Drummond, four times a winner of the Scottish Professional Championship, has been on Tour for 14 years, but amazingly his visit to the press interview area was the first of his career.

More important to the 35-year old was that he had not had to visit the PGA European Tour's Qualifying School since 1977 and again he came to what was, effectively, the last event in the battle for Tour cards just clear of the danger zone in 110th place. 'I may not have that worry, but I'd still like to make some

money,' said Drummond after a bogey-free round in which he grabbed five birdies and four times out of four got up and down from greenside bunkers.

Montgomerie was still chasing that elusive first victory of the season and had another objective too. Since joining the Tour in 1987 he had improved his money list standing each season and, after finishing fourth the previous November, needed to move up three spots on his current sixth to keep that graph going in the same direction.

McNulty, meanwhile, 'was more than delighted' to be on the birdie trail again following months of back trouble, giving credit to South African Jeff Hawkes for a swing tip that eased the pressure and to himself for sticking rigidly to a slimming programme.

Not so happy was Gary Evans. Bothered by a wrist injury for seven weeks the 23-year old withdrew after an 80, opening the door for former Walker Cup teammate Jim Payne to go £266 ahead of him in the Rookie of the Year race. He had been over £70,000 behind when August started.

First man out on a second day of much kinder weather was Cork's John McHenry, perilously placed at 122nd in the Volvo Order of Merit. When he stood on the tee at the 605-yard 18th at three over par, the halfway axe and a return to the Tour School were hanging over the 28-year old, but he smashed a magnificent three-wood second to within a foot of the hole and, hours later, the eagle three got him through with nothing

to spare. There can have been few more spectacular shots under pressure.

Glenn Ralph missed the cut, though, and two days later learnt that he would have to go back to the School, Scot Brian Marchbank taking the last card from him by less than £260.

Montgomerie still held a share of the lead at halfway, shooting a 69 to be on the nine-under-par mark of 135. But it was now not McNulty alongside him, but Spaniard Miguel Angel Jimenez, the winner of the Piaget Open only four weeks earlier, sparkling again with a superb 64.

They matched each other shot for shot in the third round, but 73s were not what they had in mind and McNulty fired his second 66 and moved into a two-stroke lead over Feherty and Jose Maria Canizares.

It had been a long while since Feherty had been a contender, but three successive birdies from the third took him ahead. McNulty levelled with a birdie of his own

on the seventh, but then came what proved to be the decisive hole, the 300-yard eighth.

McNulty, 'probably the best in the game from 100 yards in' according to Feherty, pitched too strongly and three putted. Feherty drove boldly for the green, came up just short, chipped to two feet and holed to go two clear.

It became three on the 12th, four on the 13th and on the run-in the Irishman had only one worrying moment. 'I was plugged under the lip of the bunker on the 17th and I could see the nightmare coming, 'he said. But the ball popped out and rolled to three feet.

His closing birdie was just the icing on the cake. 'I'm stunned,' said Feherty. 'I can't believe I've won again, let alone by four. I wanted to prove something to myself and I have. This was my last chance and I've always been one to take a last chance. My best has been mediocre this year, but this week I woke up. It is a fantastic feeling.'

Steven Richardson
bridges the gap.

Mark McNulty challenged
strongly for the title.

Another near miss for
Colin Montgomerie.

Madrid skyline frames
the 12th green.

COURSE: REAL CLUB DE LA PUERTA DE HIERRO, MADRID
DATE: 22-25.10   YARDAGE: 6940   PAR: 72

POS	NAME	CTY	1	2	3	4	TOTAL	PRIZE MONEY
1	David FEHERTY	N.Ire	71	65	69	67	272	£66660
2	Mark McNULTY	Zim	66	71	66	73	276	44440
3	Eamonn DARCY	Ire	68	69	72	69	278	18995
	Eduardo ROMERO	Arg	74	67	68	69	278	18995
	Colin MONTGOMERIE	Scot	66	69	73	70	278	18995
	Ronan RAFFERTY	N.Ire	71	67	70	70	278	18995
7	Derrick COOPER	Eng	72	72	67	68	279	8860
	Vijay SINGH	Fij	71	69	70	69	279	8860
	Mark ROE	Eng	69	70	70	70	279	8860
	Mark JAMES	Eng	70	73	66	70	279	8860
	Miguel Angel JIMENEZ	Sp	71	64	73	71	279	8860
	Jose Maria CANIZARES	Sp	71	66	68	74	279	8860
13	Steven RICHARDSON	Eng	69	68	70	73	280	5896
	Paul WAY	Eng	70	73	70	67	280	5896
	Des SMYTH	Ire	68	72	70	70	280	5896
	Magnus SUNESSON	Swe	69	71	68	72	280	5896
	Jamie SPENCE	Eng	72	70	68	70	280	5896
18	Peter MITCHELL	Eng	72	68	67	74	281	4766
	Sam TORRANCE	Scot	67	70	72	72	281	4766
	Vicente FERNANDEZ	Arg	72	71	70	68	281	4766
	Santiago LUNA	Sp	68	69	71	73	281	4766
	Malcolm MACKENZIE	Eng	72	66	71	72	281	4766
	Andrew MURRAY	Eng	68	73	70	70	281	4766
24	Darren CLARKE	N.Ire	70	74	66	72	282	4080
	Silvio GRAPPASONNI	It	72	72	70	68	282	4080
	Steen TINNING	Den	71	69	73	69	282	4080
	Barry LANE	Eng	71	69	73	69	282	4080
	Stephen BENNETT	Eng	69	72	69	72	282	4080
29	Adam HUNTER	Scot	71	74	69	70	284	3540
	John BLAND	SA	73	70	71	70	284	3540
	Jose RIVERO	Sp	72	68	72	72	284	3540
	Anders FORSBRAND	Swe	72	70	68	74	284	3540
33	Roger CHAPMAN	Eng	73	70	69	73	285	3120
	Phillip PRICE	Wal	73	71	71	70	285	3120
	Tony JOHNSTONE	Zim	70	71	72	72	285	3120
	Michael ALLEN	USA	73	68	72	72	285	3120
	John DALY	USA	70	71	72	72	285	3120
38	Patrick HALL	Eng	71	70	72	73	286	2680
	Carl MASON	Eng	71	71	72	72	286	2680
	Howard CLARK	Eng	71	72	70	73	286	2680
	Yago BEAMONTE	Sp	72	71	72	71	286	2680
	Brian MARCHBANK	Scot	73	69	73	71	286	2680
	John McHENRY	Ire	71	74	72	69	286	2680
44	Richard BOXALL	Eng	72	69	74	72	287	2240
	Jim PAYNE	Eng	71	71	72	73	287	2240
	Ignacio GERVAS	Sp	69	76	73	69	287	2240
	Keith WATERS	Eng	73	70	73	71	287	2240
	Danny MIJOVIC	Can	71	74	71	71	287	2240
49	Joakim HAEGGMAN	Swe	70	73	73	72	288	1760
	Ross DRUMMOND	Scot	67	76	73	72	288	1760
	Paul BROADHURST	Eng	74	68	77	69	288	1760
	Mike MILLER	Scot	77	68	68	75	288	1760
	Costantino ROCCA	It	71	73	71	73	288	1760
	Chris MOODY	Eng	71	72	72	73	288	1760
	Mark DAVIS	Eng	70	74	71	73	288	1760
56	Juan QUIROS	Sp	74	70	69	76	289	1360
	Peter LONARD	Aus	69	73	73	74	289	1360
	Sandy LYLE	Scot	74	71	74	70	289	1360
59	Heinz P THUEL	Ger	72	73	74	71	290	1160
	Alfonso PINERO	Sp	71	71	72	76	290	1160
	Kenneth TRIMBLE	Aus	72	71	72	75	290	1160
	Mark MOULAND	Wal	71	72	70	77	290	1160
	Bill MALLEY	USA	74	71	74	71	290	1160
64	Stuart LITTLE	Eng	72	71	73	75	291	1040
65	Jimmy HEGGARTY	N.Ire	70	75	75	72	292	698
	Anders SORENSEN	Den	73	72	75	72	292	698
	Peter SMITH	Scot	72	73	74	73	292	698
	Andrew SHERBORNE	Eng	74	71	72	75	292	698
69	Thomas LEVET	Fr	70	73	76	74	293	594
70	Jeremy ROBINSON	Eng	77	68	74	75	294	590
	Paul LAWRIE	Scot	71	74	75	74	294	590

LYLE'S COMEBACK IS COMPLETE

In the Volvo Masters at Valderrama Sandy Lyle demonstrated his old major championship winning form

Since the day he burst upon the professional golf scene everyone knew that Sandy Lyle had enormous talent. No matter that his swing wasn't classical and that he sometimes seemed disinterested, he couldn't half play golf, as he demonstrated by winning the Open in 1985 and the US Masters in 1988.

Victory in the 1991 BMW International Open ended the dismal run he had undergone without a victory. It lasted from mid-October 1988 to mid-October 1991. But victory in the Volvo Masters at Valderrama, when he controlled his game, kept his head and was quietly determined, showed that he is capable of returning to the heights of the 1980s.

Valderrama is as fiendishly difficult as it is exquisitely beautiful, with distant views of the Mediterranean, the Rock of Gibraltar to the east and to the west the range of hills that rears up behind Ronda. But little was as beautiful to Lyle as the sight of cheque for £110,000 and with it the chance to compete in the Johnnie Walker World Championship in Jamaica before Christmas.

He won't mind that he won it in a playoff he shouldn't by rights have reached. It took an enormous slice of luck to go his way on the 71st hole for him to tie with Colin Montgomerie over 72 holes and then defeat his fellow Scot on the first extra hole. None of that will detract from the fact that Lyle won from a field that contained every leading European save Seve Ballesteros who was at home having allergy tests. Lyle had not beaten such a stellar field in Europe for five years.

The Valderrama course that greeted contestants for the fifth Volvo Masters was similar but not identical to its predecessor. The rear half of the 15th green was relaid to make it more level. The Bentgrass areas around the greens were overseeded with rye mixture to firm them up and a collar of semi-rough was grown around the aprons to penalise a wayward shot. Everything was aimed at making it the perfect venue for the 1997 Ryder Cup.

As if all that did not make it difficult enough, the first day was blessed with the *poniente*, the west wind which blew at 30mph. A realistic par was 74 or 75 and the day's average score was 76.25. No-one went for 18 holes without dropping a shot; only two men managed to go for nine holes and they both had three bogies on the inward nine.

D J Russell, who had won a tournament in June by playing 72 holes without a bogey, had ten of them, as well as six pars and two double bogeys. His 86 was the day's highest score and he rushed to the practice ground afterwards and spent hours hitting shots while standing with his heels together. 'I hope somebody comes and joins me', he said. 'I feel silly up here by myself'.

The 16th and 17th were right into the teeth of the wind, which was so strong that Bernhard Langer and Jamie Spence needed their drivers from the tee and the fairway to reach the green of this 385-yard hole. Only two men birdied it all day and wouldn't you know they were Irishmen – David Feherty and Philip Walton. Oh yes, and Vijay Singh took a nine there, hitting his first two drives out of bounds.

No-one broke 70. Spence, captain of England's Alfred Dunhill Cup-winning team, shared the lead with Gordon Brand Junior after rounds of 70. Brand's was an up and down affair of four bogeys and five birdies and at the end of it he admitted he never felt secure. 'Playing this course is like walking along a clifftop. You are never sure that you are not going to fall over.'

Valderrama is the sternest possible test

on the Volvo Tour and it is noticeable how often the calmest golfers have done well there, men like Ronan Rafferty, Nick Faldo, and Mike Harwood. Christy O'Conner Junior is as equable as any of these, which is partly why he went round in 68 in the second round. 'It's not the length of the course, it's the toughness of club selection. If you take the wrong club you are dead. You just can't stop thinking out there. My 68 felt like a 64.'

Rafferty and Tony Johnstone joined him on this score. Feherty, Montgomerie and Lyle came in with 70s, Lyle taking the lead as the only man on par or better. 'Why have you suddenly found form?' Feherty was asked. 'Don't know, haven't a clue,' said the winner of the previous week's Iberia Madrid Open . 'It has nothing to do with practice and hard work'.

Mayhem was always in the air at this

David Feherty: the master

of his instrument.

Sequence of near disaster for

Sandy Lyle on the 71st.

*Appropriate number for
Nick Faldo.*

Eduardo Romero finished
joint fourth.

Left, view across Valderrama to the
Rock of Gibralter.

course as the players struggled with its lightning fast greens (rumoured to be 13 on the Stimpmeter) difficult rough, narrow fairways and, this year, the *poniente*. It was all too much in Saturday's third round for Mike McLean who was fined for club throwing, and it was the scene of a walkout by Dave Renwick, Jose Maria Olazabal's faithful caddie.

Olazabal berated Renwick on the ninth tee after taking a bogey five on the eighth. Renwick had had enough. He dumped the bag and Olazabal's manager, Sergio Gomez, took it over. 'I have been humiliated once too often,' said Renwick. 'When you are crying on a golf course, it is time to quit.' So he did.

Three men broke par: Johnstone, Eduardo Romero and Langer each scored 70. Lyle added a 72 and took a one-stroke lead over O'Conner, two strokes in front of Romero and Johnstone. Languishing 12 strokes behind Lyle was the tournament's hot favourite, Nick Faldo. 'You've got to play like God out there just to shoot par,' he said. Faldo, who normally does play like God, did not do so this time. Valderrama had claimed another victim.

Sunday morning was crystal clear and sunny and as the early starters were beginning their fourth rounds, Ken Schofield, Executive Director of the PGA European Tour, announced details of the

forthcoming season. Prize money would be almost £25 million, £3 million up on 1992, the 18th successive year prize-money has increased. In 1993, he said, the Volvo Tour would play 39 events, visit 19 different countries and 20 of the events would be for prize-money of more than £550,000.

Lyle, meanwhile, the tournament leader, was under attack from Montgomerie who was determined to win a tournament as he had in two of the past three seasons. He played beautifully – going out in 33, coming back in 36 and missing only two greens all day. It was good enough to tie with Lyle, who went round in 73 – surviving a huge shank on the 71st where his third shot, hit with a nine iron, ricocheted back in to play from a cork tree.

When Montgomerie snap-hooked his tee shot on the first extra hole of the play-off and the ball ended 50 yards from the tee, Lyle was as good as home and hosed. His second victory in Europe this season was a formality.

Welcome back Sandy.

Hugo Boss dresses the season's winners.

Play-off protagonists prepare, above, before final denouement, right

Big Three at the presentation.

The winner steps forward.

Twilight zone for Bernhard Langer.

Practice ground panorama.

	COURSE: VALDERRAMA, SOTOGRANDE DATE: 29.10-1.11				YARDAGE: 6920			PAR: 72	
POS	NAME	CTY	1	2	3	4	TOTAL	PRIZE MONEY
1	Sandy LYLE	Scot	72	70	72	73	287	£110000
2	Colin MONTGOMERIE	Scot	76	70	72	69	287	73330
3	Christy O'CONNOR Jnr	Ire	76	68	71	74	289	41310
4	Eduardo ROMERO	Arg	74	72	70	74	290	30660
	Tony JOHNSTONE	Zim	78	68	70	74	290	30660
6	Jose Maria OLAZABAL	Sp	75	72	73	71	291	22000
	Brett OGLE	Aus	77	72	72	70	291	22000
8	Bernhard LANGER	Ger	72	76	70	74	292	16135
	Gordon BRAND Jnr	Scot	70	74	76	72	292	16135
10	Glen DAY	USA	78	71	72	72	293	12670
	Miguel Angel JIMENEZ	Sp	73	72	76	72	293	12670
	Peter MITCHELL	Eng	73	73	76	71	293	12670
13	Steven RICHARDSON	Eng	71	74	78	71	294	10352
	Wayne WESTNER	SA	74	71	76	73	294	10352
	Frank NOBILO	NZ	74	73	73	74	294	10352
	Ian WOOSNAM	Wal	76	75	74	69	294	10352
17	Ian PALMER	SA	73	78	72	72	295	9240
18	Anders FORSBRAND	Swe	79	74	76	67	296	8725
	Mark ROE	Eng	80	71	72	73	296	8725
20	Andrew SHERBORNE	Eng	75	71	73	78	297	8370
21	Costantino ROCCA	It	74	78	73	73	298	8040
	Ronan RAFFERTY	N.Ire	77	68	74	79	298	8040
23	David GILFORD	Eng	73	75	77	74	299	7427
	Joakim HAEGGMAN	Swe	79	74	73	73	299	7427
	Robert KARLSSON	Swe	77	72	73	77	299	7427
	Nick FALDO	Eng	73	79	74	73	299	7427
27	Jamie SPENCE	Eng	70	75	74	81	300	6610
	Vicente FERNANDEZ	Arg	79	75	76	70	300	6610
	Darren CLARKE	N.Ire	73	76	76	75	300	6610
	Jose RIVERO	Sp	78	73	73	76	300	6610
	Jim PAYNE	Eng	77	73	73	77	300	6610
32	Mark McNULTY	Zim	76	74	74	77	301	5650
	Malcolm MACKENZIE	Eng	77	73	73	78	301	5650
	Jose Maria CANIZARES	Sp	74	78	76	73	301	5650
	Santiago LUNA	Sp	79	74	72	76	301	5650
	David FEHERTY	N.Ire	74	70	78	79	301	5650
	Mark JAMES	Eng	76	74	79	72	301	5650
	Rodger DAVIS	Aus	74	76	72	79	301	5650
39	Miguel Angel MARTIN	Sp	79	76	72	75	302	5050
40	Gary EVANS	Eng	75	79	77	72	303	4770
	Vijay SINGH	Fij	82	73	73	75	303	4770
	Peter BAKER	Eng	79	72	77	75	303	4770
43	Barry LANE	Eng	79	76	75	74	304	4445
	Howard CLARK	Eng	77	77	79	71	304	4445
45	Mats LANNER	Swe	80	77	74	74	305	4185
	Mike McLEAN	Eng	73	77	79	76	305	4185
47	Per-Ulrik JOHANSSON	Swe	80	73	75	79	307	3990
48	David J RUSSELL	Eng	86	75	73	74	308	3860
49	Philip WALTON	Ire	74	73	80	83	310	3730
50	Johan RYSTROM	Swe	79	83	75	75	312	3535
	Peter O'MALLEY	Aus	79	78	78	77	312	3535
52	Paul WAY	Eng	80	79	83	77	319	3340
53	Tony JACKLIN	Eng	81	83	80	76	320	3210
54	Paul BROADHURST	Eng	77	84	W/D		161	3080

Volvo 940 Turbo, 4 cyl., 121 kw (165 hp)

AMERICA'S CROWN IN THRILLING FINALE

'It's a weird game. We're going home with smiles on our faces and those other guys can't believe they didn't win. That's the dejection. And that's the excitement.'

So said Fred Couples after the dramatic, unpredictable conclusion to the final tournament of the European season, the 38th World Cup of Golf by Philip Morris at La Moraleja in a Madrid blessed by sunshine all week.

The United States sent their two leading money-winners in Masters' champion Couples and Players' champion Davis Love III and the bare facts are that they led after the first, second, third and fourth rounds to become their country's 18th winners of the event. Yet this was as thrilling a finish as there had been all year.

A gathering of 32 nations boiled down eventually to two battles. One between the favourites and the defending champions for the team title, the other between an unfancied runner and the defending champion for the individual crown. The holders couldn't quite hold on in either case.

The team contest first. Love and Couples wasted no time signalling their intention to make up for their Alfred Dunhill Cup disappointment. The former began with a putt from 35 feet and pitched to a yard at the third and Couples then holed from 30 feet on the next. Favourites they were and favourites they looked. The course, a new Golden Bear

In a dramatic finish America snatched the World Cup from Sweden

design, bit back at the 414-yards fifth. Both three-putted after Couples had a lucky escape when his topped drive skimmed the edge of the lake and came back on dry land. Love also had three putts on the seventh, but otherwise it was plain sailing. They had 13 birdies between them in the day and with Couples shooting 66 to his partner's 68 they led by two from Spaniards Jose Rivero and Miguel Angel Jimenez, with Wales and Japan joint third.

'We're not going to shoot ten under every day,' cautioned Couples and

the moment he double-bogeyed the first hole on day two the rest of the field were encouraged to believe this was no one-horse race.

Rivero and Jimenez remained the closest challengers, but defending champions Sweden moved from eight adrift to four behind thanks to an inward 30 from Anders Forsbrand. He nevertheless walked off disappointed after missing from four feet at the last for what would have been his first-ever 29.

He should worry. The following afternoon Ian Woosnam failed to hole from 14 inches on the same green – 'not my favourite distance,' he said – to leave himself two behind Australian Brett Ogle in the individual section (Forsbrand was in between them) and Wales three behind the 19 under par Americans with a round to go.

Sweden it was who were pressing Couples and Love the hardest now. They had closed to within a single shot and with Germany (for whom Heinz-Peter Thuel was round in 65 and Bernhard Langer in 66) and Spain alongside Wales on 16 under the stage was set for a fascinating final day.

It did not disappoint. Forsbrand and Per-Ulrik Johansson fell two behind with eight to play. Both then birdied the long 11th, but so did Couples and Love. Both also birdied the 406-yard 12th –

Johansson from 50 feet, his partner from ten – as did Couples after floating a nine-iron to a yard. One in it. Johansson then birdied the par three 13th as well from eight feet and when Couples three-putted the next and Forsbrand then birdied it from three feet the Swedes led by two.

Ian Woosnam and Mark Mouland in conference for Wales.

Sweden celebrate Per-Ulrik Johansson's eagle on the 16th.

Couples made instant amends with a pitch to two feet, but Love found sand and his bogey kept the situation the same with three to go. Now came the 529-yard 16th, with its green guarded by water front, right and back. Love, Couples and Johansson all made it on in two. Forsbrand, however, saw his five-iron fly 215 yards through the air, over the flag and hop into the lake. He took six, but Love took five by three-putting, Couples four by two-putting and Johansson three by making his putt for an eagle. Six and three makes nine, five and four makes nine – Sweden still two up.

The 177-yard 17th produced three threes and a two and since it was Love who hit a seven iron to five feet the gap was back to one. Sweden were still in the driving seat, though, and that did not change when Love hit his second shot to the last to 18 feet.

A successful defence looked even more on the cards when Johansson's approach covered the flag the whole way and came to rest five feet above the hole. But

Couples answered that with a pitch to 18 inches and when Forsbrand went into a bunker nothing was certain again. Forsbrand saved his par four, then stood and watched Love's putt take more twists than an Agatha Christie thriller and dive into the hole. Suddenly Johansson's putt, with Couples so close, was to force a play-off rather than to win.

A year earlier he had leapt into the air and was hugged by Forsbrand on sinking the winning putt. This time the ball dribbled past the edge and Couples stepped up to grab what for the most of the week had been an expected, but what minutes before had become an unexpected, victory. It has been said before and it will be said again: alas, Per-Ulrik.

The other victory was Australian Brett Ogle's, his first for a year and his best so far. He and Woosnam tied on 270, 18 under par. Couples finished 16 under, Love 12 under – and the Sydney golfer then made a birdie putt from seven feet on the first play-off hole to prevent Woosnam joining Jack Nicklaus as the only golfer to win World Cup individual honours three times. He will doubtless be back to try again. So, they hope, will Couples and Love at the next World Cup in Florida, when Heineken take over as the title sponsors from Philip Morris.

Decisive putt from Davis Love

on the final green.

Anders Forsbrand saves par

on the final hole.

Fred Couples on

the 15th.

Brett Ogle was

individual winner.

COURSE: LA MORALEJA II, MADRID, SPAIN								
DATE: 5-8.11			YARDAGE: 6955					PAR: 72
POS	**COUNTRY**	**PLAYERS**	**1**	**2**	**3**	**4**	**TOTAL**	**PRIZE MONEY**
1	USA	Fred Couples	66	71	70	65	272	£77,419
		Davis Love III	68	68	70	70	276	
2	SWEDEN	Anders Forsbrand	68	66	68	70	272	£38,709
		Per Ulrik Johansson	74	69	68	65	277	
3T	AUSTRALIA	Peter O'Malley	72	71	73	69	285	£24,516
		Brett Ogle	68	67	66	69	270	
	WALES	Ian Woosnam	67	69	67	67	270	£24,516
		Mark Mouland	72	70	71	72	285	
5	GERMANY	Heinz Peter Thül	75	73	65	70	283	£16,129
		Bernhard Langer	71	66	66	70	273	
6	SPAIN	Jose Rivero	66	70	71	74	281	£12,903
		Miguel Angel Jiménez	70	70	69	70	279	
7	NZ	Frank Nobilo	71	67	69	67	274	£9,677
		Greg J Turner	69	73	74	75	291	
8	S AFRICA	Ernie Els	70	69	69	71	279	£7,741
		De Wet Basson	70	74	77	66	287	
9	ENGLAND	David Gilford	74	70	72	70	286	£5,806
		Steven Richardson	69	71	71	72	283	
10	JAPAN	Kiyoshi Murota	68	72	77	73	290	£5,161
		Hirofumi Miyase	71	70	71	69	281	
11T	CANADA	Richard Zokol	71	70	72	75	288	£4,193
		Brent Franklin	69	72	71	72	284	
	CHILE	Roy Mackenzie	69	72	72	74	287	£4,193
		Guillermo Encina	71	73	67	74	285	
13	PARAGUAY	Raul Fretes	69	71	75	68	283	£3,225
		Carlos Franco	73	73	72	72	290	
14	KOREA	Sang Ho Choi	70	69	74	74	287	£2,580
		Nam Sin Park	70	71	73	73	287	
15	ITALY	Silvio Grappasonni	74	74	73	67	288	£2,258
		Costantino Rocca	73	71	72	71	287	
16	SCOTLAND	Gordon Brand Jnr	72	70	76	74	292	£2,258
		Colin Montgomerie	71	73	74	66	284	
17T	IRELAND	Ronan Rafferty	77	70	72	73	292	£2,258
		Christy O'Connor Jnr	73	72	71	69	285	
	SWITZ	Paolo Quirici	68	72	71	70	281	£2,258
		André Bossert	74	75	73	74	296	
19T	FRANCE	Michel Besanceney	72	74	73	71	290	£2,258
		Jean van de Velde	73	74	71	70	288	
	MEXICO	Esteban Toledo	71	74	68	70	283	£2,258
		Enrique Serna	73	78	73	71	295	
21	DENMARK	Ole Eskildsen	75	71	74	72	292	£2,258
		Anders Sörensen	73	74	69	72	288	
22	TAIPEI	Yu Shu Hsieh	72	72	73	75	292	£2,258
		Ter Chang Wang	72	72	74	71	289	
23	FINLAND	Anssi Kankkonen	76	73	76	73	298	£2,258
		Mikael Piltz	74	74	71	70	289	
24T	BRAZIL	Joao Corteiz	76	79	73	75	303	£2,258
		Acacio Jorge Pedro	72	73	74	67	286	
	ARG	Ruben Alvarez	69	68	71	81	289	£2,258
		Antonio Ortiz	76	72	74	78	300	
26	PHILIPPINES	Robert Pactolerin	81	78	74	73	306	£2,258
		Francisco Minoza	70	70	70	74	284	
27	NORWAY	Gard Midtvage	76	75	72	79	302	£2,258
		Per Haugsrud	71	76	72	70	289	
28	COLOMBIA	Angel Romero	73	76	71	75	296	£2,258
		Rigoberto Velasquez	70	73	75	80	298	
29T	GREECE	Vassilios Karatzias	75	77	77	77	306	£2,258
		Craigen Pappas	75	70	73	71	289	
	HOLLAND	Constant Waesberghe	73	75	75	73	296	£2,258
		Chrsi van der Velde	81	71	72	75	299	
31	H.KONG	Dominique Boulet	73	74	71	76	294	£2,258
		Yau Sui Ming	79	80	74	70	303	
32	MOROCCO	Moussa Fatmi	81	77	78	76	312	£2,258
		Mohamed Makroune	80	75	84	78	317	

INTERNATIONAL TROPHY (LEADING SCORES)							
POS	**NAME**	**CTY**	**1**	**2**	**3**	**4**	**TOTAL**	**PRIZE MONEY**
1	Brett OGLE	Aus			270			£48,387
2	Ian WOOSNAM	Wal			270			£32,258
3T	Anders FORSBRAND	Swe			272			£22,580
	Fred COUPLES	USA			272			£22,580
5	Bernhard LANGER	Ger			273			£12,903
6	Frank NOBILO	NZ			274			£9,677